W R Sorensen
July 1989
Tucson

RECORDS OF A BIBLIOGRAPHER

Selected Papers of

WILLIAM ALEXANDER JACKSON

RECORDS OF A BIBLIOGRAPHER

Selected Papers of

WILLIAM ALEXANDER JACKSON

Edited with an Introduction
and Bibliography by
William H. Bond

THE BELKNAP PRESS OF
HARVARD UNIVERSITY PRESS
Cambridge, Massachusetts

1967

Distributed in Great Britain by Oxford University Press, London
Library of Congress Catalog Card Number 67–22861
Printed in the United States of America

I conceive it, sir, a part of a library-keeper's business to know what books are extant in other libraries besides his own, and as this qualifies him the better for his place, so by that means he may prove the more serviceable, knowing what copies of an author are in his own library, and where they may be found elsewhere.

— Humphrey Wanley

Publisher's Foreword

The imprint of The Belknap Press of Harvard University Press on a book, we like to believe, has come generally to be accepted as a symbol of high quality. Thus it is proper for this volume to bear that imprint: the essays of the late and much lamented William A. Jackson about his vocation of collector and keeper of books and manuscripts are joined here to make a work of great distinction. But the imprint is in fact doubly fitting. Without Mr. Jackson it is entirely possible that there would never have been a Belknap Press of Harvard University Press.

Waldron Phoenix Belknap, Jr., of the Harvard Class of 1920, died in December 1949. He had been a close friend of Philip Hofer, the learned Curator of the Department of Printing and Graphic Arts of the Harvard Library. Mr. Hofer was, of course, closely associated with Mr. Jackson, Director of Harvard's great library of manuscripts and rare books, the Houghton. Through Philip Hofer, William Jackson came to know Waldron Belknap — a man of wealth, a bachelor, a connoisseur of the books that were the center of the existence of Hofer and Jackson. It is clear that at one time, after many talks among the three men, Mr. Belknap intended to bequeath all but a portion of his estate to the Houghton Library for the purchase of rare books to make its already outstanding collection even greater. But during World War II Mr. Belknap was stationed in England as a captain in the United States Army. He spent much time in Oxford, where he frequented the great Bodleian Library. Through it he learned more than he had ever known before of the Oxford University Press and of its eminent scholarly imprint, The Clarendon Press; and he convinced himself that his money would more usefully be spent in publishing or reprinting great books than in buying rare ones. Already stricken with the disease that killed him a few years later, he returned to the United States at the end of the war determined to draw a new will along the lines he had laid out at Oxford. He told Jackson and Hofer that he intended to maintain the Library as his beneficiary, but at the same time he explained to them that he wished his bequest used for the publication in book form of the unpublished manuscripts held by the Library.

Jackson and Hofer sensed that Mr. Belknap's wealth would be far more than enough to produce the Library's rare manuscripts as books. As dedicated collectors, they were, I am sure, disappointed by Belknap's change of aim. In their position who would not have been? But they were above all, wise and loyal servants of Harvard. Rather than agreeing with Mr. Belknap's new proposal and planning to use his gift less effectively for the Library's publications, they pointed out to him that Harvard University Press was in a position to publish the books he wanted issued and many more like them, from many sources, not just one; that the Press was established for the purpose; and that, adequately staffed as it was coming to be, it could use his largesse fully and efficiently. Mr. Belknap thereupon drew the new will which resulted, soon after his death, in the foundation of The Belknap Press of Harvard University Press.

That is the story as I understand it. I knew Mr. Belknap only slightly and never heard the facts from him. William Jackson, while he was alive, was far too reticent to describe his role adequately; the same restraint has characterized Philip Hofer to this day. So I hope I will be forgiven for the details I have left out or the misinterpretations of which I may be guilty. In any event, I can testify of my own knowledge to the effect of what was done. As Director of Harvard University Press, and hence in charge of the development of its Belknap Press, I saw the change from fear of publishing books at a loss to confidence that we could safely publish any book worth while as scholarship; that change from fear to confidence created around the Press of Harvard University a bright light which has not since dimmed and never, I believe, will. Waldron Belknap naturally deserves the credit. But I am deeply honored to have the opportunity, in this Foreword, to credit also the unselfishness, the generosity, the clear view ahead that enabled William A. Jackson and Philip Hofer to point Mr. Belknap along the path he took.

THOMAS J. WILSON

April 1967

Acknowledgements

Many people have contributed to this compilation. Foremost among them is Mrs. William A. Jackson, who gave me access to her husband's personal papers with permission to publish them, and supplied many details for the brief memoir that serves as introduction.

For permission to reprint specific articles, I am indebted to Mr. J. E. Reynolds, of the Southern California Chapter of the Antiquarian Booksellers' Association of America; Mr. H. Richard Archer, of the Chapin Library; Mr. R. J. Roberts, Honorary Secretary of the Bibliographical Society; Mr. Edwin Wolf, II, President of the Bibliographical Society of America; Mr. Frederick R. Goff, of the Library of Congress; Mr. Nicolas J. Barker, of *The Book Collector*; Mr. George McKay Schieffelin, Chairman of the Publications Committee of the Grolier Club; Mr. E. M. Dring, President of the British Antiquarian Booksellers' Association; Dr. Louis B. Wright, Director of the Folger Shakespeare Library; and Dean Andrew H. Horn, of the School of Library Service of the University of California, Los Angeles. The frontispiece portrait is reproduced by permission of Fabian Bachrach.

My colleagues in the Houghton Library have all had a share in this book, but particular contributions have been made by Mr. G. W. Cottrell, Jr., Mr. Philip Hofer, Mr. Sidney E. Ives, Miss Carolyn E. Jakeman, Miss Luise B. Mallinger, Mr. Roger E. Stoddard, Mr. James E. Walsh, and Mr. Daniel E. Whitten. I am grateful for the excellent camera work of Mr. Frank White, who made most of the photographs for the illustrations.

W. H. B.

CONTENTS

CONTENTS

Illustrations

ILLUSTRATIONS

Introduction

EARLY in 1938 there occurred an exchange of letters of great moment for the future of the Harvard College Library. The correspondents were Charles Warren, Chairman of the Visiting Committee of the Board of Overseers, and K. D. Metcalf, Director of the library. On January 7 Mr. Warren wrote as follows:

My dear Mr. Metcalf:

There has been referred to me, as Chairman of the Committee on the Library, the appointment, which is to be laid before the Board of Overseers, of Assistant Librarian in charge of the Treasure Room and Associate Professor of Bibliography. There has also been sent to me a copy of your letter to President Conant of December 23, 1937. This is in accordance with the practice of the Board that information of this kind shall be referred to the Overseer assigned to consider the affairs of the Special Department.

I judge from your letter that this is a newly created position and a newly created professorship. I should be very glad if you would write me more at length regarding the necessity for such a professorship, especially at the present time when economy seems to be a necessary watchword in Universities.

I think that it is very desirable that the resources of the Treasure Room should be more developed than they have been and that there should be someone particularly fitted to do that work. Whether, however, there is a necessity for the professorship, in connection with it, seems to me to be a matter of doubt. At least, it seems to me that the Overseers will probably want very full reasons for such a new professorship . . .

Cordially yours,
Charles Warren

Mr. Metcalf replied on January 8:

Dear Mr. Warren: —

The position of Assistant Librarian in charge of the Treasure Room and Associate Professor of Bibliography, concerning which you wrote on the 7th, is the most important of those which I mentioned at the meeting of the Visiting Committee last November (I did not at that time suggest a title for the position).

I shall try in this letter to explain the need for the appointment, but I hope it will be possible for me to talk with you personally about it later.

The greatest single need of the Library at present is for a bibliographer and scholar in the broad sense of the terms. Unfortunately we have no such man on the staff. In Mr. [William A.] Jackson, for whose appointment I have asked, we have an ideal candidate.

The new appointee should, as is indicated in his title, take charge of the Treasure Room, filling the place formerly occupied by Mr. [George Parker] Winship. The Treasure Room now has no one able to care for it adequately or to serve it properly or to select additions to it. The man in charge should be one who would interest the college men in fine books and manuscripts and give informal, if not formal, instruction in connection with them. The returns that will come to the Library as a result of interest so aroused should in the long run prove to be one of the best sources of growth for our research collections . . .

In addition to taking responsibility for the Treasure Room, Mr. Jackson, if appointed, would give bibliographical advice and instruction to graduate students who now must flounder around and waste time in getting started with their research work. He would take charge of book selection in the whole field of English literature. Here he could save a good part of his salary by coördinating our efforts and through his special knowledge of the field and of book values. He would become editor of the library publication which we hope to develop along lines which will make the Library more useful to the University, and at the same time will interest prospective donors.

Mr. Jackson is a man who would bring unusual prestige to the University. He is outstanding in his line and is one whom I am convinced the University cannot afford to lose . . .

Your letter asks specifically about the need for a new professorship. The Library staff should include, as it has in the past, at least one man with professional rank as part of his title (later there should be several of these positions). This is in connection with my effort to knit the library and the faculty together so that the latter will take full advantage of the resources of the former. The Library, to perform its proper function in the University, should be the best possible service organization, and should also take its place as a productive unit. Without men of faculty rank and calibre on its staff, this will not result. In my opinion university libraries in general, in spite of their much advertised claims of being the heart of their respective universities, have been mediocre in character, this being largely due to their not having employed first-rate men to help open their doors to the faculty and students who are doing distinctive work.

Sincerely yours,
K. D. Metcalf,
Director

The appointment was made, with results that the worlds of scholarship, bibliography, and bibliophily well know. Coupled with it was the similarly momentous appointment of Philip Hofer, a Harvard graduate of 1921, as Curator of Printing and Graphic Arts. A pair of old friends was thus transformed into a formidable professional team, each contributing his own highly specialized knowledge and abilities.[1]

As it turned out, Jackson's responsibility for book selection never regularly extended beyond the Houghton Library. Nor did he assume the role of editor of the *Harvard Library Bulletin*, although he took a leading part in its development. He helped to plan it and to secure the services of its first editor, G. W. Cottrell, Jr.; he appeared in its pages at least as often as anyone else; he fought for its preservation; and the *Bulletin's* present reïncarnation is substantially financed by the Fund contributed by friends and admirers in his memory. Mr. Metcalf's other predictions were speedily fulfilled to a degree that he himself probably did not expect. Within a few years the old Treasure Room was transformed into the Houghton Library. Jackson established courses in bibliography and book collecting for both undergraduates and graduate students. He attracted and held the nucleus of a professional staff of a caliber to suit his exacting standards. He began the search for new funds to bolster the woefully inadequate income annually available for rare books and manuscripts. His irresistible combination of enthusiasm and expertise aroused fresh support among old friends of the Harvard Library and brought into the fold a host of new friends. If anything, the pace of his scholarly labors increased. And he commenced a spectacular career of collecting for Harvard reflected in the twenty-three annual reports that were the admiration, envy, and despair of the rare book world.

How is a bibliographer-librarian of such formidable qualifications trained? Not by any common educational formula, and not by accident. Jackson perceived the outlines of what he wanted to do while still a pupil at the South Pasadena High School and set his course accordingly, at each stage of his development taking maximum advantage of the opportunities at his disposal. No Olympic athlete ever trained his muscles more systematically, more unremittingly, or to better avail than Jackson trained his eye and his mind. He regarded education as coterminous with life, and never ceased to learn and to explore. In our last conversation

[1] For Jackson's account of Hofer's collection, see "Contemporary Collectors XXIV. Philip Hofer," *The Book Collector*, IX (1960), 151–164, 292–300. Hofer's contribution to the development of the Harvard College Library deserves separate treatment of its own.

at the library I called his attention to the word "opsimath," which I had accidentally come upon in the *N. E. D.* It means "one who begins to learn late in life." Jackson was delighted, in his sixtieth year, to discover a word that characterized so perfectly his own profound belief that learning is a constant beginning.

Jackson was born in 1905 in Bellows Falls, Vermont, the son of Alice Mary (Fleming) and the Reverend Charles Wilfred Jackson, a Baptist clergyman. His father later moved to Canada and then was called to a parish in South Pasadena, California, where Jackson began his schooling. From the start the most important part of his education was extracurricular and was associated with a library. In the Public Library he read voraciously and fell under the spell of writers about books, in particular A. Edward Newton, author of the classic *Amenities of Book Collecting* (1918). It is fashionable today to dismiss Newton as an inaccurate amateur whose own collection sometimes failed to live up to the glowing descriptions he published; but he wrote with a vigor and enthusiasm that infected generations of bookmen and collectors, and he deserves honor as a pioneer of bibliophily. He was precisely the right mentor for this particular boy growing up in the next town to the newly established Huntington Library.

Jackson's connection with the Huntington began on a homely plane — he cut the grass at the house of a neighbor, Dr. George Watson Cole, who was its first librarian. At this time the great influx of students to the Huntington was far in the future. Founded in 1919, it did not officially open until 1928. Mr. Henry E. Huntington himself still inhabited the house that is now the art gallery. Cole and his staff were engaged in organizing and cataloguing Mr. Huntington's books and manuscripts. When young Jackson's interest in these matters became obvious, he received an entrée usually denied to all but a few mature scholars, and he laid the foundation for his life-long opinion that books are the only topic in the world worth continued and serious study and discussion.

Jackson graduated from high school in 1922 and, on Dr. Cole's advice, matriculated at Williams College with the class of 1927. Mr. Alfred Clark Chapin had just placed his choice collection of some twelve thousand volumes, mainly in English literature, in the college library, which became as potent a magnet to Jackson as would be the newest electron accelerator to a nuclear physicist. He was soon spending eight or more hours a day in the Chapin Library. It was a marriage of love and necessity, for a job there helped him work his way through college.

Miss Lucy Eugenia Osborne was Chapin's librarian.[2] She must soon have perceived that this was no ordinary freshman helper, fit mainly to fetch and carry and dust books. He began to take part in the descriptive cataloguing, and before long he had developed such a surprisingly sophisticated form and style that Mr. Chapin found it appropriate to have him work on a full-dress catalogue intended for publication. Jackson also hastened to enter the world of rare books in New York, then as now the chief American market: he attended his first auction, began the rounds of the shops, and breached the defenses of the Morgan Library, which was not yet open to the public.

During the summer vacation of 1924 Jackson returned to Pasadena, where he found more than ever to do in the Huntington and to discuss with its staff. In particular, C. K. Edmonds, cataloguer of early English books, and Captain R. B. Haselden, curator of manuscripts — each in his own right a remarkable character — spent many evenings of conversation with him. Back at Williams in the autumn the pace of his bibliographical work increased, and the publication of the catalogue was discussed in concrete terms.

Jackson passed the summer of 1925 in the almost hermit-like solitude of Williamstown, while the college was closed, working on the books for a salary underwritten by Mr. Chapin. An abortive diary, kept up for a few weeks only, records long days of concentrated work in the library. It also contains bibliographical maxims and shrewd self-analysis:

> [June 23] A good thing for any person who is engaged in bibliographical work to realize is the fact that there are generally several ways of approaching the same subject — when blocked on one avenue, back away until you get a clear view, outside the smoke and dust of the struggle, find a new opening and charge there.
>
> [July 6] I tried my best to untangle an ugly mess of Allots[3] today and although I kept at it for some time I didn't get as much done as I should, possibly because I was thinking too much of the pleasures of owning a great and fine

[2] For Jackson's tribute to Miss Osborne on her retirement, see *Williams Alumni Review*, XL, no. 1 (October 1947), 19–20.

[3] *Englands Parnassus* and *Wits theater of the little world*, anthologies of prose and verse compiled by Robert Allott. They are very complicated bibliographically; the revised *S.T.C.* will list four issues of the former and two of the latter — which Jackson at last properly differentiated.

library and so on. If I could only convince myself that the only way to have such pleasures is to get in and dig now — with all my heart and energy — not letting even my unconscious stray into such pleasant paths.

Cataloguing books on the scale that he had begun demanded the comparison of copies in other libraries. Jackson had already started to explore the resources at Yale, Harvard, the Morgan Library, and the Newberry in Chicago, as well as the old familiar Huntington back home. It was time for further explorations overseas. He had not asked help from his parents for his college education, but now he wondered if they could assist him to finance a trip abroad. They could, and the expedition was planned for the summer of 1926, between his junior and senior years. Their acquiescence produced a letter that was extraordinary for the clarity of its view of his future course. It is undated, but it was probably written in May or early June 1926.

Dear Father and Mother,

I have read your letters over several times and am very much pleased that you give the idea of the trip as much consideration as you do. I'll confess I was afraid that you would reject the idea altogether.

In this letter I shan't go into the financial side of the question at all because I haven't talked over my salary with Miss Osborne and so can't say just exactly what I can do.

However as to P.[ost] G.[raduate] work I have thought a good deal about it and this is about where I have come out. I shall probably stay here at Williams to get my M.A., finishing up the cataloguing of the Eng. Lit. It is even possible that I can submit the published catalogue as my thesis for altogether it represents far more toil and investigation, not to speak of thousands of decisions, the ability to maintain that 'bane of little minds,' consistency, and a grasp of bibliographical method than any ordinary thesis for the Master's Degree.

If I am allowed to do that I shall only take a few courses, and those in foreign languages, German, Italian, and Greek, and tutor in my French. (My French is so funny. I can read anything in that language, technical monographs, novels, poetry, absolutely everything that I have ever picked up with very very little stumbling, and yet although I can understand it when Joe Harsch, who returned yesterday from Paris, speaks it, I cannot somehow speak more than the most elementary sentences. The words come all right but I can't remember their order, whether you use *en* or *dans* with a particular word, anything in fact that is idiomatic. All I need to know about the language is how to read it with facility and that I hope to get without much difficulty. When I start any new language I shall be much more careful about how I get the elements of it than I was with French.)

Of course if I do that I shall be paid for the work in the Library and liberally enough, I hope, so that I can begin getting together those books that I shall later master and use, as well as pay off such things as the loan from the college which still stands but need not cause me any anxiety for I am not expected to pay it back until I have finished my education, i.e. the collegiate part of it.

After that of course I can only vaguely plan, but I hope that I can get a scholarship which will enable me to spend a couple or may be three years at Cambridge or Oxford, if it is possible to get a degree there to get it but not to let it control my whole time for I have been looking forward to that period as a time when I shan't have to feel that when I am reading what interests me most, I am using time that I ought to be spending on lessons that are of no interest to me at all. I hope then to become familiar with the literatures of all nations and all times, to read and master things that I shall never have time later to touch but which will give me a broader view-point, add immeasurably to my ability to appreciate what I do come in contact with in my latter life, in short to provide broad foundations upon which I can build whatever 'specialized' structure I later decide upon, and know that it will not be weakened by my failure to see it in its proper proportions and relations to the life of mankind. I hope to break away from the things which take so much time here, the bull-sessions, happy and profitable as they are, fraternity and extracurricular activities and the earning of money. I am sure that if I can those three years will be the happiest of my life. I don't intend to become a hermit — in fact I think I should seek the society of those from whom I could learn so much, men whose work I now admire, and men who are interested in the things that I am interested in. They are so few here at Williams.

If I didn't take a degree in England, I should probably return and spend a year in residence at Harvard to get it there.

In these plans the $500 would make little difference one way or the other.

Joe Harsch has just come over and I think I'll go out to lunch with him. When I know how I shall stand financially I shall write.

Lovingly,

William.

Apart from its professional overtones, the letter contains evidence that Jackson was enjoying a normal and active college career beyond the Chapin Library and his preoccupation with books. He joined the Alpha Delta Phi fraternity and always valued his association with it; he became editor of the college magazine, the *Williams Graphic*, whose business manager was his lifelong friend Joseph C. Harsch; he was Ivy Poet for his class at commencement; and he so far overcame his distaste for a set curriculum as to graduate with final honors in English Literature. The letter also shows that even in his college years Jackson's thorough enjoyment of social intercourse was overlaid with a sense that such things constituted an interference with his life's work and were therefore of secondary importance.

The summer of 1926 was decisive in many ways. On shipboard for England he met Miss Dorothy Judd of Honolulu, who three years later was to become his wife. He made his earliest forays into the Bodleian, the North Library of the British Museum, and the other great collections that were to become his familiar haunts. He met and quickly earned the respect of his bibliographical heroes, such as W. W. Greg, R. B. McKerrow, and Seymour de Ricci, and made the acquaintance of the coming men of his own generation, such as John Carter, Graham Pollard, and Percy Muir. And in London the Bibliographical Society published *A Short-title Catalogue of Books Printed in England, Scotland, & Ireland and of English Books Printed Abroad 1475–1640*, compiled by A. W. Pollard and G. R. Redgrave, which was the key to the books he loved most and became the bibliographical tool that he spent the rest of his life revising and enlarging. He secured a copy at once, had it interleaved, and began entering the thousands of annotations that were eventually to crowd every page.

By June 1927, when Jackson graduated from Williams College, the shape of the Chapin Catalogue had been fully determined, and it was agreed with Mr. Chapin that he should stay on, complete it, and see it into print. Instead of working toward a master's degree from Williams, he began directing his own specialized curriculum, as outlined a few years later (July 15, 1930) in a letter to Carl H. Pforzheimer, Sr.:

> While it is true, that in recent years, I have specialized in English to 1640, nevertheless I have not neglected such opportunities as I have had for keeping in touch with other fields. Though I do not pretend to be an expert in all lines, realizing that dogmatic infallibility is rather more than usually foolhardy in things bibliographical, I may state that I have paid particular attention to the study of bindings (sufficient to correct, and have it admitted, several of the ascriptions in the Huntington bindings exhibit), to English provenance marks and armorial stamps (in this I have had the assistance of M. de Ricci but have gathered and verified some hundreds of unrecorded rubbings by myself), and to English paleography especially the later court hands. I have also paid particular attention to the recognition of fakes and facsimiles and have made a practice of estimating the value of the items in the auction sales and later checking my estimates by the priced catalogues. As opportunities and circumstances have permitted I have gathered together a usable collection of reference books which I have systematically annotated after the fashion of the copy of the Short-Title Catalogue

which I showed you.[4] As a collector I have specialized in American 19th Century literature and in English 18th and 19th century prints . . .

The Chapin Catalogue itself is best described in his own words, in a letter written to Professor Karl Young of Yale, November 7, 1928:

The Catalogue is an attempt to describe by means of the most advanced bibliographical methods some 1500 volumes in the Chapin Library which were printed in England (i.e. in what is now the United Kingdom) before the year 1641, or which were printed in English in Europe prior to the same date. The Catalogue will also contain an appendix of such books as are in the Chapin Library which were written by Englishmen and first printed on the continent in Latin but which were later translated into English and are to-day regarded as English books . . . In the case of an author whose works were published both before and after the year 1641, all of the editions of his works which are in this Library, except of course modern reprints, will be described if the Library possesses a copy of at least one work by that author printed prior to 1641 . . .

Besides containing descriptions of the books in the Chapin Library the Catalogue will also describe, in many cases with facsimile reproductions, all known variant issues of those books. It will, moreover, in those instances where two or more editions of a book were printed with the same date, distinguish between them and present such evidence, bibliographical or documentary, as may be adduced to determine the order in which they were printed. For example, and this is only one of several hundred which might be cited, the early editions of Edward Halle's "The union of the two noble and illustre famelies of Lancastre [and] Yorke" were all printed in the same shop within a period of two or three years and many copies are made up from sheets of more than one edition. Because of the confusion which has thereby arisen and which has previously only been worse confounded by the attempts which have been made to distinguish between the variant issues and editions by the examination of the copies to be found in one library alone, in describing the copy of this book in the Chapin Library the copies in the British Museum, Bodleian, and Huntington libraries have all been examined and compared . . .

In the preparation of this Catalogue, a task which has consumed the better part of five years, I have not been confined to the resources of the Chapin Library and of the Williams College Library alone, but have personally examined in nearly all the great libraries of this country as well as in the British Museum other copies of the books which will be described in the Catalogue. Before the Catalogue is ready for the press I shall have spent some five months at the Huntington Library, for the purpose of comparing copies of these and related books. I have also had the assistance of a paid expert correspondent at the British Museum.

[4] See James E. Walsh, " 'The Librarian's Library': The William A. Jackson Bibliographical Collection," *The Book Collector*, XIV, no. 4 (Winter 1965), 499–510; XV, no. 1 (Spring 1966), 35–45.

It is not possible to mention here all of the matters to which particular attention has been paid in the preparation of this work; but this care has been gratifyingly productive of original and important discoveries. Attention should perhaps be called to the effort which has been made to identify the printers of anonymously printed books; and the use that has been made of the Calendars of State Papers for the discovery of the authorship and the history of the suppression of anonymous books.

Finally, besides indices of printers, publishers, engravers, provenience, etc., the Catalogue will contain what may be called a bibliographical index. By this means it will be possible to make available for general use the numerous examples and instances of printing practices and bibliographical methods which are discovered or discussed throughout the Catalogue. This index will largely supplement the recently published work of Dr. McKerrow and Miss Albright. For example, in the case of title-signatures of which Dr. McKerrow was only able to cite one example in English printing this index will contain, among others, 18 examples of this practice in the production of Wynkyn de Worde alone . . .

It is astonishing to realize that these statements were made by a man in his early twenties, and that they represented not daydreaming but solid achievement. Bibliographical work of such scope and caliber had scarcely been done before, certainly not in the United States.

The letter to Professor Young marked another step in the education of the bibliographer, for what was proposed was nothing less than that Yale University accept the catalogue as a thesis for the doctorate in English philology. One greatness of a university lies in its ability to recognize an exceptional situation: a week later Dean Wilbur L. Cross replied, "The Department of English has voted unanimously to accept as your dissertation for the degree of Doctor of Philosophy the bibliography you are preparing of the Chapin Library."

By 1929 his work on the catalogue was nearly completed. In August he and Dorothy Judd were married in Honolulu. They returned to the States to set up housekeeping in Altadena, California, the first of a series of homes over which Dolly Jackson presided with tranquillity and warm hospitality.

After some nine months, they moved to New Haven, Connecticut. Jackson thus established residence at Yale to meet the degree requirements and was also well situated to see the catalogue into print. The resources of a great library were at hand; the journey to consult books in Williamstown was not too long; and the publication itself was to originate in New Haven. Carl Purington Rollins, typographer for the Yale University Press, had already produced specimen pages, which had accompanied Jackson's application to the Yale faculty.

But 1929 was also the year when the declining stock market signaled the beginning of the great depression. Early in 1930 Mr. Chapin decided that the state of his investments no longer permitted him to incur the cost of printing an elaborate catalogue. On very short notice he canceled all further work on it. To all intents and purposes, the text was complete, and it can still be consulted in typescript at Williamstown, but it was never printed. The published record of the Chapin Library is the much simpler *Check-List*, prepared by Lucy Eugenia Osborne and issued in 1939.

Publication of the catalogue would have established Jackson's international reputation at once. To have it withheld at the last minute was a bitter blow. He faced increased personal responsibilities as well: the Jacksons' only child, Jared Judd Jackson, was born in the summer of 1930. A new position had to be sought, in a field in which there were not many openings.

The Huntington offered a job, but not at a salary sufficient to compensate for the expensive transcontinental move. Jackson began to correspond with Carl H. Pforzheimer, Sr., of New York, who owned a magnificent library of English literature, in many ways similar to Mr. Chapin's, and unsurpassed among private collections with respect to certain authors. Mr. Pforzheimer wished to publish a proper bibliographical catalogue and to enlist expert advice for further acquisitions. A bargain was struck, and in the autumn Jackson moved to New York to begin an association that lasted seven years and resulted in the superb three-volume Pforzheimer Catalogue designed by Frederic Warde and Bruce Rogers and published in 1940.

Anyone who compares this work with the unpublished Chapin Catalogue will be struck by the close similarity of method and style. The underlying principles were the same: meticulous description of each book, close analysis of its bibliographical features, a succinct résumé of its publishing history, notes on copies in other collections, and references to it in bibliographical literature. Jackson's attack was unchanged, but his knowledge was broader and deeper. He had continually enlarged his acquaintance with libraries great and small. In order to bring more information to bear on the problems of the catalogue, he spent the year 1933–1934 in England with his family — mainly to enjoy constant access to English collections but also to represent Mr. Pforzheimer in the London book market. It was his longest continuous residence abroad. He returned to the United States to complete a book that provides a standard against which all other bibliographical catalogues must be measured. In it the self-training so rigorously administered and the years of experience came to full flower.

In New York Jackson began another association of the greatest importance to him. In 1931 he joined the Grolier Club, the premier collectors' club of the United States, which had a long and honorable history and a vigorous and lively membership. The club roster included not only the tycoons of American collecting but also a good representation of younger men and coming collectors, with a liberal seasoning of able booksellers, librarians, and other professionals. The club library, then as now, was one of the most distinguished bibliographical reference collections anywhere, notably strong in books relating to provenance and book sales — matters that particularly concerned Jackson. In daily intercourse in the library and clubrooms he met men of like interests and attracted a wide circle of friends and acquaintances, who speedily recognized that along with his engaging amateur qualities he was a professional of professionals. It was at the Grolier Club that his lifelong friendship with Philip Hofer was cemented.

In addition to these private contacts Jackson made his public debut before a stated meeting of the club, on December 19, 1935, reading a paper on Thomas Frognall Dibdin. Young, tall, handsome, in full command of his subject and with enthusiasm to spare, he made a stunning impression on his audience. Next day A. Edward Newton wrote to him, "I knew that you were a bibliographer but I had no idea you could beat me to a frazzle at my own game. Your address last night was the finest that I have ever heard. I don't think there was a single fault or blemish, and I am but voicing the general opinion." Praise such as this must have been exhilarating, coming from the man whose writings had helped to start him on his way years before in the Pasadena Public Library.

Out of his friendships at the Grolier Club sprang a bibliophilic tour, planned for the summer of 1938 with Philip Hofer, Boies Penrose, and Peter Oliver. At the last moment Oliver was stricken with appendicitis and could not go. To this mischance we owe a long Dibdinian account of the trip, written by Jackson to Oliver while homeward bound aboard the S. S. "Scythia." In sixteen days the three friends had made a circuit from London through the Midlands, back to East Anglia, and then to London again, with a carefully prepared entrée to selected great private and institutional libraries all along the way.

Each of the three concentrated on his own specialties and then pooled findings and enthusiasms over dinners in country pubs specially selected by Penrose. Jackson's account shows how he could go Dibdin one better by adding accurate observation to the old master's verve and gusto. Expeditions of such felicity are likely to occur only once in a lifetime. His later bibliographical journeys in England, largely in quest of notes for the *Short-title Catalogue* and of books for Harvard, were more strictly professional. Although they were studded with social occasions, Jackson never again had the opportunity for such a convivial and sustained excursion in bibliophily.

By the autumn of 1938, when Jackson left New York for his appointment in Cambridge, his work on the Pforzheimer Catalogue was completed. It was even in page-proof, though publication was delayed for another two years. He immediately plunged into his new responsibilities at Harvard, inaugurated his famous course in bibliography, and began studying the collections and determining what could be done to build them up.

The Friends of the Harvard College Library, an organization dating back at least to 1925 but fallen somewhat into the doldrums, was revived, largely in the hands of Philip Hofer, who served as Secretary. Jackson and Hofer took their places in the bibliophilic world of Boston, becoming members of the Club of Odd Volumes, of which each eventually served as President. They also began the practice of showing the library's newest treasures at the annual meeting of the Visiting Committee. Their spirited presentation, their erudition, and the spectacular quality of their books and manuscripts soon established this as a regular custom of the Committee and helped to secure its sustained and powerful support for the activities of the library.

Space is the perpetual problem of the learned librarian; his inventory always increases and never diminishes. Rare books and manuscripts also require a controlled atmosphere for their better preservation, particularly in an urban industrial environment such as Cambridge. In 1938 the Treasure Room was on the first floor of the Widener Library, where it occupied as a Reading Room the chamber now used by the Widener cataloguing staff. A portion of the adjacent stack was shut off from the rest of the library for rare book storage. On the ground floor immediately beneath was the Lower Treasure Room, with offices for Jackson and Hofer and their secretaries. Opening off this was a locked stack for Hofer's personal collection, occupying an area that now houses computation equipment. A nearby study contained a Washington press and some type, then mainly used by the staff. When bibliographical students printed, they did so at the Harvard Printing Office in Randall Hall (which occupied the site of today's William James Hall) under the tutelage of Charles Grassinger, who had worked as compositor under Bruce Rogers. Several large tables just outside Hofer's stack provided space for study and work, and a small room with a long table served for the bibliographical seminar. Since smoking was not permitted anywhere in Widener, the now disused west door was often opened for the enjoyment of a cigarette just outside the sanctuary.

The space was barely adequate for staff and collections, but the conditions of storage were not. Jackson shortly had a rudimentary humidifying system installed in the Treasure Room stack; some of the fittings can still be seen. Nothing practical could be done about temperature, but at least the books could be saved from baking dry during the winter months of steam heat. Further expansion of the Treasure Room stack could only be accomplished at the expense of Widener's normal stack area, which was itself dangerously near capacity.

Help was at hand. At the meeting of the Visiting Committee in February 1940 the talk turned to rare books and the need to provide for them in a university library, and Arthur Amory Houghton, Jr. (Harvard 1929), volunteered to back the building of a completely new facility. His offer was accepted with alacrity. A site on the hill east of Widener was selected, and Jackson was shortly in conference with the architects, the firm of Perry, Shaw, and Hepburn. Excavation began in October 1940; the building was largely completed before Pearl Harbor Day in 1941. Early in the new year the transfer of collections began, and the Houghton Library was formally opened on February 28, 1942.

Every feature of the building received Jackson's constant and concentrated personal attention. He made numerous trips to New York to consult with Arthur Houghton at all stages of the planning, and Houghton repeatedly visited Cambridge for the same purpose. Keyes Metcalf advised on stack layout and technical library equipment, and Philip Hofer gave the benefit of his judgment in matters of design and decoration. All were determined to see that Harvard's rare books received the best possible housing.

The air conditioning system was the most advanced of its day. A new kind of cool lighting was used in display cases. The metal stack shelving was specially designed and manufactured to rigorous specifications so that it could have no possible rough edge to injure a binding. Jackson later told with pride of the hours he had spent with the blueprints tracing every possible route through the building, simply to make sure that anywhere one went one could always turn on the lights ahead and turn off those behind without retracing one's steps. This was typical of his meticulous attention to detail. The very few awkward spots of this kind that exist are mainly the result of later remodeling or of new functions not originally anticipated.

The same care went into the public aspects of the building. The double entrance staircase and porch owe something to the Queen's House in Greenwich, England, a building Jackson had seen and remembered. The light and pleasant rooms of the Department of Printing and Graphic Arts were designed according to Philip Hofer's tastes and specifications. The Keats Room at the north end of the top floor was paneled in walnut and featured an antique chandelier, the twin of one in Arthur Houghton's personal library at Wye Plantation in Maryland. At the other end of the building a room was designed in English oak for the future accommodation of the library of William King Richardson (Harvard 1880), designated for Harvard by bequest and placed in the room after Mr. Richardson's death in 1951.

Other rooms were designed around furnishings that Jackson had found. His office, for example, was focused on three enormous glass-fronted mahogany bookcases from the home of Daniel B. Fearing, angling collector and sometime mayor of Newport, Rhode Island. These housed Jackson's own bibliographical collection. A huge mahogany library table, cut down to size, became his desk, and the excess wood was transformed into a small standing desk for easy consultation of reference works.

Jackson's interest did not end with the planning and construction of the library. The building and its contents reflect his unflagging concern for its upkeep. He insisted on the highest standards of maintenance, and the custodial staff have always responded accordingly.

When the Houghton Library opened, it could be said without boasting to be the most advanced library building in the United States, if not in the world, and to a large degree its success resulted from Jackson's thought and effort. No building to rival it could be built during the war years. Since the war, even though there have been important technical improvements in air-conditioning, lighting, and other details of structure and equipment, the basic principles specified for the Houghton Library are still standard for the design of rare book libraries.

Jackson's staff was by no means expanded in proportion to the magnificence of the new surroundings. His office force consisted of a secretary, an assistant, and an accessions typist. Procedures were simple but effective. Jackson read dealers' and auction catalogues, marked entries, and turned them over to his assistant to be checked against the Harvard holdings. He did much checking himself, especially when there was an unusual press of business; even in those somewhat less competitive days, promptness spelled the difference between securing or losing a book. The checking went beyond merely determining whether or not Harvard already had the book. It also attempted to assess its desirability and appropriateness in terms of the existing collections and the literature of which it was a part. Experience told Jackson whether the price was proper or not.

The assistant also made accessions records of all currently received printed books and most manuscripts (there was no Manuscript Department until 1948), answered certain inquiries, compiled data so that Jackson could answer others, and did all manner of odd jobs from guiding visitors to setting up exhibitions. No more concentrated bibliographical training covering so wide a variety of material could possibly have been devised, as the ten men who held the post would surely testify.[5] Not until several years after World War II did Jackson acquire a second assistant to deal exclusively with the problems of the *Short-title Catalogue*.[6]

Both by necessity and by choice Jackson participated in every aspect of the library's functions. Administrative isolation never appealed to him. He resented anything that cut him off from first-hand contact with the books themselves. Moreover, there were often times when every available staff member had to pitch in to finish a piece of work. In fact, at no time could the Houghton Library be said to have been overstaffed, and Jackson himself usually went to take a hand in

[5] Jackson's assistants, in order of tenure, were W. H. McCarthy, Jr., John Alden, G. W. Cottrell, Jr., W. H. Bond, L. M. Oliver, W. B. Todd, R. E. Stoddard, K. C. Carpenter, M. J. Faigel, and S. E. Ives IV.

[6] The principal assistants on the *S.T.C.* were Miss Frederica Oldach, Miss Anne Henry (now Mrs. Irvin Ehrenpreis), Miss Janet Eagleson (now Mrs. John Critics), and Miss Katharine Pantzer.

the actual packing and transfer of any large new acquisition. Sometimes it was a one-man expedition. When it was a mass assault, nobody worked harder, longer, or to better effect than he. He even drove the rented truck transporting W. B. Osgood Field's books from Lake Monhegan to Cambridge, suffering an incredible number of flat tires (wartime recaps) as the ancient vehicle chugged across Connecticut and Massachusetts. And when it came time to move the contents of the old Treasure Room stack to the new library, he headed the crew made up of W. H. McCarthy, Jr., Miss Carolyn E. Jakeman, and one or two other stalwarts, who performed the entire back-breaking task. The same crew spent a wild last night before opening day chasing and killing mice that had found their way in during building operations.

Even before the Houghton Library was built, Jackson's collecting activities for Harvard were in full career. The detailed story of his achievement is set out in his annual reports, which began to appear in 1942 and were foreshadowed by the descriptive booklet he prepared for the opening of the library earlier that same year. For the first time he was dealing not merely with English books before 1641, or even English literature in general, but with the whole range of subjects, cultures, languages, and periods represented in a great university library. His response was quick and sure. Instinctively he sensed the important books even when he could not read a word of the language involved; and he continued his custom of rigorous self-education by seeking out and mastering the works that could best inform him about an unfamiliar field. Since all his life he required less sleep than most men, he spent many night hours gutting one book after another and filing their contents away in his extraordinary memory for future reference.

First he explored the Harvard collections in detail; then he followed the library axiom of building on strength. Certain fields, he felt, were a Harvard responsibility: for example, the leading authors of New England. He collected their published works in depth, but even more important, he set out to garner their personal papers. The current vogue for collecting literary archives did not then exist in university circles. In fact, not many years earlier a previous librarian at Harvard had declared that the library *should not* collect manuscript materials if they could be avoided.

Jackson was a pioneer in this kind of endeavor. As so often during his career, he recognized the importance of a neglected area and then persuaded friends and administrators of the validity of his judgment. In the field of New England letters, he secured from their respective trustees the permanent deposit of the Emerson and Longfellow papers; from descendants the deposit or gift of the Holmes, Lowell, Melville, Alcott, Higginson, Aldrich, Howells, and various allied archives; and from a generous donor the money to purchase the Emily Dickinson papers. These were backed up by an impressive series of archives of the great New England families whose interests were basically mercantile or financial but who also upheld the grand intellectual tradition of the region and associated on equal terms with artists, poets, philosophers, and scholars. In pursuit of such goals he was irresistibly enthusiastic, and not much on which he had set his heart ever eluded him. Jackson in full cry after a desirable acquisition was a phenomenon not soon to be forgotten.

Extremely limited income from endowed funds forced him to rely heavily on gifts in cash and in kind. Although new to raising money, he speedily became expert. By knowing the personal interests of prospective donors, he was able to bring giver and gift together in a pleasing harmony that resulted in substantial gains for the library and a glow of achievement for its benefactors. At a meeting of the Colonial Society, he once remarked, "Steve, I believe you and I are the only men here who can truly appreciate the significance of this [10th century] manuscript of Horace," which led to further conversation on the topic. Not long after, Stephen W. Phillips (Harvard 1895), had the pleasure of giving Harvard the Horace that is now MS Latin 199, one of the two earliest Latin classical text manuscripts of any substance in the United States.

In acquiring private libraries and collections for Harvard, Jackson was equally successful. Here his study of provenance and his long memory were of great value. He could walk into a library new to him and straightway begin to tell its owner all sorts of unsuspected facts about the books: who had owned them and when, what sales they had appeared in, the meaning of this armorial bearing or that classical motto, and very often the number and location of other copies. His wide experience and acquaintance in the book world frequently enabled him to put a collector on the trail of an elusive desideratum. Faced with such expertise, collectors readily agreed to designate their treasures for Harvard, and long lines of books followed this Pied Piper to the library shelves. His annual reports contain on every page the names of those who contributed so much to the success of his collecting endeavors.

Jackson's collecting was always highly selective. He never grasped merely because the object was scarce or costly — though he was sometimes devilishly ingenious at justification. The scholarly dealers learned that Harvard would give intelligent attention to the books they had to offer even when relatively obscure. They responded with the kind of support that is absolutely essential for a learned library. As far as his limited funds would allow, Jackson bought if convinced of the importance of the book for Harvard.

The test of a librarian's acquisitions is not rarity, curiosity, or monetary value. These are side issues too often mistaken for the main purpose of collecting. The real test is the use scholars make of the collections. By this standard there can be no question of Jackson's brilliant success. During his administration the number of readers in the Houghton Library increased threefold; inquiries by mail and requests for photographic services swelled to a flood threatening to engulf the staff. The acknowledgments to Jackson and the library in innumerable articles, monographs, dissertations, books, and editions on a bewildering variety of subjects provide additional evidence of the importance of his achievement.

The funds available to Jackson were limited by subject as well as amount, which led to periodic intramural encounters that were thoroughly enjoyed by all participants. For some years, until their retirement, the two Gertrudes — Miss Shaw and Miss Sullivan — ran the Order Department in Widener and had charge of assigning funds to all purchases. Since rare book purchasing depends upon so many variable factors, the librarian cannot simply count on buying so many dollars' worth of this subject or that. The books must be acquired as they can be found, a circumstance that frequently involves pounding a slightly squarish peg into a somewhat rounded hole.

Every two weeks or, in slack times, once a month, Jackson would display his new acquisitions to the two Gertrudes and exercise all his salesmanship to "sell" the books to such funds as were available. Since some funds were so restricted as to be difficult to utilize, he naturally tried to push acquisitions into them before exhausting "easy" funds of more general application. The resulting debates frequently elicited gales of laughter as he expounded new theories of flexibility for the De-grand Fund ("for French science") or exhibited a technicality to justify other dispositions. At last all would be amicably settled and Miss Shaw would enter the date and fund in pencil in her neat hand on the verso of each title page. When she and Miss Sullivan retired, Jackson began to do all his own funding, but these friendly book-flytings were sorely missed.

World War II, which the United States had entered just before the Houghton Library officially opened, quickly brought changes. Both staff and readers dwindled. Philip Hofer temporarily crossed the river to the Business School, acting as Assistant Dean to relieve a regular staff member who had departed for government service. In 1945 Jackson himself made a goodwill tour of South American libraries under the auspices of the State Department, but most of the time he remained in Cambridge, looking after the affairs of the library.

Because of the war, many of the overseas sources of ordinary current library material — periodicals and the like — were cut off. Keyes D. Metcalf wisely made the funds thus released available to Jackson, so that temporarily he had command of greatly increased purchasing power. At the same time unusual opportunities arose and competition from other purchasers diminished. For example, Jackson learned that one of the stately homes of England was reinforcing its windows against blast with sacks full of the family library, and he negotiated to purchase the books at a rate that more than permitted replacing them with sandbags — actually about two dollars a volume. Tears of bitter envy may be shed by present-day librarians upon learning that these were mostly *S.T.C.* and Wing period books in decent, though not flashy, bindings.

Some big ones also got away. Good books came up in periods of financial drought, near the end of the library's fiscal year, and donors could not always be found. In 1945 there was a chance to acquire the entire remainder of Sir Thomas Phillipps' manuscripts, numbering some 12,000 items. Philip and Lionel Robinson, the London book dealers who were negotiating with the trustees of the estate for their purchase, offered to turn them over to Harvard for a modest commission. The sum was large, though not impossible; but Jackson had not yet learned all the ins and outs of raising money. Furthermore, by the greatest of bad luck he was in the midst of his South American tour when the negotiations reached a crisis, and the collection was lost.[7] In the event, the Robinsons purchased the collection on their own account. Harvard along with other libraries and collectors has been buying individual items from it ever since, by private treaty and in the apparently endless series of auction sales it has provided. It is unfortunate to have to record a lost cause, but as Jackson said, a good bookman is never able to forget the books that have escaped his grasp, no matter what the reason. And the incident illustrates, as vividly as do all the successes spread in his annual reports, how he positively welcomed a great challenge when it offered a worthy goal.

Meanwhile Jackson's scholarly work did not flag. He kept quantities of notes on all kinds of bibliographical points and topics, and from time to time prepared articles based on his findings for journals or festschriften. By no means all of them concerned books of the *S.T.C.* period, though these remained his greatest interest. Latterly his papers were mainly directed to the *Harvard Library Bulletin*, which printed sixteen of his contributions during its fourteen-year span. A major work was *Records of the Court of the Stationers' Company 1602 to 1640*, an edition with exhaustive notes of the hitherto unpublished Court Book C, issued by the Bibliographical Society in 1957.[8] His annual reports, which he faced each winter with ever louder groans, were as scholarly as he could make them, considering the number and variety of entries in each and the relatively cramped space at his disposal. He devoted many hours of concentrated toil to the task of transforming the dry bones of the accessions records provided by his staff into the enticing account that was eagerly read by bookmen all over the world.

His great work, however, was that in which he was associated with Dr. F. S. Ferguson: the revision of the *Short-title Catalogue*, which really began with the publication of the *S.T.C.* in 1926 and increasingly occupied his time and thought as the years went by. Ferguson had seen and collated most of the early English books that passed through the London market for many years and had collected and indexed printers' marks, compartments, initials, and the like. When he retired from the firm of Quaritch, he continued at a desk reserved for him in the stacks of the British Museum, making a weekly trip to the Bodleian to check

[7] A. N. L. Munby, *The Dispersal of the Phillipps Library* (Cambridge, 1960), p. 102.

[8] Jackson joined the society in 1932 and became its Hon. Secretary for America in 1936.

points on *S.T.C.* books. Jackson, for his part, visited collection after collection on both sides of the Atlantic, recording what he saw. He assumed responsibility for consolidating and organizing the enormous mass of information, and the manscript took shape in his office.

Scholarly librarians and collectors all over the world gave unstinting help through correspondence. Of invaluable assistance was the late L. W. Hanson of the Bodleian, an old and dear personal friend of Jackson's as well as a powerful supporter of the revised *S.T.C.* Hanson took the lead in the Council of the Bibliographical Society to ensure the continuity of work on the *S.T.C.* after Jackson's untimely death.

The original *S.T.C.* was largely based on printed catalogues and secondary sources; the revision, as far as possible, was derived from personal examination of the books themselves. As a result, ghosts were laid, duplications eliminated, anonymous printers identified, and the whole corpus of information immensely refined in many ways. Titles, editions, and issues were discovered and differentiated. When published, the new *S.T.C.* will add some 10,000 entries to the 26,000 in the original, and between two and three thousand of these will be new titles.

At Jackson's death in October 1964 the revision had reached the letter *R*. For the remainder, his notes were full and usable; with the coöperation of Dr. F. S. Ferguson and under the direction of Miss Katharine Pantzer, the latest of Jackson's research assistants, the work proceeds, with the completed text expected by 1970. At every stage the information so painstakingly gathered has been at the disposal of all scholars wishing to consult it, with a freedom typifying the way Jackson shared his fund of knowledge with all competent inquirers.

During his lifetime the eminence of his scholarship received public recognition in honorary degrees from Williams College (A.M., 1938), Harvard (L.H.D., 1962), and Oxford (Litt.D., 1964); a fellowship in the Society of Antiquaries, London; and memberships in the Massachusetts Historical Society, the American Antiquarian Society, and the American Academy of Arts and Sciences. In 1946 he was nominated for the Presidency of the Bibliographical Society of America, of which — as everyone was astonished to learn — he was not yet a member. He joined, was elected, and served as President for two years. In 1958 the Stationers' Company of London honored him with their medal, and he was posthumously awarded the Gold Medal of the Bibliographical Society, London — perhaps the highest honor in the world of books.

INTRODUCTION

The bibliography course at Harvard absorbed much of Jackson's thought and effort. Its format and syllabus were entirely of his own devising. Composed mainly of graduate students in the English Department, it met once a week through both terms of the academic year in a two-hour session with a short break for tea and a cigarette. Enrollment was limited to ten or twelve at most, and some years it was much smaller.

The baptism of fire was immediate: Jackson's customary inaugural lecture, "Linked and Unlinked Books," was sufficiently different from anything the class had ever heard to bring them to a pitch of attention that never slackened throughout the year. All students were expected to master McKerrow's *Introduction to Bibliography* as rapidly as possible. With that as a common background, Jackson launched into the bibliographical stratosphere in all directions. Each session revolved about a special topic: signatures, cancels, collation, provenance, type identification, and the like. Jackson's remarks were generally informal, based partly on outline notes but mostly on actual examples chosen from Harvard collections. He demonstrated each book in turn, then passed it about the table for the students to see at close range. Few could forget this experience of examining a procession of fascinating books with perhaps the best guide in the world standing by to explain and illuminate.

Each member also had to take part in composing and printing a short text edited by the class. Producing this pamphlet provided an actual printing experience that was more valuable than reading any textbook, and their copies were greatly treasured by those who had worked on them. A high point of each year was an invitation from the Jacksons to cocktails and a buffet supper, after which all hands sat about the dining-room table to stitch the pamphlets into their covers. The size of Jackson's martinis was matched only by their excellence, and these combined with Mrs. Jackson's savory casseroles to produce a glow seldom experienced by the hard-working denizens of the Graduate School of Arts and Sciences.

The course regularly concluded with the presentation of an hour-long paper by each member. Sometimes it represented the bibliographical chapter of a doctoral dissertation, but more often it dealt with a problem assigned by Jackson. Frequently these developed into publishable form and found their way into the pages of some bibliographical journal, guided there by the good offices of the instructor, who was generous with praise and support whenever he thought it deserved.

From time to time, with the help of others in the library, Jackson also gave undergraduate courses designed to encourage embryo book-collectors. These courses never enjoyed a success comparable to his graduate course or to the earlier course in which George Parker Winship had nurtured so many future friends of the library. The fields of collecting practical for an undergraduate had certainly changed since Winship's day; almost as certainly the temper of the undergraduate body had changed. But whatever the reasons, Jackson worried about the problem. He was concerned to have the library reach as many facets of university life as possible. In his last year he devoted much thought and effort to planning a wholly new course on the history of the book, intended for the program in General Education. It was to treat books as a vehicle of art and a medium for the communication of literature, thought, and history to later generations. The course was launched in the autumn of 1964, but unhappily he did not live to see it to completion.

Jackson did much to strengthen the link between the library and the faculty, even as Mr. Metcalf had predicted when advocating his appointment. He encouraged teachers to bring their classes to Houghton and expose them to the dramatic impact of primary source materials; he staged exhibitions tied to academic meetings and courses; and he was always ready to provide bibliographical expertise and advice at need, or to draw upon his wide personal acquaintance to smooth the way for Harvard scholars wishing to consult the great libraries of the world.

Jackson's appointment carried faculty standing. From the beginning he met the Harvard community with ease on its own ground, and not merely when the topic was books and manuscripts. The first day that he entered the dining room of the Faculty Club for lunch he saw no familiar face, so he sat unbidden at the table immediately to the right of the entrance. Long custom had hallowed that table to the use of archeologists and anthropologists, but he did not know it. Shortly the anthropologists arrived; Jackson found their professional conversation as agreeable as they found his. For twenty-five years he was a welcome member of their company, lunching with them more often than not. It may not be sheer coincidence that after his death a Harvard archeologist took his place as President of the Club of Odd Volumes.

In his relations with his colleagues, his staff, his extramural friends, and his students, Jackson observed the same high standards he brought to his work. Unswervingly loyal, he expected the same loyalty in return. He was unsparing of himself in his devotion to his scholarly duties, and he could not help showing at least slight disappointment when his colleagues did not work as hard and as long as he did. Since he would forgo food, sleep, and even cigarettes to complete a self-assigned task, and regarded weekends and holidays as a time to work all the harder because no visitors would interrupt, most of his colleagues at least occasionally experienced twinges of inadequacy.

He was intolerant of dishonesty in any form, and he was absolutely enraged by double-dealing. He seldom could bear confrontation with stupidity. Occasionally a student or a reader in the library would be utterly unable to grasp a bibliographical point or procedure. One such session was enough to bring Jackson to a boil. Thereafter he generally begged some other member of the staff to deal with visits of the unwitting offender; he knew that another interview would probably make him lose his temper completely. When irritated by incompetence or ignorance, his wrath was impressive, and some never recovered from exposure to it.

Jackson placed a special value on his association with the last vestiges of male society in an equal-suffrage world. He regarded his membership in the Senior Common Room of Lincoln College, Oxford, presided over by his old friend Walter Oakeshott, as a great privilege and a pleasure. He took pride in belonging to the Athenaeum in London, the Century Association and the Grolier Club in New York, the Club of Odd Volumes and the Tavern Club in Boston, and he particularly relished the semi-annual journeys of the Walpole Society, among whose members were many of his closest friends. The Walpole's emphasis upon fine food and drink accorded completely with his ideas of the amenities of life. A sideline of the investigations during his student trip to Europe had been a note-taking tour of the wine countries, and he never lost his intense interest in a good table and a sound cellar. After a Walpole expedition, colleagues were always regaled with an account of menus and vintages only slightly less detailed than his account of books seen en route.

If books represented only one small facet of the Walpole Society's concern with antiquities, the purest bibliophily was promised him by his election in 1964 to the Roxburghe Club, the senior book collectors' club of the English-speaking world. Its foundation dates from the Roxburghe sale of 1812, which the leading collectors of Great Britain, organized by the Reverend Thomas Frognall Dibdin, decided to commemorate by forming a society. Only a few Americans have been elected to this small circle. There was a peculiar fitness in having a Dibdinian association crown Jackson's career, as it might be said to have opened it with his Grolier Club address of more than thirty years before. The one meeting of the Roxburghe Club that he was fated to attend was possibly the highlight of his last trip to England in the summer of 1964. It was held at Cambridge with Lord Rothschild as host. Jackson brought back to the other Cambridge glowing accounts of the meeting and banquet held in Trinity College Library. Election to the Roxburghe, coming in the same year as his honorary degree from Oxford, represented all that he valued most highly in the world of books and men.

Although he certainly preferred male conversation, no one could be more charming and courtly with the ladies than Jackson. And when he could be persuaded to turn from his favorite topic to other matters, his conversation lost none of its sparkle or liveliness. For many years the anniversary of the dedication of the Houghton Library was celebrated by the staff with a square dance in the Exhibition Room. While younger colleagues retired to chairs to rest their feet and mop their brows, Jackson would still be on the floor, dancing every dance with vigor and grace.

Despite his sedentary occupation, Jackson relished outdoor activity. Each autumn he cruised for ten days or two weeks off the coast of Maine with his good friends, David and Stephen Wheatland, in Steve's boat, the *Nimbus*. Starting from Sorrento in Frenchman's Bay, they usually sailed still further down east, dropping anchor in small harbors by night to bring together fresh-caught native lobsters with the vintage wines Jackson had selected in Boston. He would return, deeply tanned and relaxed, ready for the new academic year. These cruises extended in an unbroken series for twenty-four years. The important part they played in his life was properly commemorated in the citation for his Oxford D. Litt., which described him as one "qui tamen non modo lepidi libelli sed etiam phaseli celeris amore doctum Catullum aemulatur." [9]

[9] "Who was like learned Catullus in his love of both a fine book and a swift sailboat."

When Jackson could find time, he loved to tramp through such parts of the New England forests and mountains as were relatively unspoiled, sometimes camping with his son. At the library he was surrounded by bird watchers, chief among whom was G. W. Cottrell, Jr. Since Jackson respected mastery of any subject, he viewed Cottrell's ornithological pursuits with something more than tolerance. But he was less tolerant of those who simply went along for the ride. Occasionally he and Mrs. Jackson accompanied the Cottrells on the annual expedition of an irregular group called the Pawtuckaway Mountain Bird Club, some of whom knew a good deal about birds and some of whom did not. For one such trip Cottrell borrowed a stuffed tropical bird from the Museum of Comparative Zoology, and Jackson planted it in a tree a short distance from the proposed route of the explorers. His delight was unbounded at the astonishment and puzzlement of those not in on the secret and not sufficiently expert to recognize the hoax.

In fact, a boyish sense of humor was an important part of Jackson's temperament. He relished jokes ranging from the broadly practical to the highly sophisticated, even when the laugh was at his own expense. One such joke that he did not relish quite as much, however, began with the receipt by mail of a letter from an unfamiliar writer who said he had a lot of old books and wondered if they were worth anything. Unwilling to ship such bulky objects, he enclosed the title-pages, which he had torn out for the purpose — title-pages of a dozen or so *S.T.C.* books, one of them bearing an unrecorded imprint. Every effort to get in touch with the sender proved unavailing, and the effect was even more maddening when a second lot of title-pages arrived a week later. After that, silence. Not until after Jackson's death did the perpetrator reveal himself as a New York book dealer who had accumulated bits and scraps of defective books with just such a practical joke in mind. His exploit is immortalized, if obscurely, in the revised *S.T.C.*, which records the variant title-page for which no complete book is known to exist.

Jackson's own humor was often displayed at the weekly meetings of the male staff, whom he banded together under the name of the Collation Club. The club met (as it still does) every Tuesday at 12:30 for sherry in his office and then adjourned to the Faculty Club for lunch. Conversation was informal, and sometimes the meetings were further enlivened by a guest from the book world. The only time a dreadful silence fell was on those occasions when Jackson hopefully called for volunteers to mount a new exhibition.

During the summer of 1950, when he and his wife were in England, a kind of madness seized his stay-at-home staff. They leagued together to produce a burlesque library report, vying with each other to invent absurd but appropriate items. Entitled *The Haughton Library Report of Accessions for the Year 1949–50*, it was larded with the very phrases Jackson habitually used in his serious reports. It was printed by the Harvard Printing Office with identical typography. Instead of the usual *Veritas* shield, the cover bore a device drawn by Fernando Zobel symbolizing the Collation Club.

At a small formal meeting of the Club immediately on his return, Hofer placed the first copy in Jackson's hand with a short speech to the effect that it had been done to spare him the effort of composing his usual report. Jackson's jaw dropped momentarily, but he soon began to chuckle and then to roar with laughter as he read the whole report aloud. He took it for the compliment it was meant to be, although he later admitted that it made him terribly self-conscious in writing his next reports.

The *Haughton Report* typified the deep respect and affection in which Jackson was held by his staff. His ideas and ideals of professionalism pervaded the library and encouraged a vigorous esprit de corps. His colleagues held it a privilege to be associated with him, even in a minor capacity, in the development, growth, and maintenance of the Houghton Library.

But greater by far than his impact on any person or group of persons was his permanent effect on the Harvard College Library. He arrived in Cambridge superbly equipped at a crucial moment in the library's history. It was the last gasp for many important lines of collecting. He saw what had to be done, and he did it to the utmost limit of his energy and ability. Before his death on October 18, 1964, he had seen the growth of the collections for which he was responsible matched by their enormously increased use by scholars. It will take years for the resources he added to the library to be truly known and appreciated by the academic community at Harvard and in the learned world at large; and these resources will, quite literally, never be exhausted. It is a weighty responsibility for those who follow him to conserve the collections he brought together, to maintain the momentum and direction of the collecting he inaugurated, and to continue the humane administration he established.

A librarian and bibliographer of Jackson's caliber occupies very nearly the position of a public utility in the scholarly world. Throughout his career he was strategically associated with one important collection after another. This was somewhat of a disadvantage from the point of view of his own research because of the barrage of inquiries and appeals for help to which he was constantly subjected. Since he always responded generously to an intelligent query, much of his time and energy was expended on problems that were not his own. Nevertheless, the recurring theme of Jackson's work was always the revision of the *Short-title Catalogue*. In addition, he found time to complete three books — the Pforzheimer Catalogue, the court-book of the Stationers' Company, and the Dibdin check-list, the last of these published posthumously — and he completed the text for the Chapin Catalogue, even if it never saw print. His annual reports as Librarian of the Houghton Library were eagerly awaited and eagerly read throughout the world of books and libraries. His other works, many but not all dependent upon his research for the *S.T.C.*, were scattered through the pages of learned journals, festschriften, and the publications of other scholars whom he had aided or encouraged. The present selection of his published and unpublished writings, with its accompanying bibliography, is intended to serve as a monument to the man and as at least a partial record of his career in scholarship.

W. H. B.

Cambridge, Massachusetts
21 September 1966

I. William Alexander Jackson in 1937

William Alexander Jackson

Bibliography of Published Writings

1926

1. "The Williams Chapter of Alpha Delta Phi," *Williams Alumni Review*, XVIII, no. 5 (March 1926), 230–232.

1932

2. "Wayland's Edition of 'The Mirror for Magistrates,'" *The Library*, 4th series, XIII (1932–3) 155–157, illus.

1933

3. "Woodes's *Conflict of Conscience*," *Times Literary Supplement*, no. 1649 (7 September 1933), 592.
4. Letter to Christopher Morley on punctuation in the inscription on Marshall's portrait of Shakespeare in the *Poems* (1640), printed in "The Bowling Green," *Saturday Review of Literature*, X, no. 8 (9 September 1933), 95.
5. Review of R. B. McKerrow and F. S. Ferguson, *Title-page Borders Used in England and Scotland: 1485–1640* (Oxford, 1932), in *New York Herald Tribune Books*, 28 May 1933, p. 14.

1934

6. "Edward Gwynn," *The Library*, 4th series, XV (1934–5), 92–96.
7. "Counterfeit Printing in Jacobean Times," *The Library*, 4th series, XV (1934–5), 364–376.

8. G. C. Moore Smith, "Printed Books with Gabriel Harvey's Autograph or MS. Notes," *Modern Language Review*, XXIX (January 1934), 68–70, 321–322, containing many notes sent the author in letters from W.A.J. and so acknowledged.

1935

9. "Proof-reading in the Sixteenth and Seventeenth Centuries," *The Colophon*, new series, I, no. 2 (Autumn 1935), 254–260; in part a review of Percy Simpson, *Proof-reading in the Sixteenth, Seventeenth, and Eighteenth Centuries* (Oxford, 1935).

1936

10. "A Note on Robert Greene's *Planetomachia* (1585)," with Chauncey Sanders, *The Library*, 4th series, XVI (1935–6), 444–447.

11. "The Textbook of the Past," in *The Textbook of the Future and Its Forerunners, a Program for an Exhibition at the National Arts Club by the American Institute of Graphic Arts* (New York, 1936), pp. 8–9.

12. "A London Bookseller's Ledger of 1535," *The Colophon*, new series, I, no. 4 (Spring 1936), 498–509.

1937

13. "The Library of Lt.-Col. W. E. Moss," in "Notes for Bibliophiles," ed. Leonard L. Mackall, *New York Herald Tribune Books*, 7 March 1937.

1939

14. Bibliographical note in Jan van der Noot, *Theatre for Worldlings*, introduction by Louis S. Friedland (New York, Scholars' Facsimiles and Reprints, 1939), pp. xviii–xxi.

1940

15. *The Carl H. Pforzheimer Library: English Literature 1475–1700* (New York, privately printed, 1940), 3 volumes: I, pp. xli + [i],

378 + [4]; II, v + [i], 379–791 + [5]; III, v + [i], 793–1305 + [3]; illus. Limited to 150 copies.

16. "The Lamont Collection on the Spanish Armada," *Harvard Library Notes*, no. 30 (March 1940), 303–307, illus.

17. *The Harvard Library. The New York Meeting of the Associated Harvard Clubs*, 17–19 May 1940 (n.p., 1940). Pp. [8].

1941

18. "Some Limitations of Microfilm," *Papers of the Bibliographical Society of America*, XXXV (1941), 281–288.

19. "The New Rare Book Library," *Harvard Library Notes*, no. 31 (June 1941), 23–24, illus.

20. Review of *The Cambridge Bibliography of English Literature*, ed. F. W. Bateson (New York and Cambridge, England, 1941), in *The Publishers' Weekly*, CXXXIX (19 April 1941), 1676–1677.

1942

21. *The Houghton Library, Harvard College* (Cambridge, Massachusetts, 1942). Pp. 27.

22. *The Houghton Library Report of Accessions for the Year 1941–42* [no. 1] (Cambridge, Massachusetts, 1942). Pp. [ii], 32.

23. "Bibliography," a column comprising "The Fate of English Libraries," and "Historical Library of the Yale School of Medicine," *Print, a Quarterly Journal of the Graphic Arts*, II, nos. 3–4 (dated 1941, published 1942), 139–140.

24. "The Matt B. Jones Collection," *Harvard Library Notes*, no. 32 (March 1942), 95–96.

1943

25. *The Houghton Library Report of Accessions for the Year 1942–43* [no. 2] (Cambridge, Massachusetts, 1943). Pp. [ii], 32.

26. "Notes on English 'Publishers' Bindings' of the Sixteenth and Sev-

enteenth Centuries," in *Bookmen's Holiday: Notes and Studies Written and Gathered in Tribute to Harry Miller Lydenberg* (New York, 1943), pp. 483–488, illus. Also a separate paged 1–6.

27. "The Books and Manuscripts [of Grenville Lindall Winthrop]," *Bulletin of the Fogg Museum of Art*, X (1943), 71.

28. "Rare Books at Harvard," *College and Research Libraries*, V (1943), 31–35, illus.

29. Review of J. Basil Oldham, *Shrewsbury School Library Bindings* (Oxford, 1943), in *Papers of the Bibliographical Society of America*, XXXVII (1943), 322–324.

1944

30. *The Houghton Library Report of Accessions for the Year 1943–44* [no. 3] (Cambridge, Massachusetts, 1944). Pp. [ii], 32.

31. *A Paper Read at the Presentation of a Gutenberg Bible to the Harvard College Library by Mr. George D. Widener on Behalf of His Sister Mrs. Widener Dixon and Himself* ([Cambridge, Massachusetts] 1944). Pp. [ii], 11, illus.

32. "A Gutenberg Bible Presented to Harvard," in "Notes for Bibliophiles," ed. Lawrence C. Wroth, *New York Herald Tribune Weekly Book Review*, 28 May 1944.

33. "The Houghton Library," in *The Canadian Collection at Harvard University*, ed. William Inglis Morse (Cambridge, Massachusetts, 1944), pp. 12–14.

34. "Alfred William Pollard," an obituary in Herbert Reichner's catalogue 5, *Great Thinkers* (New York, 1944), pp. [3–4]. Reprinted in Brick Row Book Shop *Special List* no. 21 (1946).

35. Review of Fremont Rider, *The Scholar and the Future of the Research Library* (New York, 1944), in *The New England Quarterly*, XVII (1944), 613–616.

1945

36. *The Houghton Library Report of Accessions for the Year 1944–45* [no. 4] (Cambridge, Massachusetts, 1945). Pp. [ii], 36.

37. "The Study of Bibliography in America," in *The Bibliographical Society 1892–1942, Studies in Retrospect* (London, 1945), pp. 185–187.

38. Review of *Letters of Thomas J. Wise to John Henry Wrenn*, ed. Fannie E. Ratchford (New York, 1944), in *Papers of the Bibliographical Society of America*, XXXIX (1945), 169–171.

39. "Houghton Library, C. H. and L., 1944–1945, Reports on MSS., and Printed Books," in *The Canadian Collection at Harvard University . . . Bulletin II*, ed. William Inglis Morse (Cambridge, Massachusetts, 1945), pp. 46–51.

1946

40. *The Houghton Library Report of Accessions for the Year 1945–46* [no. 5] (Cambridge, Massachusetts, 1946). Pp. [ii], 37.

41. "John L. Clawson's Early English Books," in *To Dr. R. . . .* (Philadelphia, 1946), pp. 97–119.

42. "The Funeral Procession of Queen Elizabeth," *The Library*, 4th series, XXVI, (1945–6), 262–271.

43. "Fakes and Forgeries," excerpted by Taylor Starck from a paper delivered at a meeting of the American Academy of Arts and Sciences (n. p., 9 October 1946). Pp. 3; offset from typescript.

44. "Houghton Library, C. H. and L., 1945–46, Report on MSS., and Printed Books," in *The Canadian Collection at Harvard University . . . Bulletin III*, ed. William Inglis Morse (Cambridge, Massachusetts, 1946), pp. 47–52.

45. "J. R. Lowell and John Locke," *The New England Quarterly*, XIX (1946), 113–114.

46. Review of *American Book Prices Current, 1944–5*, ed. Colton Storm (New York, 1945), in *Publishers' Weekly*, CXLIX (19 January 1946), 330–331.

1947

47. *The Houghton Library Report of Accessions for the Year 1946–47* [no. 6] (Cambridge, Massachusetts, 1947). Pp. [ii], 37.

48. "Humphrey Dyson and His Collections of Elizabethan Proclamations," *Harvard Library Bulletin*, I (1947), 76–89, illus.

49. "The First Separately Printed English Translation of Horace," *Harvard Library Bulletin*, I (1947), 238–241, illus.

50. "The Carl T. Keller Collection of *Don Quixote*," *Harvard Library Bulletin*, I (1947), 306–310.

51. "Additions to the C. H. and L. Collections in the Houghton Library, 1946," in *The Canadian Collection at Harvard University . . . Bulletin IV*, ed. William Inglis Morse (Cambridge, Massachusetts, 1947), pp. 108–110.

52. "Lucy Eugenia Osborne," *Williams Alumni Review*, XL, no. 1 (October 1947), 19–20.

1948

53. *The Houghton Library Report of Accessions for the Year 1947–48* [no. 7] (Cambridge, Massachusetts, 1948). Pp. [ii], 37.

54. "English Title-labels to the End of the Seventeenth Century," *Harvard Library Bulletin*, III (1948), 222–229, illus.

55. "Signatures in Nineteenth-Century American Printing," *The Library*, 5th series, III (1948), 224.

56. "The Lamport Hall-Britwell Court Books," in *Joseph Quincy Adams Memorial Studies*, ed. James G. McManaway, Giles E. Dawson, and Edwin E. Willoughby (Washington, 1948), pp. 587–599.

57. "Additions to the Canadian History and Literature Collections in the Houghton Library, 1947," in *The Canadian Collection at Harvard University . . . Bulletin V*, ed. William Inglis Morse (Cambridge, Massachusetts, 1948), pp. 112–114.

1949

58. *The Houghton Library Report of Accessions for the Year 1948–49* [no. 8] (Cambridge, Massachusetts, 1949). Pp. [ii], 35.

59. "The Importance of Rare Books and Manuscripts in a University

Library," *Harvard Library Bulletin*, III (1949), 315–326. This paper, containing the quintessence of W.A.J.'s philosophy of collecting, was first delivered in a symposium in Cambridge on "The Place of the Library in a University," 30 March 1949, honoring the opening of the Lamont Library; subsequently he read it at Syracuse University, 21 November 1961, and at the opening of the Beinecke Library at Yale, 3 April 1964. It was also published as follows: in *The Place of the Library in a University* (Cambridge, Massachusetts, 1950), pp. 26–37 [from the type of the *Harvard Library Bulletin*, re-paged]; in *The Courier* [publication of the Syracuse University Library Associates], II, no. 3 (October 1962), 2–12; and as a separate entitled *Universities and Rare Books* (Syracuse, New York, 1962). Pp. 12.

60. "Humphrey Dyson's Library, or, Some Observations on the Survival of Books," *Papers of the Bibliographical Society of America*, XLIII (1949), 279–287.

61. "Canadian Literature at Harvard," in *The Canadian Collection at Harvard University . . . Bulletin VI*, ed. William Inglis Morse (Cambridge, Massachusetts, 1948–1949), pp. 98–102.

62. Preface to *The Cost Books of Ticknor and Fields*, ed. Warren S. Tryon and William Charvat (New York, 1949), pp. [ix].

63. Review of Allen T. Hazen, *A Bibliography of Horace Walpole* (New Haven, 1948), in *Philological Quarterly*, XXVIII (1949), 409.

1950

64. *The Houghton Library Report of Accessions for the Year 1949–50* [no. 9] (Cambridge, Massachusetts, 1950). Pp. [ii], 40.

65. "Sir Robert Bruce Cotton's *A short view of the long life and raigne of Henry the third*," *Harvard Library Bulletin*, IV (1950), 28–38, illus.

1951

66. *The Houghton Library Report of Accessions for the Year 1950–51* [no. 10] (Cambridge, Massachusetts, 1951). Pp. [ii], 37.

67. *A General Note of the Prices of Binding all Sorts of Books, 1669* (Cambridge, Massachusetts, 1951), a facsimile with a 2-page note. Limited to 350 copies, as a keepsake for a meeting of the Bibliographical Society of America.

68. "Tunc et Nunc: or the Pepys and Taylor Collections of Early English Books on Navigation," in *Essays Honoring Lawrence C. Wroth* (Portland, Maine, 1951), pp. 195–201.

69. "The William King Richardson Library," *Harvard Library Bulletin*, V (1951), 328–337, illus.

1952

70. *The Houghton Library Report of Accessions for the Year 1951–52* [no. 11] (Cambridge, Massachusetts, 1952). Pp. [ii], 40.

71. Appendix to Roman Jakobson, "The Archetype of the First Edition of the *Igor Tale*," *Harvard Library Bulletin*, VI (1952), 14.

72. "Did Halliwell Steal and Mutilate the Phillipps Copy of *Hamlet*, 1603?" Appendix B in A. N. L. Munby, *The Family Affairs of Sir Thomas Phillipps* (Cambridge, England, 1952), pp. 116–117.

73. "*Heuy newes of an horryble erthquake in Scarbaria*," *Harvard Library Bulletin*, VI (1952), 248–250.

74. Review of William Beattie, *The Chepman and Myllar Prints, a Facsimile with a Bibliographical Note* (Edinburgh, 1950), in *Scottish Historical Review*, XXXI (1952), 89–90.

1953

75. *The Houghton Library Report of Accessions for the Year 1952–53* [no. 12] (Cambridge, Massachusetts, 1953). Pp. [ii], 45.

76. "Three Printed English Indulgences at Harvard," *Harvard Library Bulletin*, VII (1953), 229–231.

77. "The 'Lincolne Nosegay' Books," in *Books and the Man. Antiquarian Booksellers' Association Annual* (London, 1953), pp. 25–30.

78. Foreword to Thomas Franklin Currier, *A Bibliography of Oliver Wendell Holmes*, ed. Eleanor M. Tilton (New York, 1953), pp. v–vi; reprinted with variants in *Antiquarian Bookman*, 1 August 1953, pp. 299–300.

1954

79. *The Houghton Library Report of Accessions for the Year 1953–54* [no. 13] (Cambridge, Massachusetts, 1954). Pp. [ii], 48.

80. "Printed Quire and Sheet Numbers," *Harvard Library Bulletin*, VIII (1954), 96–102, illus.

81. "Printed Quire and Sheet Numbers, II," *Harvard Library Bulletin*, VIII (1954), 363–364.

82. Review of *A Contribution to a Union Catalogue of Sixteenth Century Imprints in Certain New England Libraries* (Providence, 1953), in *Renaissance News*, VII (1954), 43–44.

83. Review of *American Book-prices Current, 1952–53*, ed. Edward Lazare (New York, 1953), in *Library Journal*, LXXIX (1954), 613.

84. Review of *Transactions of the Cambridge Bibliographical Society, Vol. I, Part V* (Cambridge, England, 1953), in *The Library*, 5th series, IX (1954), 68–69.

1955

85. *The Houghton Library Report of Accessions for the Year 1954–55* [no. 14] (Cambridge, Massachusetts, 1955). Pp. [ii], 53.

86. Foreword to *Harvard College Library. Illuminated & Calligraphic Manuscripts* (Cambridge, Massachusetts, 1955), p. [3].

87. "The Revised *STC*: A Progress Report," *The Book Collector*, IV (1955), 16–27.

88. Letter of tribute in *To Hans Nachod on the Occasion of His Seventieth Birthday* ([New York], 1955), unpaged.

89. Appendix to Roman Jakobson, "Ivan Fedorov's Primer," *Harvard Library Bulletin*, IX (1955), 40–42.

1956

90. *The Houghton Library Report of Accessions for the Year 1955–56* [no. 15] (Cambridge, Massachusetts, 1956). Pp. [ii], 54.

91. "The Belknap Press," in *Waldron Phoenix Belknap, Jr.* (Cambridge, Massachusetts, 1956), pp. 15–17. W.A.J. also chose the design for Belknap's bookplate; see p. 18.

1957

92. *The Houghton Library Report of Accessions for the Year 1956–57* [no. 16] (Cambridge, Massachusetts, 1957). Pp. [ii], 44.

93. *Records of the Court of the Stationers' Company 1602 to 1640* (London, 1957). Pp. xxiii, 555.

94. "Variant Entry Fees of the Stationers' Company," *Papers of the Bibliographical Society of America*, LI (1957), 103–110.

95. Review of Archer Taylor, *Book Catalogues: Their Varieties and Uses* (Chicago, 1957), in *The Book Collector*, VI (1957), 184–186.

1958

96. *The Houghton Library Report of Accessions for the Year 1957–58* [no. 17] (Cambridge, Massachusetts, 1958). Pp. [ii], 53.

97. "Rare Books and the Small Public Library," *Bulletin of the Massachusetts Library Association*, XLVIII, no. 2 (1958), 5–6.

98. "The Education of a Bibliographer," *Bulletin Number Three* of the Southern California Chapter, Antiquarian Booksellers Association of America (Summer 1958), 3–4.

99. "Robert Waldegrave and the Books He Printed or Published in 1603," *The Library*, 5th series, XIII (1958), 225–233.

1959

100. *The Houghton Library Report of Accessions for the Year 1958–59* [no. 18] (Cambridge, Massachusetts, 1959). Pp. [ii], 48.

101. Preface to *The Kilgour Collection of Russian Literature* (Cambridge, Massachusetts, 1959), unpaged.

102. "Parochial Libraries," *Times Literary Supplement*, no. 3,016 (18 December 1959), 747.

103. Review of Sears Jayne and Francis R. Johnson, *The Lumley Library* (London, 1956), in *Renaissance News*, XII (1959), 189–191.

104. "Lucius Wilmerding, 1880–1949," in *Grolier 75: A Biographical Retrospective* (New York, 1959), pp. 210–212.

105. "The Howe Fund, a Generation Later," *Harvard Library Bulletin*, XIII (1959), 475–477.

106. Letter on "Henry Stevens and Washington's Library," *Papers of the Bibliographical Society of America*, LIII (1959), 79–80.

1960

107. *The Houghton Library Report of Accessions for the Year 1959–60* [no. 19] (Cambridge, Massachusetts, 1960). Pp. [ii], 51.

108. "The Hofer Collection," no. 24 in the Contemporary Collectors series, *The Book Collector*, IX (1960), 151–164, 292–300, illus.

109. "Racan's *L'Artenice*, an Addition to the English Canon," with Jean Parrish, *Harvard Library Bulletin*, XIV (1960), 183–190, illus.

110. "Racan's *L'Artenice* — Addendum," *Harvard Library Bulletin*, XIV (1960), 493, illus.

111. "The Curse of Ernulphus," *Harvard Library Bulletin*, XIV (1960), 392–394, illus.

112. Letter in *PaGA*, VII (1960), 123–124, raising questions about Richard Holman's article on John Foster's woodcut map of New England.

113. Review of: Cyprian Blagden, *The Stationers' Company: a History* (London, 1960), in *Times Literary Supplement*, no. 3,065 (25 November 1960), 768.

1961

114. *The Houghton Library Report of Accessions for the Year 1960–61* [no. 20] (Cambridge, Massachusetts, 1961). Pp. [ii], 58.

115. *An Exhibition of Books Published When They Were 21 or Younger by One Hundred Authors Who Later Became Famous* (Cambridge, Massachusetts, 1961). Pp. 28. Reprinted in 1962.

116. Review of Lawrence B. Romaine, *A Guide to American Trade Catalogs 1744–1900* (New York, 1960), in *Williams Alumni Review*, LIII, no. 2 (1961), 32.

1962

117. *The Houghton Library Report of Accessions for the Year 1961–62* [no. 21] (Cambridge, Massachusetts, 1962). Pp. [ii], 52.

118. *Bibliography and Literary Studies*, a Zeitlin Lecture (Los Angeles, 1962). Pp. 16.

119. *Bibliotheca Chimaerica: A Catalogue of an Exhibition of Catalogues of Imaginary Books* (Cambridge, Massachusetts, 1962). Pp. [iv], 12.

1963

120. *The Houghton Library Report of Accessions for the Year 1962–63* [no. 22] (Cambridge, Massachusetts, 1963). Pp. [ii], 52.

121. Review of Franklin B. Williams, Jr., *Index of Dedications and Commendatory Verses in English Books Before 1641* (London, 1962), in *Renaissance News*, XVI (1963), 351–353.

1964

122. "The Early Editions of Machiavelli's First *Decennale*," with Ernest Hatch Wilkins and Richard H. Rouse, *Studies in the Renaissance*, XI (1964), 76–104.

123. "George Luther Lincoln," Harvard University Faculty Obituary Minute with Raimundo Lida, Francis M. Rogers, and Taylor

Starck, *Harvard University Gazette*, LX, no. 12 (5 December 1964), 76–7.

124. Foreword to reprint of *The Country Book-Club* (Boston, 1964), unpaged.

125. Foreword to Ruth Mortimer, *Harvard College Library. Department of Printing and Graphic Arts. Catalogue of Books and Manuscripts. Part I: French 16th Century Books* (Cambridge, Massachusetts, 1964), p. [v].

1965

126. *An Annotated List of the Publications of the Reverend Thomas Frognall Dibdin, D. D.* (Cambridge, Massachusetts, 1965). Pp. 64; illus. Limited to 500 copies.

Selected Papers of William Alexander Jackson

I

The Education of a Bibliographer

(1958)

These informal reminiscences were delivered as a talk before a meeting of the Southern California Chapter of the Antiquarian Booksellers Association of America (Bibliography, no. 98).

IT has always seemed to me that the only way a bibliographer can be trained is for him to obtain access to the kind of books which interest him, and the books, such as they are, about those books, then set to work. If he is fortunate also in having guidance of able bookmen to answer questions and set a standard, he may be saved much time and will be early initiated into the freemasonry of bookmen and the pleasures of libraries.

For myself this sort of training began early. The public library of South Pasadena had, and probably still has, a well-selected stock of books and the librarian, a sweet old lady, was intelligent about letting a small boy read almost anything, so long as it was not trash. Those were the days of Don Marquis, Christopher Morley, and the early A. Edward Newton, and I read everything of theirs I could find as well as much classic literature.

Dr. George Watson Cole, the librarian of the newly opened Huntington Library and a neighbor whose lawn I took care of, suggested that if I went to Williams College I would probably have access to more rare books in the newly founded Chapin Library than I would at either Harvard or Yale, at both of which, as was the custom then, I was entered. I took his advice and have never regretted it. The ten thousand books there have remained for me the standard copies against which all others I come across are measured — not many, I may say, are superior in condition.

During my freshman year I met such bookmen as James F. Drake and Lathrop C. Harper, the latter of whom took me to my first book-auction, the second Chew sale, where despite his whispered warning to be careful, I bought a fine copy of Buchanan's *Fleshly School of Poetry*, in the original wrappers, at less than an eighth the price I had just seen it listed in a catalogue. I still have the pamphlet, preserved in a Stikeman case which, in my pride, I had had made for it. That same year I first went to the Morgan Library, then still a private library and reputedly very difficult of access. It may be that I wrote ahead, I hope so, but my recollection is that I merely rang the bell and asked for Miss Greene. In any case, I shall never forget her kindness nor the glorious books and manuscripts which she and Miss Thurston then showed me.

To later years belongs my introduction to the libraries of Paris under the guidance of Seymour de Ricci, and to the Vatican under Cardinal Mercati; as well as the many kindnesses of R. B. McKerrow, A. W. Pollard, F. S. Ferguson, and Dr. Rosenbach, to all of whom I owe much, going back in most cases to undergraduate days. I should prefer to use such space as I have in recounting my recollections of the summer between my freshman and sophomore college years, much of which I spent at the Huntington Library.

The Huntington of those days was not very different from the present except that somehow it seemed smaller and more intimate. What is now the Art Gallery was still Mr. Huntington's home. One was conscious of the orange groves which seemed not only nearer the library but filled acres of the empty lots surrounding it. There was, of course, no reference reading room and stack. The "readers" were fewer and the staff much smaller. The lunchroom was then a single room where both staff and reader mingled. Nearly every day one found on the menu avocado sandwiches or salads made from fruit grown on the library grounds. Perhaps because there were so few readers, I do not recall any difficulty being raised as to my admission, though not a graduate student or established scholar, and once admitted I was made to feel welcome.

My parents were away that summer and, for some weeks at any rate, I lived at the Pasadena Y.M.C.A., for this was long before the Athenaeum was even dreamed of. I presume I must have used a bicycle for transportation, for the only automobile that I remember of that summer was an ancient Model T, without a top, belonging to Roland Baughman, now Curator of Rare Books at Columbia University, which on occasion took far more of the younger Huntington staff than it was designed to hold to a speakeasy in the Mexican part of Los Angeles. I suppose that speakeasy was probably a rather squalid place but in my recollection it still has an aura of romance, for it was an old saloon with a long bar and footrail. The only change it had undergone, for the swinging doors were still there, was that it had a chute built into it, down which, on a signal from a lookout, all the glasses, full or not, were whisked, being replaced by "pop" bottles before the policeman sauntered in.

The staff contained then very few library-school trained members but a larger proportion of men who had either grown up in the library under Dr. Cole or had trained themselves. These were men who were generally specialists in various fields of bibliography and worthy to rank with almost any other specialists in those fields in the country. A few of these gentlemen are still carrying on their valuable work, but I shall confine my recollections here to two of them, no longer alive, who were most helpful to me that summer.

They were both somewhat odd in many ways and had no great liking for any of their colleagues, which they expressed mainly by avoiding them. But they both had what seemed to me then vast experience in bibliographical matters and were willing to guide a beginner's steps and even to spend many long evenings of that summer talking of bookish matters. Being both of them bachelors, for the time at any rate, they could employ those evenings as they wished. The one of whom I saw the most, both at the library and in the evenings, was Cecil Kay Edmonds, who was in charge of the cataloguing of the early English books.

He had at one time been a church organist but for some years had immersed himself in the intricacies of the books in his charge. At that time, of course, the *Short-title Catalogue* had not been published and the main tools of a bibliographer working in that period were the British Museum 1884 Catalogue, Sayle, Herbert, Duff, Hazlitt, Sinker, Madan and Maitland. Mr. Edmonds' main concern was in recording the books as he found them, noting variant readings, cancels, and issue points. I doubt if he was much interested in ascertaining the causes of the variation which he found, but to this day his records of what he saw are as detailed and accurate as those of any bibliographer known to me.

It is difficult now to reconstruct what it was we spent so many hours talking about, except of course that it was all connected in one way or another with early English books. However, I do recall that one evening we debated the question of who had been the greatest of the bibliographers who had concerned themselves with those books. I believe I was then torn between William Herbert and E. Gordon Duff, while Edmonds maintained that Charles Sayle was the greatest. I did not then agree with him but I now understand much better why Sayle should have been his choice.

The other member of the Huntington staff who that summer was extraordinarily kind and helpful to me was Captain R. B. Haselden, then in charge of the manuscripts in the library. I now cannot remember anything of the Captain's military career but he had spent some years in the London world of books and in the evenings I spent with him, when not listening to his new and very grand automatic record-changing phonograph, he told me many tales of books and bookmen. Just what the stories were I now cannot recall, but the flavor of the bookish evenings still lingers.

The Captain had a nice sense of humor. One time when I asked him what particular type of manuscript interested him most, he replied with a twinkle, "Western manuscripts written before the eighth century." On another occasion I told him that I would like to have him give me a "difficult" sixteenth century manuscript to transcribe as I thought I could handle most ordinary Tudor hands. He gave me a little notebook written by John Penry. I found it difficult enough and eventually was spending day after day on it, when I had only intended a few hours. Finally, I went to the Captain with my transcript and asked him if he would mind checking it. He laughed and said if I had transcribed it, that was fine, and then showed me a passage in one of the Egerton manuscripts which stated that when this notebook was produced in court at Penry's trial no-one then could read it. (It has since been transcribed, and published by Dr. A. Peel.)

Last summer I had in my hands in the Huntington stack a unique early English book. While I was making some note of it one of the stack-pages came by and I explained to him how interesting it was and said that I had never seen it before. In a few minutes he returned with a card which showed that I had seen it during that summer so long ago. However, the moral of this tale is not that the generosity which allowed me, an undergraduate, to handle such treasures was obviously wasted because I had such a poor memory, but rather that one wonders if eager young bibliographers are now so welcome in our rare-book libraries as I was made to feel in that summer of 1924.

2

Thomas Frognall Dibdin

(1935)

This paper marked Jackson's brilliant debut before a full meeting of the Grolier Club on December 19, 1935. He delivered it at the opening of an exhibition of books and manuscripts. Hitherto unpublished, it was never prepared by its author for publication, and no attempt has been made to remove the characteristics of a paper intended for presentation viva voce.

NO apology need be made for devoting a meeting of this club to honoring the memory of the Reverend Thomas Frognall Dibdin. I have no doubt his name is familiar to all of you, and that many here tonight have read, enjoyed and collected him much longer than I have. So long as we subscribe to Frederick Locker's dictum that, "It is a good thing to read books, and need not be a bad thing to write them, but, in any case, it is a pious thing to collect them," we need not fear nor be made timorous by the scorn and ridicule of the uninitiate who ever since Dibdin's day have persisted in confusing an "unopened copy" with an "uncut one." Though there have been many fads and changes in collecting interests in the century that has more than passed since Dibdin led the pack, and set the style and timbre for what has ever since been the view halloo of book-collecting, the memory is still fresh of his enthusiasm, his ecstasy, and his contagious enjoyment of all that relates to books and their collecting or collectors.

There are many collectors and bookmen today, some of them members of this club, who whether consciously or not stem directly from the great prototype, T. F. Dibdin. It is not necessary to name any living examples but perhaps I can illustrate what I mean by reading to you a portion of the book credo of Ingram Bywater, that paragon of collectors of the classics, connoisseur of fine books, sound wine, and good silver, whose library has recently been enshrined in the Bodleian. Bywater was a scholar, a gentleman, and a collector in whose library Dibdin himself would have been very much at home. He declared — possibly with a twinkle in his eye, though we shan't admit that to the Philistine — "there are various reasons for buying books. Some people buy books for the contents and that is a very vulgar reason; and some people buy books for the binding, and that is a little better and not so vulgar; others buy them for the printing, and that is really a very good reason. But the real reason for which to buy a book is the margin! Always look at the margin!"

So long as there are men who are enraptured by the sight of a really fine copy of not necessarily a great book, men who sometimes find themselves walking out of a bookshop with a book under their arm which they had not intended to buy, whose purchase they could not very well defend, but which tempted them by something really fine in its paper or binding, its condition or its total rightness as a book — so long, I say, as there are such *Helluones librorum*, in Dibdin's phrase, gluttons of books, some of his rapture, his delight, and his spirit is still inflaming men's hearts and desires.

I am not going to bore you with a formal biography of Dibdin; you will find an excellent, though brutal, one in the *Dictionary of National Biography*, or better yet his own *Literary Reminiscences*. Dibdin was born in the year of our Independence and he died in the tenth regnal year of Victoria, i.e., he lived through the later part of the reign of George III, the Regency, George IV, William IV, and the beginning of the Victorian era. Perhaps I can place him for you by saying that when he went to Oxford it was the unreformed university that he knew (which may well explain his scholarship — but of that more later). As a young man in London he joined the militia formed to defend Albion from the invasion of Bonaparte. He lived through the period of agitation concerning electoral reform, Welsh disestablishment, and the Corn Laws. Through it all, of course, he was a staunch Tory, as was wellnigh universal among the clergy of the established church. The great period of the Bibliomania which he did so much to stimulate and to celebrate was during the inflation which followed Waterloo. The Sykes sale of 1824 might be said to be the apogee of that movement, just as the Kern sale was of our more recent if equally specious prosperity. But let us hope that we will not have to pass through as large a segment of the curve of depression as did mid-eighteenth century England before we return to more normal times, for it was not until the George Daniel sale of 1864 (more than a decade after Dibdin's death) that books were as eagerly competed for as they had been in the teens of that century.

The London that Dibdin knew was Nash's London. Kensington, where he first lived, was as remote from Bedford Street or St. James's as Virginia Water is today, and as rural. He was the first rector of St. Mary's, Bryanston Square, when it was built by the Crown authorities of the Marylebone estates to accommodate the parish then rapidly filling with the homes of prosperous middle class merchants attracted by the proximity of the newly opened Regents Park. The London Institution in Albemarle Street, where Dibdin delivered a course of lectures on English literature, was for that time a combination Town Hall Club and Chatauqua — a place where the leisured middle classes sought to obtain culture painlessly or, at any rate, as comfortably as might be since the lectures were usually an hour and a half to two hours long. It was the beginning of the Age of Humanitarianism, the emancipation of slaves, and the organization of what were then called eleemosynary institutions. The great Quarterlies formed the major staple of the reading pabulum of that day, and their influence and authority is hard for us now to appreciate. Dibdin's England was the England of Scott, of Keats and Shelley, of Byron, Southey, and Cowper. It was also the England of the Industrial Revolution, though Dibdin himself was so thorough a Tory that he never lost his faith in the land and all the established things for which that word stands. In a word, it was the England of *Evelina* and Barsetshire that Dibdin knew.

And in that England our hero lived, a clergyman of the Church of England. As in political circles sinecures were still dispersed — you will recall that Thomas Grenville enjoyed during most of his life a handsome income from the sinecure office of Chief Justice in Eyre South of Trent, which he devoted mainly to the accumulation of the magnificent library that he finally bequeathed to the nation, instead of to his nephew as he had formerly intended — so in the Church pluralism was still practised. And Dibdin was a pluralist — Vicar of Exning, with a curate in charge, Vicar of St. Mary's, and in his later years one of the Royal Chaplains. In fact, he was, according to the gossip of the time, a promising candidate for advancement to the Episcopal lawn and gaiters. It cannot be denied that Dibdin sought ordination as a last resort. A letter is in the case over yonder from the Bishop of Winchester appointing the date of the ceremony and acknowledging that in Dibdin's case there were certain ameliorating circumstances which made it possible to advance the date — Dibdin had presented the Bishop with a copy of the second edition of his *Introduction to the Classics*. Still, though he may not have been born to the calling and only entered it after he had failed at the law, it is unfair to our hero to say that his bookish interests and activities prevented him from performing his clerical duties in a manner sufficiently satisfactory according to the standard of those days. It was well into Victorian times before fox-hunting parsons and four-bottle curates were regarded as anomalies.

Perhaps I can illustrate the contemporary attitude toward clergymen by telling the story of a civil action brought in the spring of 1812. Its only connection with bookish matters is that the defendant was Sir Mark Masterman Sykes — the Lorenzo of the *Bibliomania*. The plaintiff was the Reverend Randolph Gilbert, a clergyman you will note but not, so far as I can ascertain, a book collector. It seems that at a dinner some three years before — apparently it was toward the end of the dinner and the bottles had all been emptied — an argument arose concerning the probable success of the allied armies against Napoleon. Sir Mark declared that Bonaparte had not a hundred days to live. The Reverend Gilbert took him up and offered to wager: he would pay a hundred guineas to Sir Mark if the Frenchman was dead before the hundred days were passed; but if not, Sir Mark was to pay him one guinea per day as long thereafter as Bonaparte should live. The amiable baronet could do nothing less than take the wager, and though his friends tried to persuade the clergyman not to offer the wager, the only answer they could get was that he would withdraw the bet if Sir Mark would ask him to, which of course Sykes could not do.

Of course, Napoleon lived on, and for nearly three years the defendant continued to pay the stipulated sum. Finally he stopped payment, and the lawsuit was the result. Counsel for the plaintiff cited the fact that, though immoral, being on the life of a man, the wager was legal. They recalled the case of the Earl of March (later Duke of Queensbury) vs. Mr. Pickard, who had bet on the lives of their respective fathers, and that wager had been supported by Lord Mansfield. And in answer to the objection that Bonaparte was an enemy of England, a case was cited which had been upheld by the courts of a wager made during the protectorate that Charles Stuart would return within a year, which considering that Cromwell was the *de facto* head of the government was treason, though legal in the court. The lawyer for the defendant cited the evidence that the bet had been made in a moment of excitement and he concluded: "I know not whether the Rev. Clergyman frequently attends the church where we are commanded to pray for our enemies, but the plaintiff has a most cogent reason for being devout in that part of the service, viz. an annuity of 365 guineas a year."

My point is, if a clergyman of that time could so take advantage of the patriotism of such an amiable and ardent gentleman as Sir Mark undoubtedly was without being unfrocked, then that generation was one which would view lightly the bibliographical zeal and devotion of the Reverend T. F. D. In fact, I am not prepared to admit that Dibdin was not, for that time, a conscientious and able cleric. There can be no question of his ability as a preacher. In the case over yonder is a clipping from the *Gentleman's Magazine* which Dibdin himself preserved among the papers which after his death his widow presented to Dawson Turner. It is a letter from a constant attendant at the evening services which Dibdin conducted for some seven years at the Brompton Chapel, around the corner from the Brompton Oratory — "Hortry" as the busmen now call it. There had been some remark passed on Dibdin's translation to the parish of St. Mary's, and his former parishioner wrote in his defense to Mr. Urban. According to that letter, Dibdin had by his attractive voice and message built up the attendance of the chapel from the thirty or forty which was normal when he came, to an average of three or four hundred. Indeed, it is unlikely that he would have been made a Royal Chaplain if his pulpit manner had not been better than average. From all that we know of him it appears that he exhibited the resonant voice and charm of person, if not the stature, of his famous uncle, Charles Dibdin, the actor and song writer.

He was in considerable demand as a charity and visitation preacher and he published nearly a dozen volumes of sermons. These last are among the most difficult of Dibdiniana for the collector, and the absence of some of them here forms the only serious gap in the exhibition. Besides these there are one or two legal broadsides which in 1836 Dibdin himself supposed had completely disappeared. He had no copy and neither have we, nor do we know of the existence of any.

Probably I should not overemphasize his devotion, for Dibdin tells the story on himself that shortly after *The Lady of the Lake* was published he read the first two Cantos (not in a sotto voce) on a Saturday evening, with the result that when he preached a charity sermon the next morning, two-thirds of his voice was gone, and the congregation in consequence requested that "a gentleman in the possession of lungs might be engaged on a future occasion."

It is my own opinion, however, that Dibdin would have been a better bibliographer, at any rate a better writer about bibliophily, had he not been so much a man of religion. For instance, he did his best to spoil a thoroughly interesting book, one of his best, *The Library Companion*, by so frequently recollecting his cloth and thereby injecting rather irrelevant moral reflections. In the preface he declares, "From the beginning to the end, I have never lost sight of what I considered to be the MOST MATERIAL OBJECT to be gained from a publication of this nature; namely, the imparting of a *moral feeling* to the gratification of a *literary taste!*"

But enough of this! Let us turn to Dibdin the bibliographer. By bibliographer I mean not his anecdotal volumes but the more technical writings on books — his *Introduction to the Classics*, the *Althorpe Catalogues* and his magnificently printed edition of Ames's *Typographical Antiquities of Great Britain*.

Alexander Dyce — no mean scholar himself but one who had evidently not fallen under the spell of Dibdin's charm, who did not appreciate his lovable companionship in what Dibdin calls "library comforts" or his ability as a raconteur — once said of our hero, "He is an ignorant pretender without the learning of a schoolboy, who published a quantity of books swarming with errors of every description." If we grant this pre-Macaulay schoolboy the ability to read, not accurately but tolerably easily, both Latin and Greek, and a retentive but not very dependable memory, Dyce's strictures are, I am afraid, on the whole deserved.

For example, the *Introduction to the Classics*, at least in the first edition (it was later considerably expanded and rewritten as the author gained experience and knowledge from his acquaintance with the Spencer and Grenville books), is merely a paste-pot tabulated compilation from Edward Harwood's *A view of the various editions of the Greek and Roman classics*, together with notes on copies then, or recently, listed in London booksellers' catalogues. His edition of Ames is little better, despite the regal splendor of its illustration and, in the large paper copies, its amplitude of margin. It is a reprinting of Herbert's edition of Ames, which was for its time — the last decade of the eighteenth century — an amazing bibliographical achievement. Herbert spent the last years of his life annotating and correcting his work, and his own copy, interleaved and expanded from three volumes to six, was purchased by Dibdin when he determined to re-edit the book. Dibdin's edition amounts merely to this: it is a not very accurate reprint of the first two volumes of Herbert with lives of Ames and Herbert prefixed as well as a long and somewhat muddled note on the art of engraving and a life of Caxton. In the text Dibdin has introduced rather trifling additions, mostly concerning literary merit or lack of it, a few notes on books unknown to Herbert, as well as certain notes, literally clipped out of Herbert's annotated copy and turned over to the printer. (I have been reading so much of Dibdin of late that I cannot here resist a footnote to say that that copy thus mutilated is now kept behind the door of the Keeper's office in the British Museum. It was once in New York, having been bought by Lenox from Bohn, who had acquired it from Dibdin. It went back to England as the result of a trade arranged through Stevens by Panizzi.) The result is a book which is unmistakably Dibdinian in style and flavor — Herbert was so self-effacing a person that throughout his book wherever he had occasion to mention the first person singular, which was not often, he insisted that the printer use a lower-case *i*. But it is not a book that the bibliographer uses very much except for such items as are not in Herbert.

I am not going to bore you with a long recitation of errors, but it is not fair to Dibdin to condemn him as a bibliographer without some proof. And therefore I shall select several examples which, perhaps you will accept my word, are typical. For example, in the *Typographical Antiquities* Dibdin devotes a plate to reproducing what purports to be the first page of Machlinia's edition of Canutus' *Treatise on the Pestilence*. But instead of being an aid to those interested in the book, it is merely a puzzle. The upper part of that page is taken from a unique copy of Wynken de Worde's edition in the Cambridge University Library and the lower part from the unique copy of Machlinia's edition then in Triphook's possession and later in the Spencer library. To make such a botch must have entailed considerable trouble and perhaps a modicum of genius.

The high-water mark of his ineptitude was reached, however, in his edition of More's *Utopia*. In his introduction, after describing the various editions and doing a rather workmanlike job, he finally comes to the edition of 1639, of which he says: "This edition is, in truth, one of the most erroneous extant. It has everything of Robinson's translation but its accuracy . . . the type, paper, and text are equally wretched." Seven pages farther on he says, apparently without any appreciation of his folly, "The text of the present edition [i.e., the one he is editing] is printed from Alsop's of 1639 [i.e., the one he has so justly condemned], as being the most convenient edition for the compositor to execute."

Usually, however, the person who turns to Dibdin for information finds a more baffling kind of error — and sometimes it entails considerable search to ascertain whether or not Dibdin is confused or careless, or whether he really had seen such a book as he describes. For example, in the *Library Companion*, Second Edition, p. 526, he declared: "Lord Spencer lately purchased of Mr. Triphook a copy of the first folio of Lord Herbert's book [*Henry VIII*], on LARGE PAPER; the only copy of the kind which I remember to have heard of." Now that is certainly categorical and circumstantial enough, no loose ends lying about, and one might perhaps be pardoned for putting it down on Dibdin's authority that at least one Large Paper copy of the first edition is known. However, a little experience with the man will make one wary, and therefore we need not be surprised if in looking in the Rylands Catalogue we find that no copy of the first edition is there listed although there is one of the third edition, 1672. Pursuing the matter a bit farther, we find that three years before Dibdin made that statement, Triphook, the dealer he mentioned, bought at the Bindley sale, Part IV, Lot 847, a copy of that third edition of 1672, which was described as on Large Paper. And finally, when we find that the Rylands copy is the Bindley-Spencer, we are perhaps justified in thinking that our hero of this evening is not a particularly shining example of bibliographical accuracy.

But if he is not a great bibliographer, then why, in Heaven's name, should we hold him in such affectionate memory? I think the answer is because Dibdin was a great lover of books! He so whole-heartedly enjoyed everything which in any way was connected with books and their collecting. He loved the sight and feel of them. He loved even the smell of a library — he called it the fragrance, nor was even daunted by the odors of paste and glue and raw leather of a bindery. The sound of the auctioneer's hammer was as pleasing to his ears as was good bookish talk around a well-filled library table or around the same article of furniture in the dining room. Not only was he a lover of books but he was also a lovable fellow. Whatever may have been his shortcomings as a clergyman, he was a good practicing Christian. There was no malice in him and his cheerful good nature refused to harbor any venom against those who insulted or mistreated him. He was a staunch friend, and his friends were, for the most part, faithful to him. Very few, if any, lovers of books who knew him personally could resist the charm of his bookish talk, and they supported him in his extravagant publishing ventures as long as they lived — for most of them were his senior.

And much of the charm of his character and talk he managed to put into his books. A Frenchman once said of the *Tour* that it would have been a capital volume (actually it is three volumes) had there been no letterpress. But no real lover of books would agree with that. Sir Walter Scott, with a more just appreciation of his merits, wrote to Dibdin: "All Bibliomanes must remember you long, as he who first united their antiquarian details with good-humoured raillery and cheerfulness." Now raillery and cheerfulness, though pleasant things in themselves, are not necessarily passports to Parnassus. But, with all due deference to that great Scotsman as a writer of books and reader of them, too, he was not inoculated with the true bibliomaniacal serum, for though the library at Abbotsford is indeed a respectable accumulation of books, it is not the library of a book-collector. As proof of this assertion I offer you not the printed catalogue of the Abbotsford library, which, as collectors, I assure you you would find extraordinarily dull, but — and here I hope if there are any Scott infatuates present they will close their ears against this blasphemy — Sir Walter sealed his own exclusion from the ranks of the foreordained (shall we call them?), despite the accolade of his membership in the Roxburghe Club, by actually inscribing in his own copy of Harry Maule's *History of the Picts*: "Very rare, therefore worth a guinea; very senseless, therefore not worth a shilling." Consequently, Scott's palate, I think you will agree, was not one which could appreciate the full flavor and quality of our hero's bookish effusions. Full of raillery and extravagance they sometimes were, it cannot be denied, but they also teem with passages expressive of the most rapturous enjoyment of bibliomaniacal pleasures — experiences which may still be vicariously shared by his readers. Though not perhaps a great writer, he possessed the faculty in common with Pepys and Boswell of being able to communicate the sensations of a bystander, so that today we can relive that memorable scene in St. James's when the Valdarfer Boccaccio was sold or breathe again the excitement of hunting by candlelight for Black Letter nuggets in the York Minster library at midnight.

Dibdin was not a great writer in the sense that Scott, whom I have just maligned, was. And I can believe that there are people to whom his style might even be nauseating. It is frequently bespattered with a grotesque slang — "saucy margins," "creamy papyrus," etc. His rhapsodies are freqently disfigured by an insane riot of words which might almost be charged with savoring of bibliomaniac quackery, and sometimes, I will admit, his hyperbole borders on the absurd. For example, and this is not the worst passage that might be cited but rather a typical one, referring to the Advocates Library at Edinburgh, Dibdin wrote: "That Library is the first shrine at which I should kneel, if fate ever carried me to that most interesting capital. My friend David Laing, Esq., the erudite and able secretary, would, I feel persuaded, help me up in case I fell — or was taken with too long a swooning fit of delirious rapture."

But usually he does better than that, and sometimes he rises to considerable heights. I wish there were time to read the whole of the unpublished letter, exhibited in the case over yonder, which Dibdin wrote to Heber from Ratisbon when he was making his Tour — it was written *currente calamo* but rings true throughout.[1] Speaking of the *Epistolae ad familiares* of Cicero (1467), he says: "though upon paper, large, white, stiff and triumphant!" I do not think that the beauty of an unwashed Sweynheim and Pannartz has ever been more perfectly expressed. But enough of his style — if you have any bookish instincts in you and you do not know his books, I think you would find pleasure in reading them.

Before I say a few words about the exhibition, perhaps you will permit me to discuss briefly what Bibliomania, as Dibdin practiced it, was and what his contemporaries thought of it. In this case on my left you will see that the Beau Brummel of the cult was not left to his own devices. The *Library Companion* was parodied by no less a person than De Quincey, and rather cleverly too. *The Confessions of an Oxonian* by Thomas Little has a chapter lampooning the pursuit. I don't believe

[1] [Reproduced in facsimile in Jackson's *An Annotated List of the Publications of the Reverend Thomas Frognall Dibdin, D.D.* (Cambridge, Massachusetts, 1965).]

it has ever been pointed out, but I think there is some reason for attributing that book to Thomas Moore. The style would seem to support such an attribution, and the name Thomas Little, not otherwise known, seems a plausible pseudonym for Moore.

It puzzled our hero and, I am afraid, caused him considerable chagrin that the Quarterlies, those great arbiters of intellectual taste of that generation, never once deigned to notice his publications. In one of the cases near the end on the left are bundled together all the reviews of his works which came to Dibdin's notice. The slightly condescending review which the *Gentleman's Magazine* gave of his *Reminiscences* was perhaps the most satisfying of them all, and yet as one reads Dibdin's manuscript commentaries on these reviews, one cannot help but feel that it was not only his writer's vanity which was offended by those which were published but rather was he hurt by the failure of his contemporaries to appreciate the viewpoint of a bibliomaniac.

The true bibliomaniac is rather humble about his pursuit — he is content to enjoy it quietly with his fellows as an end in itself. At most, he may contend that his preoccupation with condition, editions and issues, points, and all the other arcana of book-collecting frequently is of considerable importance to sober scholarship. But when he is charged with the belief that the margin of a book, however ample, contains the whole pith and marrow of a book, and that he never spares even a little time for a survey of the text — and such a charge from Dibdin's day to the present, is still leveled at him — then he may well feel that his critics have completely misunderstood him. There are many bibliomaniacs who are also students of books, but insofar as they are bibliomaniacs, their concern is with books qua books, not with books as vehicles of ideas. For example, the collectors of Black Letter Lore, as it was called in Dibdin's day, have undoubtedly performed a very great service to literary scholarship in illustrating and elucidating the period, but as bibliomaniacs their primary interest was in the books themselves, and they would have been hardly less keen about them had they been merely bibliographical rarities and not documents of considerable scholarly importance.

It has been charged against the bibliomaniac that his concern with title-pages and colophons, his fastidiousness about condition, is like studying the wards and handle of a key instead of thrusting it into the lock and opening the door. But I do not think that simile is a just one. That is not the province of a bibliomaniac. Dibdin himself was not infrequently led to place a higher estimate on the typographical merit of a book by the sight of a particularly well-preserved, well-bound or fine paper copy of it. Such a copy, the delight of a bibliomaniac, presumably should be no better in the eyes of the scorner than a scrubby, unkempt, foxed, and wretched specimen for which a bookseller can think of nothing better to say than that it is a "students" copy. And yet, I leave the decision to you. It is utterly impossible not only to appreciate the full typographic merits of a book from such a copy but even to have any adequate conception of what sort of impression the book made upon the generation which saw its production.

If you will turn to the books exhibited here you will find some examples of early nineteenth century printing which, by the quality of their paper, the blackness of the ink, and the beauty of their presswork, will give you an adequate means of forming a favorable impression of the books printed by Bulmer and Bensley and their contemporaries. Dibdin spared no cost in having his books well printed and elaborately illustrated. On four of them he spent more than £20,000, and he was the first man in England to pay a hundred guineas for a single plate.

3

A Description from the Unpublished Chapin Catalogue

(1929)

This specimen page prepared for the Chapin Catalogue may serve as a fair sample of the whole work. Since it is only a trial page, it is not free from typographical errors, and the printer ventured to use *f* instead of long *s* in the next to last line — details that Jackson would have attended to had the book gone on to publication.

II. Trial page for the unpublished Chapin Catalogue, 1929

[MORE, *Cresacre* (or *Christopher*)]. (1857-1649.) D. O. M. S. The life and death of Sir Thomas Moore. [Antwerp, 1631?].

D[eo]. *O*[ptimo]. *M*[aximo]. *S*[acrum]. | THE LIFE AND DEATH OF | SIR THOMAS | MOORE | Lord high Chancellour of | England. | WRITTEN BY | *M. T. M. and dedicated to the Queenes | most gracious Maiestie.* | [ornament] |

4to. (186x144 mm.) Straight grain niger morocco, extra, inside dentelles, gilt edges, by Lloyd, Wallis & Lloyd.

Collation by signatures: ✠[4]; A-Hhh[4]; total 220 leaves.

Collation by pagination: title-page, as above, recto [✠]; verso blank; dedication to Queen Marie Henriette, signed M[agister]. C[resacre]. M[ore]. E[boracensis?], recto ✠$_2$-verso [✠$_4$]; preface, pp. 1-10; text, pp. 11-432.

First edition. Wood describes this book as "incomparably well written." Previous to the publication of Hunter's edition in 1828 it was usually ascribed to Cresacre's elder brother, Thomas, who died in Rome, April 11, 1625, and indeed that ascription is not without foundation by reason of the initials which appear on the title, and the referencer to the late deceased author as "eldest sonne by descent, & heire by nature ot the family of that worthy Martyr."

The assignment of this book to "Douai or St. Omer" by the Short-Title Catalogue was probably a conjecture based on the Catholic nature of the book. But such books were also printed at Antwerp and a comparison of the types and ornaments used in the present with those in a number of books known to have been printed at both Douai and St. Omer has failed to reveal any connection with those presses. Whereas, though it cannot be connected with any one printing house at Antwerp, it can be shown that the ornaments used in this book were also in use in Antwerp at about the same time.

"Deo Optimo Maximo Sacrum" is the received version of "D. O. M. S." It is a common inscription over the doors of churches in Ireland. It also heads the inscription on Thomas More's tombstone in Rome as quoted by Hunter and Hearne (Appendix to his edition of "Johannis Glastoniensis Chronica" 1726) and Anthony à Wood. The book is regarded as a "monumentum" and therefore the gender ot the adjective is neuter.

One of the copies of this book in the British Museum has the first sheet cancelled and another title, from a new setting and with a different ornament, inserted with stub appearing between [A$_4$] and B$_1$.

Huntington C. L. p. 298. Hoe Cat. III (1903) p. 194. Gillow V p. 95. Huth Cat. III p. 997.

BUNYAN, *John* (1628-1688). The Pilgrim's Progress. London, for Nath[aniel]. Ponder, 1681.

The Pilgrim's Progrefs. From this world to that which is to come: delivered under the similitude of a dream, wherein is difcovered the man-

4

A Dibdinian Tour

(1938)

Jackson wrote this journal-letter to Peter Oliver, who had been prevented by an emergency appendectomy from joining him, Philip Hofer, and Boies Penrose on their tour of the English collections. Previously unpublished, the letter should be set beside Boies Penrose's account, "An Indiscreet History of a Bibliographical, Picturesque, & Antiquarian Tour," which appeared in *The Colophon*, N.S. III (1938), 490–512.

S. S. Scythia
[1 August?] 1938

Dear Peter,

It is not possible for me to tell you properly of our tour. Even if I wrote dozens of pages I could hardly give you a full account of its manifold delights, of the books and manuscripts we saw — many of them so magnificent that I could with difficulty go to sleep at night from excitement, of the people who were everywhere so kind to us, of the many magnificent houses with their furnishings in every way, sometimes, the equal of the books, and of the England through which we passed. Nor can I begin to tell you of our talk which continued briskly, if not brilliantly, throughout the whole tour and ranged over every subject under heaven. I have not laughed so heartily or so much for years and both Boies and Philip said they had not felt so carefree and young since leaving Cambridge. Perhaps you may judge of our pleasure in the trip when I say that we are all determined to repeat parts of it again and hope to make such tours annually.

The dinners at the Athenaeum were really superb. We had a private dining room with well trained waiters. I believe I have sent you the menu for the first dinner and I have asked Boies to send you that for the second which was, if anything, slightly the better. Parenthetically I may say that including sherry, decanters of port and whiskey, cigars, and everything, the two dinners cost only fifteen pounds. At any restaurant with food of that quality it would have been at least double. Our guests enjoyed them, obviously, almost as much as we did and the conversation was very general and of good quality even though few present had ever met most of their fellow-diners. On the whole, we felt that such evenings were ones we should never forget and well worth all the trouble and work their arranging cost. We were unfortunate in not having several interesting guests (see enclosed list) [1] as our dates conflicted with those of other dinners.

Our tour officially started Friday morning [July 15] when we hired a Daimler and started off in good time for Windsor. On the way Boies took us on a slight detour to see a Jacobean library room in a church at Langley. We could only peek at it through the window, but later, at The Combe, saw pictures of it and regretted that we had not had time to find the sexton. At Windsor, Morshead, the King's Librarian, was awaiting us and after showing us the Doll's House, for the benefit of small Frances who was with us that day, took us to the library. Our stay there was very limited but we saw, besides the great monuments of Gutenberg and Caxton, several very fine bindings, royal copies of this and that, including the dedication copy, Eliza's, of *The Faerie Queene*, and an example of a tympanum cut-out for rubricating, possibly sixteenth century. Morshead showed us some amusing royal dedications, particularly a most obsequious one of Disraeli to Victoria and, as contrast, a very curt one of Tennyson to the same, and a more usual one of Dickens. He also showed us a book on the Life of Victoria (up to her Marriage) by Miss Strickland. It contained the Queen's penciled comments throughout and, according to Morshead, these remarks were sent to the publisher who withdrew the book so that the copy we saw is said to be the only one issued in that form.

We were forced to hurry on as Canon Deane at St. George's Library was leaving in a few minutes for the weekend. He was very kind to us, however, and gave us a hurried glimpse of the collection there which

[1] [The guests at the first dinner were Lord Rothschild, Harold Williams, Hugh Sinclair, John Steegeman, W. R. Tyler, Jr., and George Clutton; at the second, W. R. Tyler, Jr., Byam Shaw, Paul Sachs, A. Gray, and W. S. Lewis. Also invited but unable to accept were Simon Nowell-Smith, John Sparrow, John Carter, Sir Stephen Gaselee, C. B. Tinker, Kenneth Clark, Geoffrey Keynes, Fred Norris Robinson, and Shane Leslie.]

appears to contain a very miscellaneous lot of books mainly theological of the sixteenth and seventeenth centuries. I managed to list a few, including a Mohawk book printed at Cambridge, 1656, which I do not recall seeing before. However, the most striking thing of all that I recall seeing was a volume containing the complete printed ballots for the election of Pope Innocent XI, 1676. I suppose such things do exist elsewhere but it was most interesting as showing how the majority refrained from voting until a distinct trend appeared and then climbed on the bandwagon! Our time there was all too short and I hope some time to return to check the shelves and to take rubbings of some of the unrecorded armorial stamps which I saw there. One good long day should suffice unless unexpected treasures should be revealed.

After Canon Deane, a most amiable person, had to leave, we were shown St. George's Chapel which, to me, is the equal of King's C. C., and where we first saw the handiwork of Professor Tristram of Oxford. The chapel has been very thoroughly reconditioned and gives the appearance of having been almost completely rebuilt, although very carefully and piously. I forgot to say that while in the Castle we were shown the state apartments including the room with eight Holbeins, four first rate, and we also had a glimpse of the Holbein drawings. At the time we were there the vast collections of drawings were being "expertized" and so we were not permitted, had our time allowed, to see them.

We lunched very well at the White Hart and then proceeded to Eton where after several tries we found the Library and spent some time examining the exhibition cases with the assistant librarian. He is relatively ignorant but is doing an excellent job of caring for the bindings. Most of the good books there were the gift of an eighteenth century Etonian, — Story, and just as we were going I found two shelves containing mainly Jacobean plays bound in eighteenth century calf, perhaps two hundred. These should be checked, though I suppose Greg has been there. That library is open to undergraduates on Sunday afternoons and is housed in fine eighteenth century rooms.

We also had a glimpse of the School Library where we saw the Gray MSS. and the Shelley Rome notebook which Shane Leslie and one of his Churchill cousins gave after graduation. He told me that when the idea of giving a Shelley MS. occurred to them they put an advertisement in the Daily Express saying that two Eton graduates wished to acquire a Shelley MS. for Eton and would be happy to entertain offers. Lady

Shelley replied and offered them the notebook for ten pounds which they then thought outrageously expensive!

On our way back we stopped at Hampton Court and had a quick glimpse of the galleries there and also of the Mantegna cartoons.

Phil and I dined together that evening at the Athenaeum and had a final glimpse of Goldschmidt at midnight. Saturday morning we all took an early train for Taunton and on the way down Boies gave of his unrivaled knowledge of English topography and exhibited his interest and knowledge of railroads by recounting stories of their development and speed and by clocking our own time showed us how really fast we were going although without any of the usual discomforts of great speed.

I shall not try to tell you all we did while at The Combe. You know it and West Somerset as well or better than I. You also know what a gracious host Boies is and his enthusiasm for his country and his knowledge of English domestic architecture! Under his guidance we saw a number of Elizabethan and Georgian houses which we inspected very nearly as thoroughly as if we were intending purchasers. We met the owners, Boies's friends, who in some cases were as interesting as their domiciles. We dined at Dunster Castle where we were shown the Chippendale room and the Elizabethan room, the family portraits, the muniment rooms, and the few books in the library of interest, including several MS. genealogies acquired by Geoffrey Luttrell at the Luttrell-Pendarves sale in 1936. We also dined at Nettlecombe where we were shown all the mantels and other features recently uncovered, as well as the library, where we found some volumes of interest as well as one or two unrecorded Trevelyan stamps. The Wolseleys are taking great pains to bring out the best in the house and have made remarkable progress since I saw the place in 1934. We spent a pleasant hour at the Westminster Bank seeing Boies's Caxtons and MSS. and odd times looking at the books at The Combe. Altogether, his own library is much the finest in that part of the country and it, together with the house and Boies's hospitality, made the weekend a memorable one.

Tuesday morning we were off quite early in Boies's new Daimler 15, our bags strapped on in back and the 1/4-inch Ordnance maps handy under the front seat. We were due at Thirlestaine House, Cheltenham, at 11 o'clock and were very nearly on time although it was difficult to pass by the libraries of Bristol which some day we should see. The Phillipps Collection, which at one time numbered nearly 40,000 MSS., is now housed, as it has been since the 1850's in a nabob's palace which occupies a full block in the center of Cheltenham. Mr. Fenwick was awaiting us and had arisen from a sick-bed to receive us. He had brought out some fifteen MSS. to show us, including some very fine examples of humanistic MSS., several French and German romances in lettres batardes, etc. He also showed us the picture galleries of which not much need be said except of one room which contains some dozens of Catlins which, I presume, are rather good of their kind, though to me the most interesting thing about them was that they should be there at all — buffalo hunting on the Kansas plains being about as remote from Cheltenham as anything one could name. Fenwick was adamant in refusing to acknowledge our hints that we should like to see his library — we didn't, and, so I'm told, neither has anyone else.

After a hasty sherry and biscuit which came just in time to save Boies's sense of what is fitting regarding nourishment and the regularity thereof, we hastened on to Malvern to the Dyson Perrins collection. What we saw there was so very fine that, I'm afraid, we have rather forgotten the MSS. at Cheltenham, which without that immediate comparison would not have seemed so inferior and which when we saw them appeared to us to be of such great interest that only our completely empty stomachs and our appointment in Malvern induced us to leave.

Perrins' house, Davenham, is also in the heart of the city but on the side of a hill and instead of an eighteenth century Indian nabob's is a nineteenth century Worcestershire sauce nabob's house. Mr. Perrins is a little wizened fellow with a very cordial manner, a good sense of humor, and extremely good taste in books. His Italian illustrated fifteenth and sixteenth century books and his MSS. have been catalogued and are known, but it is not so well known that he has also very fine French, German, and English books as well. While there I managed to make a list of all his English books but missed seeing the French and German ones while doing so. However, I did see many of his Italian books and his MSS. The Gorleston Psalter which he showed us was one of the high points of the trip — ranking with the Benedictionale at Chatsworth. His English books include copies of all the books printed at Worcester by John Oswen in 1549–1550, a number of news-tracts of the 1590's which once belonged to Humphrey Dyson and, curiously enough, the 1631 edition of *The Shepherd's Kalendar* of which copies are also in the Metropolitan and Hofer collections. His other English books are mainly liturgical — from the Gott collection — or Caxtons and W. de Wordes. His MSS. are kept in a vault which for quality could match its contents with any collection of its size anywhere known. His books fill two other rooms and include a fine reference library. Nothing has been added to the collection for nearly fifteen years, as I'm afraid Mr. Perrins now collects Worcestershire china of which he owns the factory and of which he collects the rarest types — i.e., pre-eighteenth century. When we left Philip was making all sorts of resolutions and mental commitments about acquisitions at "The Dyson Perrins Sale, Sotheby's 19XX" and Boies was muttering "there's lots of plunder left in England." I'm afraid I was just breathless with admiration at the condition of the copies and, in general, the acumen of their selection.

We stayed that night at the Abbey Hotel. Boies made our reservations throughout the tour and, with only one exception, did very well by us. I may as well digress here and discuss our "invariable custom" which was that when arriving, usually about 7 o'clock, we would wash and then join, in one or other's room, for a glass of whiskey and a general relaxing conversation regarding the day. Then at dinner we took turns ordering such wines as the place afforded, never failing to find something quite worth drinking.

The next morning early we started off for Shrewsbury through lovely rolling country, keeping mainly to back roads and not stopping until we arrived at the school, again slightly late, where Mr. Oldham, the librarian, an ex-master, awaited us. He did the honors very well, showing us first a bit of the school which is a nineteenth century plant on a bluff overlooking the town and the Severn, with lovely broad lawns and not ugly buildings. He then took us to the library which although in a new building still has some of the feel of an old one for the room is paneled and some of the cases are old. It is a sixteenth century foundation and contains some very good early books including a unique volume of advice from Sir Henry Sidney to the Admirable Crichton, his son Philip, an alumnus of the school. Oldham let me have a list of the *S.T.C.* books in the library so we spent most of our time looking at the bindings of which they have a considerable number and talking with Oldham. I think we should all like to go there again with more leisure. There are, for example, nearly a score of unique early English books there as well as some hundreds of others.

Oldham joined us for lunch. At his suggestion we went to a "restaurant" instead of to the local pub, much to our regret. After lunch we wandered about Shrewsbury for nearly an hour seeing the old School, and some of the old streets, and the "Museum" which was not much except that in the courtyard were several pieces of good lead work. We had quite a long, and rather dreary drive through the industrial Midlands, Macclesfield, etc., to Peover Superior near Knutsford, about fifteen miles outside Manchester. We stayed at a place called the Bells of Peover which was almost in the grave-yard of the village church but turned out to be a road-house for Manchester "cits" and the only poor pub of our trip.

When we arrived shortly after ten next morning at the Rylands Library, Dr. Guppy immediately welcomed us and took us into the incunabula vault where we spent a very happy hour and a half seeing literally scores of rarities from block-books to Caxtons. We examined the Valdarfer Boccaccio (some notes in which Guppy promised to have photostated in return for a photostat of my auctioneer's notes on Blandford's payment), we saw and handled many rare Sweynheims, Jensons, and even Costeriana. Never before have we seen such an array of "Morocco by C. Lewis" or so many sound and magnificent copies of Dibdinian classics. We also spent some time in the Bible and Aldine rooms and finished off with a half-hour in the MSS. room where we saw a very fine Spanish Beatus, some good text MSS. and several very fine Oriental MSS. We also saw the case of bindings where Roger Payne's work can be seen in perhaps its finest flower and certainly in greatest profusion, including the book upon which he was working when he died, with the second volume finished by another hand. We looked over the exhibition, "Transmission of the Bible," with great interest. Certainly no place else could it be duplicated except perhaps in the B.M. and there the Coptic fragments recently identified could be overbalanced by the Codex Sinaiticus. Guppy was so proud of his library, as indeed he might well be, and so convinced that every book in it was the finest copy known, that it was a pleasure to look at the books with him even though we could see that the strain of showing them for hours on end tired him considerably.

After a substantial but late lunch in a Manchester chop-house we separated, Boies and Philip going to the Whitworth Institute and I to the Chetham Library. The Chetham was a complete contrast to the Rylands. Instead of nineteenth century Gothic, furnished in mahogany and brass, it is Jacobean oak, still well preserved and very well furnished with fine fireplaces, splendid presses much in the manner of Duke Humphrey's room, and some thousands of seventeenth century books in original calf. The attendant did not seem to think it possible for me to browse but finally after I had asked to see the ballads, including the Martial one from the Heber collection, the only one of the Daniel-Heber collection I had not seen and handled, he offered to ask the librarian to send me a set of the 6-volume catalogue which he has since done. I want some time to return there and search the collection for it has the smell of good hunting.

We left about four for a long dreary drive through the Yorkshire black moors, Huddersfield, Leeds, etc., to York. The city we left and the towns through which we drove were smoky and terrifying in their drabness, but when we arrived at York it was still light and the old city soon made us forget the Industrial Revolution and all its hideousness. After dining at our pub, the Station Hotel, a huge but very good hostel which Boies rightly assured us was quite unlike its name, we wandered around the Minster and through the old part of town, looking in the windows of the antique stores and seeing what we could find of the narrow old lanes. We were due to meet Canon Harrison under the great tower at 10:30 the next morning, so before that time Boies went to the Railway Museum from which he seemed to have obtained considerable pleasure and Philip and I went to the Treasurer's House behind the Cathedral. It has recently been given to the National Trust and is a magnificent piece of reconstruction. The fabric itself is much as it was in the eighteenth century with a fine façade, an Elizabethan hall, and several fine staircases and room after room furnished in the period of its paneling — and superbly furnished in keeping with the quondam residence of Lord Strafford when Lord President of the North. Altogether, it alone would make a trip to York well worth while.

Prebendary Harrison, the librarian, an odd, foolish little man, who knows his Crockford verbatim but considers himself a bit above doing any real work in his library, was most cordial to us and insisted on talking generalities and stupid anecdotes when we wanted to see the books. Boies was rather disgusted with the disorder and squalor of the library and soon left to see the Five Sisters when Harrison locked Philip and myself in the library for an hour or so. He, among other things, told us of the sale of the books in 1931 to Rosenbach and assured us that Dr.

R., because of his great love of the central tower, gave a philanthropic price for them. To prove it he showed me a list with the prices attached which I copied. It is an extraordinary document and a puzzling one. The total sum paid was, I think, very generous, but why it was apportioned as it was can only be conjectured. It is a long story which, if you are interested, I'll tell you some day. Philip was entranced with an English stamped binding which has tools signed "H H" and most certainly is in Holbein's manner. He took rubbings of it while I fussed about with odd things here and there. As I had already checked the printed catalogue (some of the titles there listed are not now in the library or at any rate have not been found) I made no attempt to list things in general but spent my time looking at some of the rare York printed books and trying to find my way about.

After a hurried visit to the antique stores and lunch we set out for Wentworth Woodhouse, Earl Fitzwilliam's mansion near Rotherham. Aside from a very few books which we knew to be there, all we found was a complete surprise for we had heard nothing of the house or its contents. The house itself is immense, built in the Vanbrugh manner, very Palladian, with portico and huge white marble hall almost a cube. The Van Dycks, Romneys, etc. were very fine, especially the wonderful portrait of Strafford and his Secretary. The furniture was in keeping and included several incredible mirrors, some fine Chinese Chippendale, and many impressive vases. Apartment after apartment which we went through contained treasures which deserve better treatment than this slight sketch. The painters were at work in the three rooms of the library when we arrived so that in one room we saw nothing while in the other two we worked under difficulties. The Caxtons were locked up in a glass case and we could merely look at them through the glass, because the Comptroller whom his Lordship had written would show us the library was off playing golf. There also was the unique Rastell edition of *The Widow Edyth* and an unrecorded *Medicines for Horses* by W. de Worde, of which we saw copies also at Lincoln and Chatsworth. We also found shelves of bound volumes labeled "Tracts" and "Miscellanies" among which Boies found a copy of Raleigh's "Report of a fight in the Azores (Revenge)," and I listed some dozens of good pieces. Philip took several rubbings of Wentworth stamps for me and altogether we had a profitable but tantalizing time.

We stayed the night at a very good pub on the Great North Road at Barnby Moor and were off in good time to meet Canon Kynaston under the tower at Lincoln. Kynaston is a dear old fellow who is very keen on his library and has it all very well arranged so that we soon saw everything which we asked to see and found many other fine books as well. The library, or rather, the old library is housed in a long gallery-like room by Wren. It has a good deal of charm and one might profitably spend a week there working through the books. I found, by chance, a list of books sold by the Dean and Chapter about the time they sold the Lincoln Nose-Gay. Kynaston let me take his marked *Short-title Catalogue* and Saturday and Sunday evenings I listed all 1400 of the English books in the library. Kynaston joined us for a very late lunch and then we wandered about the town, saw the Museum, etc. We enjoyed the comfort of the White Hart, which was much the most expensive of our pubs. Sunday we were pretty fagged and spent the morning writing letters and resting and just before lunch called on some friends of Boies's a few miles out in the country. After lunch we saw Tattershall Castle, a tremendous pile of brick with fine fireplaces in the chambers and the air of having been well designed by an architect of taste instead of just built by the local masons. Kynaston joined us again that evening and we became quite fond of the old boy.

Monday was, perhaps, the most thrilling day of our trip. In the morning we went to Welbeck Abbey, the seat of the Duke of Portland. After trying at several lodges we finally found the proper entrance and reached the Abbey by driving through the stables into a glass roofed court where the coal was stored and the "offices" of the staff were. Mr. Francis Needham, his Grace's librarian, met us by appointment. The first thing we saw were some rails running through a basement corridor which, we were informed, were used in bringing the food from the kitchens to the dining room. We then began a tour through the vast building; altogether we saw some hundreds of the very nearly a thousand portraits which hang there. Particularly memorable was a gallery of horses by Stubbs, painted for the Duke of Newcastle, the hippographer, and the fine Van Dycks in the dining room. One small Elizabethan bedroom we were shown was a gem of fine old paneling. There was a small library completely furnished in the large eighteenth century color-plate folios. They made quite a show but we were not allowed much time to examine them. The large library is in the old riding school of the D. of N. above mentioned and is a well proportioned room with some, but not many interesting books. I saw, for example, a large-paper Gulliver, and several rows of books which belonged to the Duchess of Portland. There was a copy of the catalogues of her sale with interesting, I believe, notes, and several fine James II bindings. I managed to find several stamps to rub, but on the whole the library was disappointing as we had been warned. We had several glimpses of the landscaping which was very fine and were taken to the plate room where we gaped unabashedly. Along with stacks of silver and gold plates, dozens of hollow pieces of all sizes, cups massive or fine or both, some tankards over two feet high which must have weighed hundreds of ounces, Goodwood cups, inkstands of great beauty, truly masterpieces of the silversmiths, we saw several Restoration and William and Mary toilet sets with mirrors, and a case of historical pieces, Henry VIII's jeweled dagger, Mary, Queen of Scots' jewel, and the chalice from which Charles took communion before going to the scaffold — these mainly, if not all, were from the Duchess of Portland's collection.

We also were shown a feature which amused Boies very much and which, indeed, was rather grotesque while at the same time stupendous, viz., the vast tunnels, one over a mile long which the late Duke had excavated. There was one room attached to the house which was dug for him. It is now occasionally used as a ballroom and is completely lined with huge Rysbracks and similar portraits, but it would serve equally well for a rugger field or for indoor flat races. We were also shown his chef d'oeuvre, which fortunately he did not live to roof over. It is now used as the site for formal sunken gardens and several tennis courts are almost lost in the middle of it.

After a quick but excellent lunch at Rowsley (the Peacock, a particularly fine angler's pub which would make an agreeable place to stay were one so fortunate as to spend several days at Chatsworth) and a glorious drive through the Dukeries, we were admitted to the park of Chatsworth and drove into an interesting and very imposing courtyard. The mansion is beautifully situated in the English fashion with a curtain of woods behind and formal gardens with a fine sheet of water and a distant prospect of rolling green hills which was achieved by the very ducal gesture of moving an entire hill which intervened. The house is built of a lovely yellow grey stone and, except for a hanging garden effect on one side, gives the appearance of being Palladian. However, originally it was Elizabethan but by a series of accretions now contains a fine central court on which galleries which were added in the 18th century look. These corridors avoid the usual necessity in these houses of going through the rooms themselves but they are built on such a generous scale and are so well furnished that it is mainly by name that one can distinguish them from the older apartments. When the fourth side of the court was filled in it was discovered that one wing was 14 feet longer than the other. Instead of shearing the excess off, that end was made with a graceful bulge which seems so right that one would think, until told, that it was planned that way. In fact, throughout the entire house there are countless evidences of taste superior to mere rules, daring almost beyond mortal courage and yet invariably successful. The only instance that failed, at least if a cursory glimpse does not make criticism an impertinence, is in the hanging of the pictures in several of the saloons which are without frames, let-in, flush with the walls, in a most striking and unusual manner but one which results, it seemed to me, in making them merely a part of the ensemble like the drapes or a door.

But I must return to the books which were the object of our visit. They occupy one great room with gallery, several smaller rooms and wall after wall of the corridors and number something like 100,000. The small room where the English drama was formerly kept is now filled with a fine selection of reference books, and in a gallery outside the great library is the library of Lord Burlington, the amateur architect and virtuoso. I had not known that it was there but it appears to contain a superb collection of the older books on the subjects which interested his Lordship. On either side of the door as one enters the library are ranged the great folio incunabula, in the most superb condition and lavish binding, mainly of the Spencerian type but even finer in general effect than those we saw at Rylands. In a large octagonal table case are kept the small quarto rarities, such as the decade of unique W. de Worde romances from the Roxburghe collection, the unique pieces from the Dampier collection, etc. I soon discovered that the librarian for the years before the war, Mr. Strong, had made a great many additions to the collections since the Lacaita catalogue was published. Particularly he had bought judiciously at the Ashburnham sale and I there found a number of books which in the Pforzheimer Catalogue I had mentioned as untraced since the Ashburnham sale, e.g., two Skeltons, etc. I found that a typed list of these additions was available and I spent my time checking it through for the more important 1640 books. However, I could not resist looking at some of the other treasures that were making Philip's temperature rise and which Boies would occasionally bring over to my table with the request "Look at this curious old book," and I turned to see some stupendous rarity which Boies had found only deliberate understatement and a twinkle in his eye could describe. We all looked breathlessly at the Benedictionale of St. Ethelwold which might well be described as the greatest MS. which now exists in private hands. That was a great experience but even more memorable, because quite unexpected, was the sight of an Aldine Petrarch on vellum with illumination throughout, *en grise*, each canto in a different luminous color and of the finest possible workmanship by Clovio. Philip spent an ecstatic hour with the 178 Claude Lorraine drawings and kept breathlessly telling of them afterwards.

As we drove away that evening all three of us were talking at once — defying all communists to see such a house as that we had just seen and not to acknowledge that there was something that the capitalist system had produced that no civil servants, no committee, and no board of trustees could ever equal. We were so thrilled that we protested that even marquises would, in the future, receive only a distant nod from us. With many a remark on the pleasures of "duking" we finally reached Grantham, and the George, tired but very happy. It was the greatest day of a series of very memorable days.

Next morning we drove across the fens to Norwich where we put up at the Maids Head and then set out for the Castle Museum where Miss G. V. Barnard awaited us. She spent the whole afternoon taking us from one museum to another and, though none of us enjoyed being "conducted," she made it possible for us to see far more than we ever could have found for ourselves and we are much indebted to her. In the first place, Norwich has some four or five museums. The largest is The Castle, which is a very good example of an English provincial museum with a few rooms of local paintings, a large section of Roman remains and various cases of local silver, china, etc. There they have a small shrine devoted to Sir Thomas Browne, but it contains nothing very remarkable of printed books. There was a case of MSS. which also contained one or two printed things, particularly a volume printed at Norwich in the 1560's by Solempne. Then we went to the deconsecrated parish church of the Pastons, which is now an ecclesiastical museum and where we found an exhibition showing the development of the English Bible. It contained most of the usual printed editions, Great, Bishops,

Authorized, etc., and several rather superior MSS. After that we saw a museum of Norfolk industries where there was another Solempne, an early nineteenth-century binder's shop, and a room of old games which amused Boies very much. To continue with the museums, but not in the order in which we saw them, we were shown The Strangers' House, which is a sixteenth-century flint house erected by the Lord Mayor at the time of the incorporation of the city. It contains nearly a score of rooms furnished in the various periods since the middle sixteenth century and very well furnished too. The Victorian room is quite a gem and the whole is far more effective than one would ever expect to find in an out of the way corner like Norwich. We were also taken to the Public Library which the librarian informed us was the first public library to be built in England under the Penny Rate Library Act. It is obviously much too crowded and we saw no books except a few MSS. which the library acquired at the Gurney sale in 1935 and which were once bound with Pforzheimer's Macro *Respublica* MS. However, the librarian promised to send me a copy of the printed catalogue which he said contained some hundreds of 1640 English books. We had a delightful hour in the cathedral, a remarkable Romanesque structure with cloisters that have recently been restored, the bosses being very effectively painted by Professor Tristram. Then Miss Hagge Scott took us to the library where we rummaged happily for some time. The library is in disgraceful order but we found a Rood, several rare W. de Wordes, etc. It was impossible to search the shelves and, without opening every volume, one could not be sure what treasures we overlooked because we found by chance several volumes on the shelves which surpassed in interest and value some of the books which were stored in the vault. Before dining we toured some of the antique stores and afterwards strolled in the lovely Georgian Dean's Yard and I swam in the pool at the Samson and Hercules. Norwich is a most interesting city and one to which I hope some day to return with more leisure.

Wednesday morning we sped down the "autobahn" to Cambridge. I have neglected to record that throughout the trip Boies exhibited the extent of his German vocabulary by interlarding nearly every sentence with German nouns, every castle was a "schloss," etc. It added a slightly foreign aura to our entourage and several times when he and Philip were bandying Deutsche in some narrow provincial lane we were probably taken for a group of Herr Schicklegruber's outcasts. Boies had, with much regret, to leave that noon for Somerset, so, after a half hour looking over the astounding array of MSS. in the exhibition at Trinity College, Mr. Adams took us over to Magdalene to meet Mr. Turner, the librarian of the Pepysian. None of us had ever been there before and all of us just ached to be allowed to rummage in the cases. That, however, is not the custom there and we were content to be shown the things for which we asked. Pepys's naval interests led him to collect many English books on navigation and travel which Boies may have another chance to see. Before we left I arranged to examine the manuscript catalogue the next day. When I had spent an hour or two with it I decided that it was too carelessly made to be worth checking and that I should be, in many cases, guessing at the editions and entering more errors into my *S.T.C.* than I hope is usually the case. Adams lunched with Philip and me and then I returned to Trinity to check their 2,000 Early English books while Philip went on to the Fitzwilliam. I met him there at five and had a hasty glimpse of its varied treasures before going to have tea with the new director, Louis Clarke. His house contains a number of good drawings, particularly a fine Fragonard, any number of Augustus John and several very fine pieces of furniture, needlework and silver. He was a most entertaining host and I wished that the task I had set myself at Trinity was not so lengthy that I might have returned to the Fitzwilliam with Philip the next day. That evening Phil and I strolled about the town after a leisurely dinner at the University Arms and next morning we made an early start — Philip at Corpus and the Fitzwilliam, and I at Magdalene and Trinity. After a late tea we packed our bags and took a cab to Merton Hall, the tenth century Pythagoras School, which Lord Rothschild has made into a most attractive home. The gardens adjoin those of St. Johns and Trinity and one facade looks like a street of sixteenth century half-timbered houses. Inside, it is furnished in modernistic beige, not at all badly done, although a great opportunity was lost. Our host had not returned from golf but we were expected and sipped cocktails and strolled in the garden until he turned up. The cocktails were without question the only ones I have ever had in England which were worth remarking. At dinner Rothschild appeared in a white silk dressing gown and red velvet slippers with embroidered coronets. Lady Rothschild, a gracious and beautiful blonde, was, as seems always to be her habit, very chicly gowned, while Philip and I, who had lugged our evening things a thousand miles for that one evening, were denied the chance to change, as the Rothschilds insisted that they always dined informally. Informally or not, we dined in Lucullan state, with Mouton

Rothschild, Chateau Rothschild, and some exceptional brandy. We then adjourned to the library where until nearly two the next morning we saw such an array of eighteenth century books and MSS. as nowhere else exists. Their condition was enough to make one's mouth water and both Philip and I, as red morocco case after case revealed its contents, lost much of our condescension to the relative modernity of the period. The ardor and success with which Rothschild has gathered his books may, indeed, be worthier of a greater field of endeavor, but that he has done a useful work and one which needed doing, at least once, is indisputable. The next morning Rothschild after breakfast walked with us through the gardens to Trinity where I finished my task and then hurried over to the University Library where later Philip joined me. There Creswick showed us a few of their great treasures, such as a presentation copy, on lavish vellum of Tunstall's *De arte arithmetica*, Pynson 1522, the Gutenberg Bible from the Young bequest, a volume of unique tracts, English c.1550, from Corpus, all unrecorded but soon to be published in a catalogue Creswick is doing, etc. After a tour of the library we had to return to Merton Hall for lunch and Creswick took us through the private walks in the meadows.

We lunched leisurely, and very well, afterwards sitting in the garden until train time. Our trip was over and we had the pleasant feeling of complete satiety which was not wholly due to the excellences of the lunch but, in a large measure, arose from the myriad memories of books, people, pictures and buildings which had filled our eyes and stirred us so deeply for just two weeks of concentrated pleasure. As I look back over what I have written you I see that not only have I omitted such pleasant interludes as our half hour at Tewkesbury and our obeisance to Milton at Ludlow Castle, but I have failed miserably in my attempt to convey the wealth of interest in some of the collections we saw. However, perhaps from these notes you can have some taste of our simpler, as well as our grander experiences. I cannot tell you fully how sorry I am that you could not join us but now that your offending vermiform appendix is plucked out, that at least will never prevent you joining us in the future if we should be so happy as to be able to make another such tour — And that, Peter, will be the constant hope of

Your servant,
Bill Jackson

5

Counterfeit Printing in Jacobean Times

(1934)

This is one of Jackson's earliest essays in bibliographical analysis based on typography (Bibliography, no. 7).

THAT patented books, particularly ABC's, catechisms, and primers, were fraudulently imitated by some of the more unruly of the London printers in the sixteenth century is well known from the Stationers' records, though the particular editions so produced have not been identified and perhaps no longer exist. There are also several instances of reprints of theological or political tracts which retain the original date of impression, sometimes also the original imprint, though apparently produced at a considerably later date.[1] But in these latter instances there was usually no attempt made to imitate the ornaments of the original, the printers being content if they were able to conceal their own identity.

These two classes of surreptitiously produced books have been, with some partiality, excused on the grounds that the first was the result of economic oppression and the printers responsible for it were fighting for the freedom of the press; while the second was the natural concomitant of religious and political tyranny. There is, however, a third class of fraudulent printing which may prove to have been much more prevalent than has yet been suspected, viz. the counterfeit printing of popular copyright books. *Doppeldrucke* of this kind are not unknown in any period since the time of the Lyonnese Aldine forgeries, but their existence in English Jacobean printing has not apparently been previously

[1] An example of this type of reprint, which does not appear to have been detected, is one of the three editions of Selden's *History of Tythes*, 1618 (*S.T.C.* 22173), which from the orthography and type is obviously the edition said by Anthony à Wood to have been reprinted in 1680.

A. Eld

B. Eld

C. Creede

D. Eld

E. Creede

F. Eld

H. Eld

G. Creede

I. Creede

J. Allde

L. Allde

K. Windet

M. Windet

III. Genuine and counterfeit ornaments

observed. In the present paper three instances of this practice are discussed, of which the first two appear to be wholly fraudulent, while the last may have been produced to deceive the retail purchaser rather than to defraud the owner of the copyright.

Wither's Abuses Stript and Whipt, *1613*

There are four editions of this book dated 1613, all of which purport to have been printed by George Eld for Francis Burton. Copies of all of them may be consulted in the British Museum and Harvard Libraries and they may be distinguished by the variations noted in the *Short-title Catalogue* (Nos. 25891–4).[2]

Of three of these editions (*S.T.C.* 25891–2 and 25984) there can be no doubt that George Eld was the actual printer, for they each contain at least a half-dozen ornaments and initials used by him both before and after this date.[3] The other edition (*S.T.C.* 25893), though stated in the imprint to have been likewise printed by Eld for Burton in the same year, was not printed by Eld but by Thomas Creede. It is a very close reprint of what appears to have been Eld's first edition (*S.T.C.* 25892).[4] Nevertheless, it may be condemned as counterfeit not merely because of the fact that its imprint is false, for that might be explained as the blind following of copy by a careless compositor; but rather because in it all of the eight ornaments and initials, including even Burton's device on the title, have been faithfully recut. In some cases, so closely have the originals been imitated, even the cracks and other defects are reproduced.

The anonymous forger was a skillful craftsman, but his handiwork may be distinguished without difficulty from the originals by variations in outline and shading. Moreover, he could not resist a not unnatural impulse to fill out with new filigree the corners and apexes of the designs, e.g., in the tail-piece on verso X8, at the top right-hand corner, where

[2] It has been stated that the Dyce copy is of another edition, but an examination of it shows that it is a copy of *S.T.C.* 25893.

[3] The urn head-piece on recto B7 of *S.T.C.* 25894, as also the half volute tailpiece at the end of the same, originally belonged to Valentine Simmes, but apparently either late in 1607 or early the following year Simmes disposed of his printing materials, for after that time they may be traced in the hands of George Eld, Felix Kingston, and Henry Ballard.

[4] It is possible that Burton anticipated a large sale and commissioned Eld to print two editions simultaneously. Some of the readings appear to point to such an explanation, and the two apparently genuine cuttings of Burton's device (see below and Plate III) lend support to such an explanation.

the original (Plate III, H) has a limp row of beads, he has introduced a sharply cut ribbon-end (Plate III, I). That particular block was used openly by Creede several times in 1615, e.g., on the title of Beaumont's *Cupid's Revenge*.

It has been thought worthwhile to reproduce in Plate III several of the forged blocks together with the originals from which they were copied in order that an opportunity might be given to appraise the degree of accuracy then possible for a copy. Presumably the method used by the cutter of these forgeries was the very simple one of pasting an impression of the original face-down upon a block, scraping the paper away until the design showed through, and then cutting as usual. The results indicate that the identity of two cuts cannot be established merely by a comparison of measurements and observation of the similarity of defects, cf. particularly the initial T (Plate III, D, E).

There are three cuttings of Burton's device (Plate III, A, B, C) of which the first two may be presumed to be genuine, for the first was used in *S.T.C.* 25892 and the edition of 1617, while the second was used on all the other genuine editions as late as 1615. The third is the forgery used by Creede in *S.T.C.* 25893 and, by a curious mischance, is the one reproduced in McKerrow, *Devices*, No. 364.

Apparently, though this counterfeit edition was sufficiently close to escape detection by the bibliographers, it was probably the one to which the following entry in the unpublished *Liber C* of the Stationers' Company applies: Fol. 38a, 1 March 1614–15. "It is also ordered that Raffe Mabb, Wm Bladon, Geo: Gibbes and Fran. Constable shall pay for printing of a booke called (Abuses stript & whipt) being the Copie of Fran. Burton wch is Contrary to the order of this house. iijl that is to say 15s a peece . . ." But if that entry does refer to this forgery then evidently Creede succeeded in concealing his connection with it, for no mention can be found of any fine being exacted from him about that time.

Bacon's Essays, *1613*

There are three editions of the *Essays* all purporting to have been printed for John Jaggard in 1613. They may be distinguished by the spelling of the word "Attorney" on their titles: "Atturny," "Aturney," or "Atturney." There were no succeeding editions, except the Edinburgh piracy, until 1624. This, by itself, might be attributed to bad

THE
ESSAIES
OF Sr FRANCIS
BACON Knight, the
Kings Atturny Ge-
nerall.

¶ His Religious Medi-
tations.

¶ Places of Perſwaſion
and Diſſwaſion.

Seene and allowed.

Printed at London for *Iohn Iag-*
gard, dwelling at the Hand and Starre
betweene the two Temple
Gates. 1 6 1 3.

THE
ESSAIES
OF Sr FRANCIS
BACON Knight, the
Kings Aturney Ge-
nerall.

¶ His Religious Medi-
tations.

¶ Places of Perſwaſion
and Diſſwaſion.

Seene and allowed.

Printed at London for *Iohn Iag-*
gard, dwelling at the Hand and Starre
betweene he two Temple
Gates 1 6 1 3

THE
ESSAIES
OF Sr FRANCIS
BACON Knight, the
Kings Atturney Ge-
nerall.

¶ His Religious Medi.
tations.

¶ Places of Perſwaſion
and Diſſwaſion.

Seene and allowed.

Printed at London for *Iohn Iag-*
gard, dwelling at the Hand and Starre
betweene the two Temple
Gates. 1 6 1 3.

A. "Atturny" Edition: Jaggard

B. "Aturney" Edition: Beale

C. "Atturney" Edition: Beale

IV. Genuine and counterfeit title pages

judgement upon the part of Jaggard, since the editions before 1613 and after 1624 appeared at regularly spaced intervals or at ones otherwise accountable, were it not that the three 1613 editions are obviously designed to appear, at any rate so far as their titles are concerned, identical (see Plate IV).

It is now customary to regard the editions of the *Essays* which bear Jaggard's imprint as pirated, but there is no evidence whatever to support such a view except the *argumentum ab silentio* that Jaggard made no entry for the book in the Stationers' Register. On the contrary, despite his family's unsavory reputation, evidence may be adduced to show that he had a right in the title and that he maintained it for his widow [5] transferred "her estate" in the copy, 24 February 1626 (Arber, IV, 151). The simplest explanation is that in 1606, when Jaggard published his first edition of the *Essays*, he bought the rights, without registering transfer, of Humphry Hooper who had made the original entry for the book and published the first three editions of it. That would explain why Hooper, who was still active, did not publish any edition of the *Essays* after Jaggard's first and, also, why he did not register a transfer to someone else or object to Jaggard's publication. Moreover, it should be recalled that whatever the origin of Jaggard's "estate" in this copy may have been, it was presumably bona fide for he did not attempt to conceal his connection with these editions as his brother did in his Shakespeare piracies.

On 12 October 1612 (Arber, III, 499) William Hall and John Beale, who were in partnership at that time, entered without transfer Bacon's *Essays* and printed an edition dated the same year. The fact that that edition was presumably authorized by Bacon himself and that besides a new dedication and considerable alterations in the nine previously published essays it had twenty-nine new ones added, evidently caused the publishers to regard their edition as an entirely new publication which they could protect by entry. In 1612 Jaggard also republished the old Hooper text in an edition which retains the original dedication to Sir Nicholas Bacon,

[5] In the Stationers' unpublished *Liber C*, Fol. 87^{a}, 22 June 1625, occurs the following entry: "Vpon hearing of the matter betwixt m^{rs} Jaggard & m^{rs} Barret Concerning the printing of the lo:verulams Essayes. It plainely appeared that the booke lately printed by m^{rs} Barret [i.e., the first "complete" edition, 1625] is m^{rs} Jaggards proper Copie wth some alteracons and addicons therevnto. And therefore (the matter being put to the table by Consent of both pties) It is thought fitt and so ordered That m^{rs} Barret shall give vnto her the said m^{rs} Jaggard ffiftye of the same bookes in quires. And m^{rs} Barret is not to printe yt any more wthout her Consent, onely so much as is not m^{rs} Jaggards she may printe at her pleasure." [This was later published in Jackson's edition of the court book (Bibliography, no. 93), p. 178.]

although he was dead, and, as originally issued,[6] ended on recto G7 with the word "FINIS." The publication of Beale's edition with four times as many essays naturally made Jaggard's unsalable. Jaggard, however, was able to force Beale (Hall was now dead), presumably by reason of his prior rights obtained from Hooper, to resign his title to the new essays and to permit Jaggard to add them to the unsold copies of his 1612 reprint of the Hooper text. This was effected by canceling G7 and 8, the latter a blank, and printing the new essays, together with the page of text in the cancellandum, as sheets H–O.

There is no record of Beale's transfer of his rights, whatever they may have been, to anyone else. Therefore, it is probable that Jaggard, by threat or purchase or both, induced Beale to cede to him all his claims[7] to the newly published essays and that Beale, perhaps irritated by the legal, but nonetheless harsh, appropriation of his copy, evened the score by surreptitiously reprinting Jaggard's book. Certainly no other hypothesis appears to account for the fact that an examination of the three 1613 editions, which are all reprints of the Beale 1612 text, shows that the "Atturny" edition, which is nearest in orthography to Beale's of 1612, was printed by William Jaggard; while the "Aturney" and "Atturney" editions, which while close reprints are removed from the 1612 edition in that order, were both printed by John Beale.

Under normal circumstances one might assume that when Beale transferred his rights to Jaggard he reserved, as was frequently done, the right to print one or more editions. But in this case, it was not the first[8]

[6] The only recorded copy of the first issue is the Pittar copy now in the Folger Library, but the Jolley-Corser copy of the second issue now in the British Museum has leaves G7 and 8 uncanceled.

[7] In 1639 Beale printed and published an edition of the *Essays* under his own name. His right in the title was disputed 12 August 1639 (Court Book C 167a) when the book was still in press and 2 September "as he still proceeds in the printing . . . the Barr & Spindle of his presse [were ordered to be taken down]" (167b). The 3 October 1639 (168a) Beale was fined "Twenty nobles . . . & more ouer to be suspended from the Cort as an Assistant." The 7 October 1639 (168b) he was ordered to "bring in the Impression" and 4 July 1640 (172a) he made submission. The decision of the court concerning the "Right" in this title is not recorded, but it may be observed that while Haviland, Hodgkinson, and Whitaker were the only ones whose claims were mentioned in the proceedings noted above, according to the registered transfers, J. Smethwicke, J. Parker, and T. Lownes had rights in the Essays also. [In Jackson's edition of the court book cited above, these passages occur on pp. 326–328 and 334.]

[8] If one considered only the three 1613 editions, the normal rule of progessive modernization of reprints would reverse the order, which is based upon the relationship of these editions to their common source. Dr. Pollard set forth the interesting theory (*The Library*, 4th series, IV [1923], 7–8) that the order of these editions might be determined by their spellings, which, on the assumption that Bacon's would be "*less* archaic — more modern — than that

1613 edition which Beale printed. Moreover, if Beale printed his two 1613 editions at Jaggard's charge, why was it necessary to make such an apparent effort to facsimile the title of the edition printed by William Jaggard? And, finally, why three editions dated 1613 and no others until 1624?

If that is actually what occurred, and it seems the only explanation of the facts, then it would seem that Beale's opinion of Jaggard's powers of observation was not very high, for his editions are only superficial counterfeits of their prototype and, except for their titles, bear marks of his work on almost every sheet. Nevertheless, there is no record that his fraud was ever discovered.

Hayward's Henry IV, *1599*

There are four editions [9] of this book dated 1599 and purporting to have been printed by John Wolfe. The fact is, however, that not one of the four was printed by Wolfe, although there is no reason to doubt that one of them was printed for him. These editions are sufficiently distinguished in the *Short-title Catalogue* (Nos. 12995–7[a]). They all have the same collation and all contain the same list of errata, though, except in the earliest, the errors are mostly corrected in their texts.

The uncorrected edition (*S.T.C.* 12995) was printed by Edward Allde. It has Wolfe's device, McKerrow No. 294, on the title and McKerrow-Allde [10] head-piece ornament No. 4 on recto A3 (Plate III, J), and tail-piece No. 2 on recto V3 (Plate III, L), while the factotum on recto A2 and the "Apostle" A on recto A3 are to be found in Allde's edition of Norman, *The New Attractive* (1596), recto B7 and A2, respectively. There is no reason to doubt that this edition was printed by Allde for Wolfe, or that it is the edition [11] of which Wolfe testified

of the printers," he would arrange in the order here listed. Curiously enough his theory holds true in this case even though the copy used by William Jaggard was neither Bacon's holograph nor even a manuscript copy of his original but, demonstrably, Beale's edition of 1612.

[9] Mr. H. R. Plomer examined some seventeen copies and set forth a list of variants which he found in an interesting paper in *The Library*, 2nd series, III (1902), 13–23. He was mistaken, however, in his opinion that they are all mere variations of a single edition. Copies of the four editions may be seen in the Huntington Library.

[10] *The Library*, 4th series, X (1929), 121–162.

[11] At his trial Wolfe stated that he was ordered by the Archbishop of Canterbury to cancel the dedication to the Earl of Essex and that he had complied with the order for the copies of this edition, some six or seven hundred, which still remained on hand. That he did so is substantiated by a letter of Chamberlain's to Carleton, 1 March 1599. Nevertheless, such copies are now remarkably scarce, presumably through having been discarded as imperfect, but Prof. C. B. Judge has recently acquired a copy of this edition, according to his tran-

"never any boke was better sould or more desired that ever he printed then this boke was."

The next edition (*S.T.C.* 12996) was, from the evidence of the ornaments, printed by John Windet, or possibly by his successor, William Stansby. It, likewise, has Wolfe's device, McKerrow No. 294, on the title. This device, after Wolfe's death, passed to Windet, Wolfe's successor as printer to the City of London, and was used by him in Marston's *Wonder of Women* (1606), Greville's *Mustapha* (1609), and elsewhere. The ornaments and initials used in this edition are all very closely copied from those used by Allde in the prceeding edition. The factotum on recto A2 occurs in Daniel's *Tethys Festival* (1610), printed by Windet; the "Apostle" A on recto A3 in Stansby's edition of Johnson's *Seven Champions*, Pt. II (1626), and the floriated T on recto A5, in Stansby's edition of Cortes, *The Art of Navigation* (1615). The headpiece on recto A3 (Plate III, K), copied from McKerrow-Allde No. 4, and the tail-piece on verso V3 (Plate III, M), copied from McKerrow-Allde No. 2, have not been found in any of the books printed by Windet or Stansby which we have examined.

There are large paper copies of this edition in the British Museum (Grenville), Lambeth (Archbishop Abbot), and Harmsworth (Augustine Vincent-Sheldon-Scott-Heber-Britwell) Libraries, of which the Grenville, which measures 9¼ × 7 inches, is the tallest. As it is the only edition of which L.P. copies are known, it was presumably issued with the connivance of the author who, in the dedication of his *Lives of the Ill Norman Kings*, reports that Prince Henry "questioned, whether I had wrote any part of our English Historie, other then that which had been published, which at that time he had in his hands . . ." It is possible that, after the accession of James, the author, still mindful of his examination at the hands of Justice Coke (see *Library*, XI (1930), 212–224) but desirous of having copies for presentation to those who might assist him in his ambition to become tutor to the Prince of Wales and a member of James's projected Chelsea College, induced Windet to counterfeit the original edition so that he might present copies as "one of a few remaining." Such an explanation is, of course, highly conjectural, but it is difficult otherwise to account for such a phenomenon as a L.P. counterfeit.

---

script of the title, in which the dedication leaf is canceled; see his *Elizabethan Book-Pirates* (Cambridge, Massachusetts, 1934), pp. 42–43n.

The third edition was printed by Bernard Alsop. It is a careful reprint of the preceding editions except that for Wolfe's device is substituted a block of type-ornament. Alsop employed in this edition two, possibly three, of the blocks which were originally used by Allde, viz., the head-piece and "Apostle" A on recto A3. The factotum on recto A2 may also be Allde's, though Creede, Alsop's predecessor, had one which is difficult to distinguish which he used in his edition of Greene's *Groatsworth* (1596). The floriated T on recto A5 may be traced in frequent use in both Creede's and Alsop's work from 1593 on, but from the extent of its deterioration in this impression it is apparent that this edition was printed after it was used in Alsop's edition of Phaer's *Aeneid* (1620). The tail-piece at the end, the only one of the ornaments in this edition which is not similar to those used in the earlier ones, is the same block used by Creede in his counterfeit edition of the *Abuses* (Plate III, I).

In the fourth edition (*S.T.C.* 12997[a]), though a paginary reprint of the earlier ones and with the same date and imprint on the title, no attempt was made to imitate the ornaments and initials. This edition was printed by one of the succession of printers who occupied a shop in Cow Lane near Holborn Conduit, viz., William White, John White, Augustine Mathews, or Marmaduke Parsons, according to the date at which it was printed. The ornaments are to be found in their work; the tail-piece at the end, for instance, was used by William White almost with the regularity of a device. The date, however, cannot be established with certainty, but it is not unlikely that this edition was printed as late as 1638 or 1639, for a copy in the library of Sir R. Leicester Harmsworth has on the title a contemporary signature dated "April 1639" and there are copies of this edition in the possession of F. S. Ferguson, Esq., and the Huntington Library with a cancel title with imprint reading: "London. | Printed for William Sheares and are | to be sold at his Shop in Coven-Garden neare | the new Exchange. | MDCXXXIX. | ."

It is difficult at this distance to gauge the political significance of this *History*, though it should be noted that when reprinted for Sheares in 1642 it was more likely intended to sell as a political pamphlet than an historical one. However, the "deposition scene" had, apparently, no great terrors for James, as witness its introduction in the fourth edition of *Richard II* (1608), and, after Elizabeth's death, the Earl of Essex might be remembered with impunity, as is testified by the replacement of the canceled original setting of the *Voyage to Cadiz* in the unsold copies of the 1598–1600 Hakluyt.[12]

The copyright in this title can be traced without a break until 1639 [13] and yet there is no means of connecting any of the owners of the rights, after Wolfe, with these counterfeit editions. It is improbable, however, that publishers of that day would continue to pay out sixpences to register the ownership of the copyright of a book which was completely "dead" and, therefore, we are probably not far wrong if we account for the retention of the false imprint and the evident care taken to imitate the original Wolfe-Allde edition by suggesting that the publishers disposed of these counterfeits as belonging to the "scarce original edition." This same theory provides a plausible explanation for the retention of the "Middlebourgh" imprint in the seventeenth century editions of Marlowe's *All Ovid's Elegies* as well as for several other instances where the meager respect for authority on the part of Jacobean printers has had to account for otherwise anomalous imprints.

[12] Copies of the Hakluyt are known with the original setting intact, canceled, and also replaced with the stubs showing. Evidently not enough copies of the canceled setting were preserved for there is a second printing, apparently contemporary, which sometimes occurs. The third setting described in the *Church Catalogue* and elsewhere is obviously a late eighteenth or early nineteenth century reprint.

[13] Originally entered by Wolfe (9 January 1599, Arber, III, 134), transferred by his widow to C. Burby (14 April 1603, Arber, III, 232), acquired without entry by W. Welby (the list of copies, Arber, III, 420–421, which Mistress Burby transferred to him is obviously not accurate for it includes more titles than the thirty-eight for which a fee was paid), transferred by him to T. Snodham (2 March 1618, Arber, III, 621), by Mistress Snodham to W. Stansby (23 February 1626, Arber, IV, 153), and by him to R. Bishop (4 March 1639, Arber, IV, 459).

6

The Funeral Procession of Queen Elizabeth

(1946)

After he published this article, Jackson discovered three more titles for the list at the end. These have been added without comment in the present reprint (Bibliography, no. 42).

AFTER lying in state for nearly a month, Queen Elizabeth's body was brought from Whitehall to the Abbey Church of Westminster for burial the 28th day of April 1603, accompanied by a magnificent procession ordered by the heralds. Sir John Fortescue, the Master of the great Wardrobe, was paid [1] the sum of £3,000 to be employed in defraying the charges of the funeral, and, according to Stowe,[2] "the citie of Westminster was surcharged with multitudes of all sorts of people in their streetes, houses, windows, leads, and gutters, that came to see the obsequie . . . there was such a generall sighing, groning, and weeping, as the like hath not beene seene or knowne in the memory of man, neither doeth any history mention any people, time, or state, to make like lamentation for the death of their soueraigne." The stationers of London were not slow to cater to this popular emotion and within the year printed nearly two score [3] of commendatory poetical laments and funeral sermons.

Both Chettle and the anonymous poetaster who wrote "A mournefull Dittie, entituled Elizabeths losse" urged the leading poets of the day to join the chorus, the former referring by means of allusive names to Spen-

[1] F. Devon, *Pell Records. Issues of the Exchequer during the reign of King James I* (London, 1836), p. 3, 16 June 1603. There is a reference, however, in *N. & Q.*, 3rd series, V, 434, to an Exchequer document which indicates that Sir John was paid over £17,000 "for the funerall charges of the late Queen," but that sum apparently included debts due at her death.

[2] J. Stowe, *Annales* (London, 1631), p. 815.

[3] See Appendix.

ser, Daniel, Chapman, Jonson, Drayton, Shakespeare and others, while the latter calls upon them by name:

> You Poets all braüe Shakspeare,
> Johnson, Greene,
> Bestow your time to write
> for Englands Queene . . .
> Returne your songs and Sonnets
> and your sayes [layes?]:
> To set foorth sweete
> Elizabeths praise.

These poets were not persuaded, and the quality of the memorial verse that was printed is such as to make the reading of much of it tedious indeed. However, our concern is not with the elegiac lamentations but with the relationships, one to another, of the descriptions of the funeral procession which are included in the volumes written by, or attributed to, Henry Chettle, Richard Niccols, and Henry Petowe.

On 25 April — that is, three days before the funeral — Thomas Millington was granted a provisional entry,[4] conditional upon the Archbishop of Canterbury's or the Bishop of London's licence, for "A book called *Englandes Moarninge garment* . . . To which is added *the true maner of her ymperiall funerall* after which folowith *The Shepherdes spring songe of enterteynement of king James &c.*" Evidently Millington changed his plans and instead of including a general account of the funeral he decided to limit his description to the procession alone, for on the day of the funeral he was granted another provisional entry [5] for "*The proceding at the funerall of the high and mightie Pryncess Elizabeth . . . from the palace of Westminster called Whitehall to the cathedrall church of Westminster* 28. *Aprilis* 1603." Nevertheless, when Valentine Simmes printed for him *Englandes Mourning Garment*, he used in the title, except for minor variations of spelling and the substitution of "for" for "of," the same phraseology as that in the entry in the Stationers' Register on 25 April and referred to ". . . the true manner of her Emperiall Funerall" and not to "The proceding . . ." or, as the printed heading (recto F2) has it, "¶ The order and proceeding at the Funerall . . . from the Pallace of Westminster called White-hall: To the Cathedrall Church of Westminster: the 28. of April. 1603."

[4] Arber, III, 35.
[5] Arber, III, 35.

This undated volume, of which the imprint reads "¶ Printed at London by V. S. for Thomas Millington, and are to be sold at his shop vnder saint Peters Church on Cornhill.," is usually attributed to Henry Chettle. He is certainly responsible for the "Mourning Garment," a pastoral in rather pleasing verse and prose which occupies recto A3–verso F, for as Ingleby pointed out, in a signed address "To the Reader" (verso F3), he blames the printer for an error which occurs in the "Mourning Garment," saying ". . . imagine I can write English, and make not the fault mine." It is probable that he also wrote "The Shepheards Spring Song" (recto [F4]–verso G), but "The order and proceeding at the Funerall" (recto F2–verso F3) was presumably prepared for the press by the publisher, Thomas Millington, who may have copied a list prepared by the Heralds and possibly printed for them. At any rate, very shortly after, Millington states in an address "To the Reader" signed with his initials and prefixed to *The True Narration of the Entertainment of his Royall Maiestie*,[6] for which he and Cuthbert Burby made entry 9 May, that the names of the recently knighted gentlemen that "the Heraldes haue in register, are duly set downe," so it is apparent that Millington had access to the Heralds and their records.

In that regard he was more fortunate than we are today, for the records of this funeral procession in the library of the Heralds' College are at the moment inaccessible to us. Nevertheless, we do have the engraved reproduction of Camden's roll drawing[7] of the procession (Additional MS. 5408) made for the Society of Antiquaries, *Vetusta Monumenta*, III (1799), Plates 18–24. A comparison of the order of the mourners as given by Camden with the order as given by Chettle shows that the source for this printed text can hardly have been the Clarenceux King at Arms' drawing, for not only does he omit a good deal which Camden includes, such as the "Poore men of Westminster in nomber .xv." and the "Officers to the Lord Maior of London," and alters the order,[8] as in putting the French Ambassador between the Lord Keeper and the Archbishop of Canterbury instead of following them as depicted by Camden, but he includes several mourners[9] not shown by Camden, as

[6] *S.T.C.* 14433 and 17153.

[7] Additional MS. 35324(7) is another roll drawing, colored, with names of the principal figures written against them as in the Camden roll.

[8] The misplacing of "The Banner of Ireland" may be a compositor's error, for that line is entirely in italic type and is inserted out of place, following two other similar lines.

[9] The section in Chettle from the Sergeants of the "Pantrie" to the "Gentlemen vshers

"Two Quirries leading a horse" following "The Standerd of the Greyhound" and the yeoman of the "Pastrie." He likewise makes other changes which may be merely errors in copying, such as 240 "poore women" instead of 266, "foure Noble men" to bear the Canopy instead of "6. Knights," and "A Sergeant at Armes" following Rouge Dragon instead of "2. Sergeants."

It has been stated [10] that this book was first issued without the "Shepheards Spring Song," but while it is true that five of the eleven known [11] copies lack it, it is called for on the title and there is no reason to think that those copies which now do not have it were originally published without it. Evidently the book sold rapidly, for Millington soon called for a second edition to be printed. The type of the first three sheets had already been distributed, so they had to be entirely reset and, even though the text was enlarged by almost two pages of new matter, the whole was compressed so that it collates A–F^4 instead of A–F^4, G^2 (the last possibly blank, or possibly used for the duplicate printing of sig. G).

The imprint of this second edition reads: "Imprinted at London for Thomas Millington, and are to be sold at the signe of the Crane in Paules Churchyard by Walter Burre. 1603." Just why Millington chose to use an agent for the sale of this edition is probably beyond proof, but we may conjecture that it may have been because he was not in good health, for his last recorded transaction occurred early in June 1603 and it is possible that he was a victim of that summer's plague. In any case, this second edition is very uncommon, only three copies [12] being traceable.

The first three sheets of this new edition Millington gave to Mrs. E. Short [13] to set up, with some few additions to the text, such as the paren-

---

and waiters," including fifteen persons or categories, is omitted in Camden, which may be due either to the loss of a segment of the roll or merely because the engraver, intentionally or not, left it out.

[10] Henrietta C. Bartlett, *Mr. William Shakespeare* (New Haven, Connecticut, 1922), No. 281.

[11] British Museum (Fillingham-Heber and Baldwin-Grenville, the latter lacking sig. G); Bodleian (Malone); Huntington (Halliwell-Huth); Folger (Walpole-Britwell-Halliwell and Harrison-Halliwell-Locker, both lacking "Spring Song"); Harvard (Halliwell-White, lacking "Spring Song"); Pforzheimer (Perry-Jones-Clawson); Newhailes (Sotheby's 24 May 1937, lot 83 [untraced], lacking "Spring Song"); Yale, and Mrs. Donald F. Hyde. [Jackson later located two more copies — at Edinburgh University, and at Shakespeare's Birthplace, Stratford-upon-Avon.]

[12] Huntington (Bridgewater); Folger (Wiper-McKee); and Trinity College, Cambridge. [Jackson later located a fourth copy at Corpus Christi College, Oxford.]

[13] Although the signatures of sheets B and C are in James Roberts' peculiar manner, i.e., the first leaf of each sheet with letter only followed by a period, the owner of the vase-with-birds ornament on recto A2 cannot be identified. However, the large initial M, also recto

thetic references to Queen Mary, recto B, lines 15–16, "(setting by her affection to Papall religion, wherein shee was borne and liued)" and verso B, lines 3–6, "for the true shepheards indeede, that suffered in her time by the malice of Romish Prelates, prayed hartily for her euen in the fire, and taught the people to obey her gouernment: but such as rayld at her," which do not occur in the first edition. By the end of the third sheet, despite these and other additions, something over an extra page of the text of the first edition had been compressed into Mrs. Short's share of the new one by the simple expedient of adding two lines to each full page. As at least some of the type for the remainder of the book was still standing in Simmes's shop, he evidently was commissioned to complete the new edition. This he did by using some of the old setting, but, with more lines to the page, and by omitting some of the leading, he managed to save two more pages by the end of the "Mourning Garment," which he concluded on recto [E4] instead of verso F as in the first edition.

For "¶ The order and proceeding at the Funerall" Simmes used the original setting of the heading, but the text was so corrected and amended [14] that he had to reset it entirely, although he managed to end each page, omitting Chettle's comment on the errata, as it ended in the first edition. The major additions were the names of the bearers of the seven standards and of the great embroidered banner of England, as also of the cofferer and the almoner, none of whom were given in the first edition. In this edition the "Fifteene poore men" and the "Officers to the Maior of London" are added, but the "Two Quirries leading a horse" and the Lancaster herald are omitted, the number of poor women is altered to "260" and an attempt, only partly successful, is made to describe more accurately the entourage of "The liuely picture" and of the "Chiefe Mourner." The "Sixe Earles assistants" who accompanied "The liuely picture" and who were omitted in the first edition are mentioned, but the "Gentlemen Pensioners houlding their Pol-axes heads down

---

A2, has not been traced in any work of his. It belongs to a series copied after an alphabet designed for Robert Estienne and made originally for Henry Bynneman, later in the hands of Henry Denham, and finally in those of Peter Short. Several of these initials, but not this one, were used by Short in P. Rosseter's *A Booke of Ayres* (1601). As Short died sometime during the year 1603, it may be that the printer was his widow, Mrs. Emma Short. Another copy of at least part of this series, including the letter M, but without the double-rule borders, was in use at this time by Felix Kingston.

[14] The title of this second edition somewhat enigmatically states: "To which is added the true manner of her Emperiall Funerall. With many new additions, being now again the second time reprinted, which was omitted in the first Impression."

wards couered with blacke" are placed incorrectly with the "Gentlemen of the priuie chamber" instead of with "The liuely picture" as in the first edition, and the chief mourner's train, which in the first edition is incorrectly "supported by maister Vicechamberlaine," is now described properly as "caried by two Countesses," but the "Two Erles assistants to her" who are recorded by the first edition are unaccountably omitted in the second. Having saved three pages and only having needed to save two, Simmes was able to use the extra page (verso F2) for a list of the bearers of the twelve "Bannerols," [15] leaving the last two leaves for the "Spring-Song."

On 7 June 1603 the clerk of the Stationers' Company recorded [16] of Matthew Law: "Yt is ordered that he shall presently pay xx^{s} for a fine for printinge contrary to order A book called Englandes mowrning garment beinge Thomas millingtons copie. And that he shall bring into the hall as forfayted by thordonnance all such numbers of the said bookes as nowe remayne in his handes vnsold which he say[th] are 100 . . . he brought in 3 quarterns [i.e., 75] or thereaboutes and v^{s} of the fine is gyven back to him — paid xv^{s}." The book which Law was then fined for printing is evidently Henry Petowe's "Elizabetha quasi viuens, Eliza's Funérall. A fewe Aprill drops, showred on the Hearse of dead Eliza. Or The Funerall teares of a true hearted Subject. By H. P. London Printed by E. Allde for M. Lawe, dvvelling in Paules Church-yard, neere vnto Saint Austens gate. 1603." It contains, following a two-page "Induction," eight sonnets and six pages of "The order and formal proceeding at the Funerall" which is substantially the text of that part of Chettle, except that it has interpolated verse passages printed in italic. The order of the procession appears in the Petowe to be an eclectic text compiled from both the Chettle editions with some independent readings unrelated to either of them. However, Law's misdemeanor in the eyes of the Stationers' Company was not the sin of plagiary but the printing of an "entered" copy.

Before going further into the matter of the text, however, we should first make note that there are two genuine editions of the Petowe, as well as a third "manufactured" one which has hitherto been accepted as genuine. The first edition, of which only two copies are known,[17] reads

[15] The name of the bearer of the fourth, Lord Rich, is left blank.

[16] Arber, II, 836.

[17] *S.T.C.* 19805 [renumbered 19803.5 in the revised *S.T.C.*]. The uncut Lamport-Britwell copy is now in the possession of Mr. and Mrs. Donald Hyde of New York, and I wish to

in the eighth line of the title, "Subject," and as both the surviving copies lack the second leaf of the first sheet,[18] which presumably contained a dedication, that edition was apparently issued with the initials which occur on the title as the only indication of authorship. The second edition, which reads in the eighth line of the title, "Subject," is a paginary resetting except for some five pages,[19] which are from the same type as the first edition, apart from a few minor alterations. This edition is not so rare as the first [20] and contains a dedication to Richard Hildersham (sig. A2) which is signed "Henry Petowe."

The other, sophisticated, edition is known only by the Reed-Heber-Britwell-White copy now at Harvard. It collates A–C^4 and is made up of sig. [A]-B3 from the second edition and sig. [B4]–[C4] from Richard Niccols's *Expicedium* (1603), another description of the funeral procession which is discussed later. It was bound by Lewis in 1833 for Heber, who has queried, in a note, whether the Bibliotheca Anglo-Poetica copy is perfect, since it is described as containing only twenty pages. Ironically, when John Payne Collier described this copy in the Heber sale catalogue,[21] he wrote: "In this Poem by Petowe there are no plagiarisms, nothing that any body else would consent to own." There can be no question but that this is a "manufactured" copy, for not only are the last five leaves from the same setting as the Niccols, but the chainlines and watermark prove that sig. B and sig. [B4] are not conjugate.

The description of the funeral procession in both editions of Petowe contains characteristic elements of both editions of the Chettle text, as well as others which seem to indicate an independent source. For example, while the bearers of the banners are not named throughout and the "Two Querries leading a horse" [22] is included as in the first Chettle, the fifteen poor men are mentioned and the number of poor women is 260, as in the second Chettle. The error of the second Chettle concerning

express my gratitude for their great kindness in lending it for examination. The other copy, the Griswold-Huntington, has been examined for me by Mr. Herman R. Mead of the Hunting Library, to whom my thanks for this and many other courtesies are due.

[18] In the Lamport copy half a watermark occurs on signature A3 and the remainder is not present. In the Huntington copy the watermark is divided [A] and [A4].

[19] Recto and verso A3, and verso B, verso C, and recto C2.

[20] *S.T.C.* 19804. Copies are in the British Museum, Bodleian (Malone, with both settings of sheet B), Folger (B. A. P.-Rice-Britwell-Harmsworth), Huntington (Halsey), and Harvard (Smith-Huth-Jones-Clawson).

[21] Heber, IV, 1834, lot 1808.

[22] ". . . Horse." in second Petowe edition.

the "Gentlemen Pentioners" is repeated, but the "Officers to the Maior of London" are omitted as in the first Chettle. The statement that the poor women, the messengers, the yeomen, and the clerks went "foure by foure," which occurs in both the Chettle editions, is omitted in both the Petowes, while an entirely new and, judging from Camden's drawing, erroneous description of the choir is given in both the Petowe editions, "Gentlemen of the Chappel in Copes, hauing the Children of the Chappel in the middle of their company, in surplices, all of them singing."

The second Petowe edition, while mainly a literal reprint of the first, contains some corrections, for the most part taken from the second Chettle, as, for example, the names of the cofferer and almoner. But it also contains some independent corrections, as, for instance, the name of the Vice-chamberlain and the correct information that the Canopie, which was entirely omitted in the first Petowe, was borne by six knights instead of the four noblemen of both Chettle editions. On the other hand, the first Petowe, like the second Chettle, includes secretaries for the Italian tongue, which are omitted by the first Chettle and the second Petowe.

The third and final work to contain a description of this funeral procession is the anonymous "Expicedium. A Funeral Oration . . . Written: by Infelice Academico Ignoto. Whereunto is added, the true order of her Highnes Lmperiall Funerall. London Printed [by Edward Allde] for E. VVhite, dvvelling neere the little north doore of Paules Church, at the signe of the Gun. 1603." J. P. Collier was the first [23] to ascribe this work to Richard Niccols on the basis of a contemporary note on the title of his own copy, "R. Niccols wrote this. J. B. 4 July 1603." That copy cannot now be traced, but it appeared in Collier's sale,[24] and as the Spencerian verse the volume contains is similar to the signed work of this author, there seems no good reason to dispute it.

There is only one genuine edition of this piece, for the edition listed in Pollard and Redgrave, *Short-title Catalogue*, No. 18519, is another "manufactured" edition. The genuine edition collates: A–C^4 (sig. A blank except for signature; sig. A3, in some copies, signed "A") and is not very common.[25] The manufactured edition is again known only by

[23] John Payne Collier, *A Bibliographical and Critical Account of the Rarest Books in the English Language* (London, 1865), II, 32.

[24] Sotheby's, 1884, lot 879.

[25] *S.T.C.* 18520. The British Museum has two copies, one the Grenville, and others are

one copy,[26] viz. the Corser (VI, 1871, Lot 86)–Pearson–White copy now at Harvard. It contains sig. [A2]–[B3] of the genuine edition followed by sig. [B4]–C2 from the second Petowe edition. It is in a Mackenzie mid-nineteenth-century binding, from which it was possible to remove quire B to photograph the watermarks of the two leaves B and [B4], which should be conjugate if this were not a sophisticated copy. Fortunately, there can be no doubt whatever that they are disjunct.

The Niccols description of the procession is headed "The True Order and formall proceeding at the Funerall . . . ," but it is a barefaced plagiary of the second Petowe edition, including the interpolated verses, with additions derived from the second Chettle. For example, it gives the names of the bearers of the banners, and also of the Bannerols, including, however, Lord Rich's name as the bearer of the fourth Bannerol.[27] It also makes some slight changes, such as altering the "Officers to the Maior of London" of the second Chettle to "Chiefe Officers to the Lord Maior of London." White certainly infringed on Millington's rights, and it is hard to guess why he was not detected and punished, unless it was because Millington died about that time and Law was, of course, in no proper position to object to White's theft of his text.

It would be informative if one could show that both these "manufactured" editions had the same origin, but they cannot be traced in the same hands until they were separately acquired by the late William A. White, long after they had been bound by different, identifiable binders.

Appendix

The surviving pamphlets and broadsides memorializing Queen Elizabeth would be even more numerous if one included all those which are concerned mainly with welcoming King James and which do not refer to the Queen in their titles, as in the case of many listed by Nichols, *Progresses of James I* (1828), I, xxxvii–xli. The majority of the items which properly may be called memorials are referred to by E. C. Wilson, *England's Eliza*, pp. 370–93, although the following list contains one or two not mentioned by him and several not included in the *Short-title*

in the Bodleian, Huntington (Bright-Britwell), Chapin (Corser [II, 1869, lot 351]-Huth) and Harvard (Sotheby's [July 1888, lot 96]-White) Libraries.

[26] *S.T.C.* 18519. The British Museum and Chapin copies belong to the genuine edition.

[27] The Huntington copy reads, instead of "Lord Rich," "Lord Compton," which is an obvious error as he carried the second Bannerol.

Catalogue. Many of these pieces, however, follow the usual line: "The Queen is dead, long live the King!"

S.T.C. 4493 Cambridge University. *Threno-thriambeuticon*. 4°. Cantabrigiae, J. Legat, 1603.
S.T.C. 5121 Chettle, Henry. *Englandes mourning garment*. 4°. V. S. f. T. Millington [1603].
S.T.C. 5122 —— [Anr. ed.]. 4°. [E. Short and V. Simmes] f. T. Millington, to be sold by W. Burre, 1603.
S.T.C. 5256 Churchyard, Thomas. *Sorrowful verses*. s.sh.fol. [1603].
Colville, John. *Oratio funebris*. 8°. Paris, ex typ. S. Prevosteau, 1604.
Davies, John, of Hereford. *Lo here her type*. s.sh.fol. Are to be sould by R. Daniell [1603]. Verses below a portrait of Elizabeth engraved by Francis Delaram after Nicholas Hilliard. Lemon No. 101.
S.T.C. 7589 Elizabeth, Queen. *A mourneful ditty*. s.sh.fol. f. T. P. [1603?].
S.T.C. 7594 —— *The poores lamentation*. 4°. f. T. Pavier, 1603.
S.T.C. 7598 —— *Sorrowes ioy*. 4°. Cambridge, J. Legat, 1603.
S.T.C. 7604 —— *Tumulus Elizabethae*. 8°. [n.p., 1610?].
—— *Weepe with joy*. s.sh.fol. V.S. f. E. Mutton, 1603. Lemon No. 108.
S.T.C. 10798 Fenton, John. *King James his welcome*. 4°. f. T. Pavier, 1603.
Gordon, John. *Elizabethae reginae manes*. 8°. excud. J. Norton, 1603. Copy in Bibliothèque Nationale, Paris.
S.T.C. 12057 —— [Anr. ed.]. 4°. imp. T. Man, 1604.
S.T.C. 12678 Hall, Joseph, Bp. *The kings prophecie: or weeping joy*. 8°. T. C. f. S. Waterson, 1603.
S.T.C. 14422 James I, King. *Englands welcome to James*. 4°. f. E. W. a. C. K., 1603.
S.T.C. 14423 James I, King. *An excellent new ballad, showing the petigree*. s.sh.fol. f. E. W. [1603].
S.T.C. 14671 Johnson, Richard. *Anglorum lacrimae, in a sad passion complayning the death of Q. Elizabeth*. 4°. f. T. Pauier, 1603.
S.T.C. 15189 Lane, John. *An elegie upon the death of Elizabeth*. 4°. f. J. Deane, 1603.
Mavericke, Radford. *Three treatises*. 4°. I. Windet, 1603. Copy in Folger Library.
S.T.C. 18251 Mulcaster, Richard. *In mortem . . . reginae Elizabethae*. 4°. pro E. Aggas, 1603.
S.T.C. 18252 —— *The translation of certaine latine verses*. 4°. f. E. Aggas, 1603.
S.T.C. 18511 Newton, Thomas. *Atropoion Delion*. 4°. f. W. Johnes, 1603.
S.T.C. 18520 Niccols, Richard. *Expicedium*. 4°. f. E. White, 1603.
S.T.C. 18586 Nixon, Anthony. *Elizaes memoriall*. 4°. T. C. f. J. Baylie, 1603.

S.T.C. 19018 Oxford University. *Oxoniensis Academiae funebre officium.* 4°. Oxoniae, J. Barnesius, 1603.

S.T.C. 19805 Petowe, Henry. *Elizabetha quasi viuens.* 4°. E. Allde f. M. Lawe, 1603.

S.T.C. 19804 —— [Anr. ed.]. 4°. E. Allde f. M. Lawe, 1603.

S.T.C. 19806 ——*Englands Caesar.* 4°. J. Windet f. M. Law, 1603.

S.T.C. 20388 Primrose, Diana. *A chaine of pearle.* 4°. f. T. Paine, sold by P. Waterhouse, 1630.

S.T.C. 20587 R., R. *Post nubila sudum.* 4°. Oxoniae, ap. J. Barnesium. 1603.

S.T.C. 20778 Raymond, Henry. *The maiden queene.* 4°. I. W. f. J. Browne [1607].

S.T.C. 21364 Rowlands, Samuel. *Ave Caesar.* 4°. [W. White] f. W. F. a. G. L., 1603.

S.T.C. 21497 S., H. *Queene Elizabeths losse.* 4°. T. C. f. J. Smythicke, 1603.

S.T.C. 24918 W., T. *The lamentation of Melpomene.* 4°. W. W. f. C. K., 1603.

S.T.C. 26040 Wright, Thomas. *The passions of the minde. With a treatise occasioned by the death of Q. Elizabeth.* 4°. V. Sims f. W. Burre, 1604.

7

Variant Entry Fees of the Stationers' Company

(1957)

As a young man, Jackson eagerly wanted to meet Sir Walter Greg, a distinguished member of the older generation of English bibliographers. In this paper he added a long footnote to one of Sir Walter's later works (Bibliography, no. 94).

IN his Lyell Lectures [1] Sir Walter Greg has provided students of English publishing practises of the century following 1550 with much that is new and far more that is for the first time accurately set forth, written with the clarity and precision which are to be found in all his work. So inevitable is it that this small volume will become the main guide to future students of the subject, that when, very occasionally, some of the statements in it may seem rather less than final it is more important than is usually the case to call attention to them.

When discussing the fees paid at the time of entrance of a book in the Stationers' Register,[2] Sir Walter, after citing fees ranging from fourpence to twenty shillings, and considering several explanations for this variation, finally concludes, "But there are seemingly insuperable objections to any explanations on these lines [such as size, importance of the book, or fees to outside licensers], and since I have no satisfactory solution to offer, I will refrain from further conjecture." It is probably true that no "satisfactory" explanation can be set forth for all the

[1] W. W. Greg, *Some Aspects and Problems of London Publishing Between 1550 and 1650* (Oxford, 1956).

[2] Greg, *London Publishing*, pp. 38–39. The manner of entry in the various record books is admirably described, pp. 21–38.

recorded variant fees before 1582, when apparently they were fixed at fourpence for a ballad and sixpence for a book. However, besides the minimum fee of fourpence for small books and ballads, it can be demonstrated that during this period the normal fee for books of twelve sheets and over was one penny for three sheets. Sir Walter refers to an entry [3] by John Wight in 1559 of John Ferrarius' *A woorke touchynge the good orderynge of a common weale*, for which he paid fourpence with the added note "And at the fynysshynge of the sayde boke he shall paye for euery iij leves a pannye." To this note Arber has a misleading gloss: "4*d*. would at this rate, be the fee for 24 pages," for the word "leaf" was used by the stationers of that day interchangeably for "sheet," as, for example, in *Court-Book C*, p. 15, 6 August 1605: "Thoms Purfoote thelder Shall haue the woorkmanship of printinge one leafe of the prymers for the company," i.e., one sheet of a two-sheet *The A.B.C. with the catechisme.*[4]

It seems probable that other factors than the number of sheets contained in the books were at times involved in the calculation of the fees. We must remember that the men who set these fees were professional printers and would be aware of the various means by which these charges could be circumvented, as for example by using paper of a large size.[5] It seems also probable that allowance was made for the use of large type for the text as well as for the use of "white" letter, as roman type was usually called at that time, presumably because size for size more text could be set in a given area in roman type than in black-letter. In some instances the variant fees recorded present bibliographical evidence that is of utility if only in confirming hypotheses otherwise established.

The fees for nine books are cited by Sir Walter as illustrating the diversity of the charges. Let us examine them one by one, but, for reasons which may become apparent, in the reverse order of his listing. First, Sir Geoffrey Fenton's *Certaine tragicall discourses* (1567) (*S.T.C.*

[3] Arber, I, 97.

[4] An edition dated 1605, collating A^8, B^4, with an unrecorded "TP" device of Purfoot on the title, is in the Harvard Library. This division of work was often employed by the warehouse keepers of the English Stock to prevent a printer from overprinting, and keeping for his own profit, copies of almanacs and other patented books belonging to the Stock.

[5] In this they were probably wiser than the Commissioners of Stamp Duties who introduced in 1712 a tax per sheet on newspapers without specifying the size of the sheet; see *The Library*, 4th series, XXII (1942), 126–137. A postal rate based on the sheet, established in the United States in the middle of the nineteenth century, produced newspapers almost the size of bed sheets.

10791), for which Thomas Marsh paid, at two different times, fees totalling two shillings fourpence.[6] It is a quarto in eights collating $*^8$, $**^2$, A-Pp^8, Qq^2, or a total of seventy-nine sheets, which at the rate of three sheets per penny leaves one sheet over. The next example is the second edition of *A myrrour for magistrates* (1563), for which Sir Walter cites only the fee of fourpence paid [7] for "the ij^{de} parts of [the] myrror of magestrates." Thomas Marsh had, however, a few days or weeks before paid [8] another fee of fourpence for "the myrror of magestrates," and in 1559 he had paid [9] sixpence for his original entry for the first edition published that same year. The first edition is a quarto of twenty and a half sheets, and so the original fee was apparently at the usual rate of three sheets per penny with two and a half sheets over. The 1563 edition is not a mere reprint of the first edition for it contains a new "second part" with eight new tragedies as well as Sackville's "Induction." The new material occupies just twenty-four sheets for which the two 1563 fees, totaling eightpence, work out at exactly three sheets per penny. Had no copy of the 1559 edition of this book survived, it would have been possible from an examination of the 1563 edition to deduce from the fees paid for it what was contained in the earlier edition. The next book listed is an edition of Thomas Tusser's *A hundreth good poyntes of husbandry* entered by Richard Tottell in 1561–1562,[10] of which no copy can now be traced unless it be the copy in the Eton College Library lacking its title. W. C. Hazlitt, however, described [11] a copy of a 1562 Tottell edition as being a quarto of forty-eight leaves. Tottell paid a fee of fourpence, which is exactly three sheets per penny.[12]

The identification of the next book, cited by Greg as "a translation of Josephus," is obviously wrong: though the entry reads "this boke of Josephus," it actually refers to Peter Morwyng's translation of Joseph Ben Gorion's *A compendious history of the Jewes commune weale* (1558), which is an octavo of thirty-six sheets for which Jugge paid only

[6] Arber, I, 343 and 356.

[7] Arber, I, 208.

[8] Arber, I, 207.

[9] Arber, I, 97.

[10] Arber, I, 179.

[11] William Carew Hazlitt, *Handbook* (London, 1867), p. 618. Owen Rogers was fined two shillings in 1562 (Arber, I, 184) for printing an edition of this book, "beynge master Totteles," and the Eton copy might be his.

[12] John Day had entered the book in 1557–1558 (Arber, I, 78) and so Tottell must have acquired his rights from Day.

fourpence.[13] On the same day that Jugge entered this book he made two other entries, one for two unidentified books which Arber conjectures were parts of the same book, for which he likewise paid only fourpence, and also for Joannes ab Indagine's *Briefe introductions vnto the art of chiromancy* (1558), an octavo of sixteen sheets, for which he paid the same fee. On the grounds that the same fee was exacted for books of sixteen and thirty-six sheets, that the titles are given in the vaguest possible way — the Indagine is "the boke of palmestrye" — it would seem possible that the entry was made before these books were printed and that Jugge would be required to pay the rest of his fee when the number of sheets could be calculated, as in the case of John Wight cited above, but no second payment is recorded.

The next book is Raphael Holinshed's *Chronicles of England* (1577), two huge folio volumes which after much effort were finally issued by a family syndicate. John Harrison and George Bishop, his partner, paid a fee of one pound for the entry,[14] the largest fee recorded anywhere in the Register. The two volumes, with certain canceled leaves, contain 741 sheets, which at three sheets per penny accounts for all but twenty-one sheets. It is possible that the clerk compounded for a round figure in the case of this enormous publication. On the other hand, it may be that the syndicate produced for inspection and gift to the company (a copy was demanded, as was customary, in addition to the fee) a copy which lacked the table: A-M^4, N^2 of the second volume, or twenty-three sheets, either because the table was not yet printed or else in order to save the sevenpence involved. In this connection one should remember both the casual reasonableness of the Stationers' "baker's dozens" and "extra copies," and the fact that a sixpence then would purchase a very good dinner.

The four remaining books do not fit the pattern of a normal fee of three sheets per penny (although one of them comes very near to it), but it is possible to suggest reasons why they should be charged more or less than the normal fee. For example, the next two books are both printed in roman type. The first of these is Thomas North's translation of Plutarch's *The lives of the noble Grecians and Romanes* (1579), which is a large folio — copies are known nearly thirteen inches tall — printed in a pica roman letter which obviously contains many more ems to the sheet than most books of the period. It consists of 298 sheets for

[13] Arber, I, 77.
[14] Arber, II, 329.

which Thomas Vautrollier and John Wight paid a fee [15] of fifteen shillings or about one and two-thirds sheets per penny. On the same day the Plutarch was entered Thomas Norton and Thomas Vautrollier paid a fee of thirteen shillings for the next book, Geoffrey Fenton's translation of *The historie of [Francesco] Guicciardini* (1579), a folio of 303 sheets, printed in roman letter, which is very slightly less than two sheets per penny. The difference between the charge for the Plutarch and that for the Guicciardini may be due to the size of the paper, and consequently of the type page, in the two works.[16] There are very few books of this period for which large fees are recorded which were printed in roman type [17] so that one cannot be certain that the type was a factor in the fee charged.

The next book is John Calvin's *The institution of christian religion* (1561), a folio of one hundred and thirty-seven sheets for which Reginald Wolfe and Richard Harrison paid three shillings and fourpence [18] which at the rate of three sheets per penny leaves an overplus of seventeen sheets. The collation of this book is somewhat complicated, there being five alphabets of which two only are nearly complete, with several different sized quires, and this might just be a case of miscalculation. The last book, Greg's first, is the 1570 edition of Alexander Barclay's translation of Brant's *The ship of fooles*, a small folio of one hundred and seventy sheets for which John Cawood paid a fee of half a crown [19] or a rate of more than five sheets per penny. An examination of the book, however, suggests a possible explanation of this anomalous rate, for most of the text is verse printed in a great primer black-letter with a very large amount of white paper, so that if the normal charge was based on a sheet of solid pica type then this book was properly given a lower rate.

It may well seem that if one has the temerity to suggest an explanation of a phenomenon such as these variable charges for entries one should at least produce an hypothesis which explains most, if not all, the ex-

[15] Arber, II, 351.

[16] The type page in the Plutarch covers an area of 455 sq. cm., whereas in the Guicciardini it covers 364 sq. cm. or a difference of 25 percent.

[17] The only example that has been found on a cursory examination of these records is the entry for Edward Dering's *XXVII. lectures, or readings, vpon part of the epistle to the Hebrues*, 1576 (Arber, II, 302), a quarto in eights printed in roman type and containing sixty-three and a half sheets, for which Luke Harrison paid two shillings fourpence, or a rate of two and a quarter sheets per penny.

[18] Arber, I, 153.

[19] Arber, I, 360.

amples, and yet, as we have seen, five out of the nine instances so far discussed do not conform to the normal and can only be explained by what may well be regarded as ingenious, though reasonable, guesses. However, if we take not a random sampling but every title listed on a given page of the Stationers' Register, for example Arber, II, 329, the page which contains the Holinshed discussed above, for which a variety of fees ranging from fourpence to the twenty shillings of the *Chronicles* were paid, we shall find rather more reassuring results. Of the nine books entered there, one, John Bradford's *Godly meditations* (1578), has no fee recorded, and two were charged the minimum fee of fourpence because in the case of the Luther (*S.T.C.* 16989) it consists of only six sheets, and in the case of the Nausea (*S.T.C.* 18413) of only five.

The others, however, all conform reasonably closely to the norm, if we may include the Holinshed: the Grange (*S.T.C.* 12174) has eighteen sheets for which sixpence was paid; the Keltridge (*S.T.C.* 14920) has thirty-seven sheets for which twelvepence was paid, leaving an extra sheet; the Wotton (*S.T.C.* 5647) has forty-four sheets for which sixteenpence was paid, which amounts to two and three-fourths sheets per penny; [20] and the Bourne (*S.T.C.* 3432) has thirty-five sheets for which twelvepence was paid, which is again one sheet off. The only remaining book entered on that page is the Appian (*S.T.C.* 713), which has ninety-two and a half sheets for which a half crown was paid, or an overplus of two and a half sheets. This fee is of some bibliographical significance because in the beginning Henry Bynneman by himself apparently intended to publish merely the first part of the book, "the Romaine Ciuill warres," and a copy in the Carl H. Pforzheimer Library has an otherwise unknown cancellandum title with only Bynneman's name in the imprint referring solely to the first part which ends with the death of Sextus Pompeius. Bynneman's plans, however, were altered, and a second part containing the civil wars to the death of Antony and "the Romanes

[20] The number of sheets in this book was taken from Hazlitt's *Handbook*, p. 679, which gives 176 leaves, information evidently derived from J. P. Collier. However, since the above was set up, it has been possible to see a microfilm of the Sion College copy, a quarto collating A–Y^4, Z^2, Aa–Qq^4, or 38½ sheets, which amounts to less than two and half sheets a penny. More than an eighth of the book is set in roman with a small quantity of two-column verse in italic. The book was divided between two compositors or presses, and it is possible that an error in casting-off gave the impression that the last two of the five histories into which the book is divided would occupy as many sheets as the first three, which would have given a total of at least 45 sheets, and that the fee was paid before the book was completed. The Sion College copy does not appear to belong to a condensed second edition.

expeditions against forraine Nations," published by Ralph Newberry in partnership with Bynneman, was added. The first part contains fifty-two and a half sheets, whereas the second part contains just forty. From the fee charged it is apparent that the change of plan was made before the Clerk of the Company recorded the payment of the half crown, and therefore it is not surprising that only one copy has so far been traced with the uncanceled original title.

Random checking of the fees recorded in these early years confirms the probability that the normal fee was calculated at the rate of three sheets per penny. It is not unlikely that should someone have the leisure to compare all the entries of these early years with such of the books then entered as can now be traced, he would be able to be much more categorical about such matters as whether the entries were often made before the books were in print, and whether leading, size, or kind of type were factors in the calculations of the fees, as well as many other particulars of entry-practises concerning which we have too little evidence as yet even to speculate.

V. Gwynn binding on *Chronicon Monasterii Reicherspergenis* (1611)

8

Edward Gwynn

(1934)

Provenance, the study of the descent of books and collections from owner to owner, always fascinated Jackson. His earliest published essay in this field is followed by four more of later date (Bibliography, no. 6).

CALF-BOUND volumes bearing the name EDWARD GWYNN,[1] stamped in gold on their upper covers, and the initials E G on their lower, are familiar to all who have to do with sixteenth- and seventeenth-century books.[2] In Bishop Stillingfleet's collection now in Archbishop Marsh's Library, Christ Church Cathedral, Dublin, there are at least thirty-eight volumes so stamped, and scattered throughout the libraries of England and America there are probably several hundred others. The most important of the books thus distinguished is the Goetz Wrisberg — Perry — Folger volume which contains the nine 1619 Shakespeare Quartos and is the only known complete collection of them still in its original seventeenth-century binding. Next to it would probably be ranked the unique vellum copy of the Wynkyn de Worde edition of *Helyas Knight of the Swan*, which at the end of the seventeenth century belonged to Sir Paul Methuen, was sold by his descendants at Christie's in 1899, passed then to the Hoe library, and now belongs to the estate of the late Mrs. C. H. McCormick of Chicago.

[1] To H. J. B. Clements, Esq., the writer of this note is indebted for generous help and advice, as also to F. S. Ferguson, of Messrs. Bernard Quaritch, Ltd.

[2] The stamping was apparently done with separate tools and not with a block, since in one or two instances the letters overlap and frequently are differently spaced. However, most of the books appear to have been stamped by the same binder, if not at the same time, for the tools used are, with one or two exceptions, the same. [In 1964 Jackson purchased for the Harvard College Library a volume bound for Gwynn; see Plate V.]

VI. The arms of Edward Gwynn

It is not unlikely, however, that the library in which these two books were once associated contained others of equal rarity, if not importance, for their bindings, though attractive to the taste of collectors of today, would probably have been discarded by nineteenth-century connoisseurs had they passed through their hands to be replaced by the "morocco liveries" of Lewis or Bedford. Likewise, although most of the seventy-odd examples of Gwynn books which I have listed are English books printed before 1640, if the array in the Marsh Library is a typical fragment of the collection, it probably contained rather more foreign books than English.

The names of most seventeenth-century English book-collectors are familiar today usually because their owners were eminent for rank, scholarship, or literary attainments. Edward Gwynn, on the other hand, is to the historians of English book-collecting merely a name, although from the fact that he owned a copy of Maunsell's *Catalogue* [3] it may be fairly deduced that, whatever the recognizable remains of his library may be, he was an intelligent collector of books.

But it is possible to identify him and to fill in a somewhat shadowy outline of what sort of man he was, for one of his books, now in the possession of Messrs. Bernard Quaritch, Ltd., has emblazoned on its title the arms [4] reproduced in Plate VI, which are inscribed "Insignia, Edwardi Gwynn: Gentilitia, Medii, Templi, Socii."

In the *Middle Temple Records* (II, 529) appears the admission, 23 November 1610, of "Edward Gwynne, of Furnivalles Inn, gent., son and heir of Thomas Gwynn,[5] late of London, gent., deceased, specially;

[3] Now in the possession of Dr. A. S. W. Rosenbach.

[4] Quarterly of six. 1 and 6 argent, a chevron between three Cornish choughs sable, a crescent for difference. 2 azure, a lion rampant or, a crescent for difference. 3 argent, three spear-heads sable. 4 gules, a lion rampant between three roses argent. 5 sable, five lozenges, one, three and one, in dexter chief a trefoil all or. Crests, 1 between two spear-points upwards or, a Cornish chough sable, a crescent for difference. 2 A lion's gamb argent holding a lozenge or. Motto, Rore tonatis. These arms occur on the title of a manuscript (Phillipps, No. 8922) entitled *Medulla Parlamentalis* and evidently written and bound for Gwynn in 1622. The first coat and crest are those of Sir Rhys ap Thomas (see College of Arms MS. Vincent Collection 181, 174 B), whose illegitimate son David founded the house of Gwynn, of Taliarus, in Caermarthenshire, which according to Dr. Lawrence Buckley Thomas (*The Thomas Book* [New York, 1896], p. 20), became extinct about 1650, in the seventh generation. The fifth coat and second crest are those of the Essington family (see note 5).

[5] Among London pedigrees in *Miscellanea Genealogica* (5th series, III [1918–19], 167) may be found an incomplete pedigree of Edward Gwynn, who is there described as "Deputy to Thomas Spencer, Custus [*sic*] Brevium of the Court of Common Pleas." His father was Thomas Gwynn, Esq., Gentleman Usher to Lady Frances, daughter of Charles Brandon,

bound with John Paris and Alexander Chorley, gents.; fine 3*l*." On 24 June 1631 he was made an Utter Barrister (*op. cit.*, II, 781) and on 28 October of the same year was fined "as usual for absence from commons during the . . . reading" (*op. cit.*, II, 785).

Furnival's Inn, an appendage of Lincoln's Inn, has no printed records, but in the minutes of a council of the latter held 22 May 1626 (*Black Books*, II, 261–2) it is recorded that "Edward Gwyn and Alexander Chorley, two gentlemen of Furnivall's Inn, have been admitted by the Principal and Ancients of that Society in an extraordinary and unusual manner into two chambers in the Garden Buildings there. In consideration of their charges in building, the admission is confirmed for their joint lives and the life of the survivor, with power to nominate a third member of that Society in place of either of them, with immunity from ordinary forfeitures. They shall pay a rent of 5*s*. yearly to the Treasurer of Lincoln's Inn."

Just how commodious were the "chambers and sellars," as a later note describes them, which, with his friend Chorley, Gwynn built in the garden off Holborn, we shall probably never know. Jacobean oak, however, and walls covered with books solidly and soberly bound in new English calf, with here and there a vellum-bound one and a few in earlier black "divinity" calf and several in brown morocco, English Lyonnese style, must have made an imposing if not a cheerful sight. At any rate, it was there that for nearly two decades the two friends lived and the library was housed.

In 1645 Gwynn made a nuncupative will which is preserved at Somerset House (Admon. w. Will, 18 Pembroke) and reads:

> Memorand that Edward Gwynne of ffurnevalls Inn London Gentleman being of perfect mind and memorie, wth an intent to settle and dispose of his estate did in the Moneths of Aprill May and June Anno Dni one thousand sixe hundred fortie five or one of them make and declare his last Will & Testament Nuncupative in manner and forme followinge (vizt) I have but few kindred and to them I have given theire Pedegree in my life time wch is all I intend to give them, but all my goods chambers and bookes in ffurnevalls Inn and els where I give and bequeath vnto Alexander Chorley gent. All wch or the like in effect . . .

---

and wife to Henry Gray, Marquis Dorset; while his mother was Katherine (1553–1598), daughter of Robert Essington, one of the Bridgemasters in London. Thomas Gwynn was the son of William Vaughan, of Berain, Co. Denbigh, whose wife was Margaret Gwynn, who was presumably descended from David, the son of Sir Rhys ap Thomas.

This will was not proved until 12 February 1649–1650, though it is probable from its form that Gwynn died not long after he made it.[6] However, it was not until May 1650, possibly because before that date the legatee could not be sued, that the council of Lincoln's Inn appears to have discovered that the nominal rent of five shillings per annum which Gwynn and Chorley had covenanted to pay in 1626 was twenty-four years in arrears! The debt was not paid for several weeks more (see *Black Books*, II, 386, 388, and 392).

Alexander Chorley, the legatee and apparently lifelong friend, for it was probably he who forty years before had stood sponsor at Gwynn's admission to the Middle Temple, was the second son of William Chorley of Chorley, Lancashire. He was "the first Protestant in the line," the father of at least fourteen children, and the ancestor of most of the surviving Chorleys (see John Wilson, *Verses and Notes* (1903), pp. 25–26). He was admitted to Lincoln's Inn, 19 October 1648 (*Register*, I, 258), presumably at an advanced age for his eldest son was born in 1611, but the date of his death [7] and the existence of his will cannot be established. It is therefore impossible to ascertain whether he retained Gwynn's library intact or what disposition he made of it. Since several of the books [8] occur in libraries collected mainly in the 1670's and 1680's, it is probable that Gwynn's books were dispersed about that time or possibly not long before.

[6] The delay was presumably caused by litigation on the part of the disinherited relatives, but no suit against the legatee by anyone bearing the name of Gwynn, or of any person listed as having married a London Gwynn during the early part of the seventeenth century, can be traced in the Chancery Rolls.

[7] From the fact that the Chorley pedigree in the Visitation of Kent, 1663–1668, is signed by his second son, Thomas, it might be inferred that Alexander Chorley was then dead; see *A Visitation of the County of Kent, Begun Anno Dni. 1663, Finished Anno Dni. 1668*, ed. Sir George John Armytage, Harleian Society Publications, LIV (London, 1906), p. 35.

[8] Some of Gwynn's books, but not all, have written in ink on the front flyleaf in an early hand an "r" above, and separated by a bar from, a Greek ε. The significance of this mark, and whether or not it was Gwynn's own, have not been discovered, but apparently it was introduced before the library was scattered.

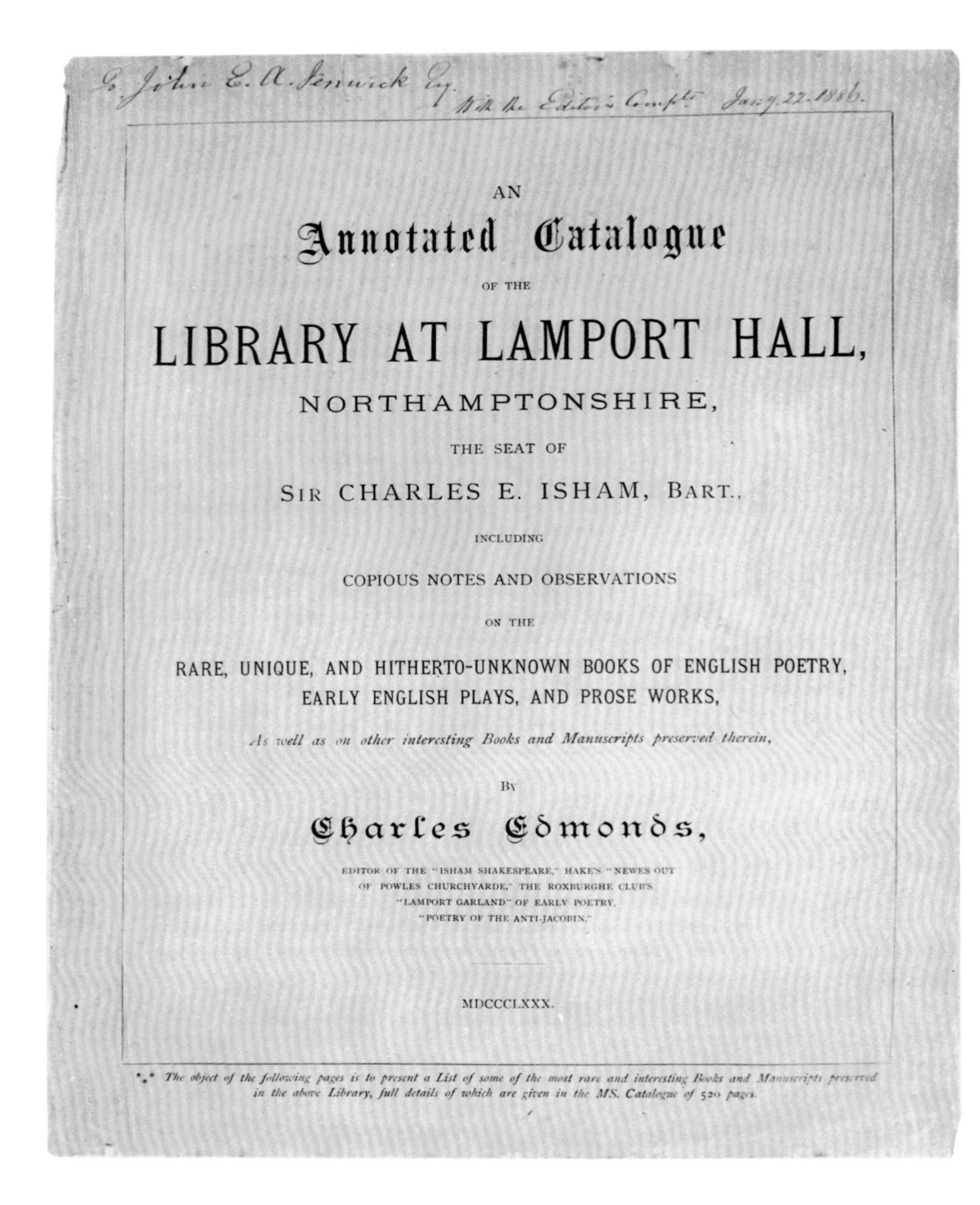

To John E. A. Fenwick Esq. With the Editor's Compts. Jany. 22. 1886.

AN

Annotated Catalogue

OF THE

LIBRARY AT LAMPORT HALL,

NORTHAMPTONSHIRE,

THE SEAT OF

SIR CHARLES E. ISHAM, BART.,

INCLUDING

COPIOUS NOTES AND OBSERVATIONS

ON THE

RARE, UNIQUE, AND HITHERTO-UNKNOWN BOOKS OF ENGLISH POETRY,
EARLY ENGLISH PLAYS, AND PROSE WORKS,

As well as on other interesting Books and Manuscripts preserved therein,

BY

Charles Edmonds,

EDITOR OF THE "ISHAM SHAKESPEARE," HAKE'S "NEWES OUT
OF POWLES CHURCHYARDE," THE ROXBURGHE CLUB'S
"LAMPORT GARLAND" OF EARLY POETRY,
"POETRY OF THE ANTI-JACOBIN."

MDCCCLXXX.

*** *The object of the following pages is to present a List of some of the most rare and interesting Books and Manuscripts preserved in the above Library, full details of which are given in the MS. Catalogue of 520 pages.*

VII. Prospectus for the Lamport Hall Catalogue, 1880

9

The Lamport Hall-Britwell Court Books

(1948)

This essay was written for a volume in memory of Joseph Quincy Adams, Shakespearean scholar and long-time director of the Folger Shakespeare Library. Three minor revisions by Jackson in the book-list at the end have been silently inserted (Bibliography, no. 56).

CHARLES EDMONDS, of Willis and Sotheran, announced in a letter to *The Times* for Friday, October 4, 1867, the discovery of an unknown edition of *Venus and Adonis* (1599), as well as of a copy of *The Passionate Pilgrime* (1599), of which last only one other copy was then known. After mentioning these two books, his account continues:

> The circumstances under which the discovery was made are very remarkable. No one, not even the respected owner (Sir Charles Isham) of this precious volume and of several other rare and valuable works printed about the same time, was aware of his possessing such literary treasures, till my professional examination a few days since of the books contained in the old library at Lamport, in Northamptonshire, brought them to light. There, in a back lumber room, covered with dust and exposed to the depredations of mice which had already digested the contents of some of the books, and amid hundreds of old volumes of various dates and sizes, the far greater part of which are of very trifling value, I discovered a little collection of volumes contemporary, or nearly so, with the work in question, the very sight of which would be sufficient to warm the heart of the most cold-blooded bibliomaniac. In this same place they had remained uncared for and unexamined for a period exceeding the "memory of the oldest inhabitant." It was impossible to ascertain why they had been banished from the large library below stairs, which among a considerable quantity of common and now comparatively valueless books, contains some of great rarity and value. The majority of these, as was shown by documents which I had the privilege of examining, and many of which had the original cost prices affixed, were

collected by Sir Justinian Isham, the fifth baronet, a gentleman of great literary acquirements, who built the library and altered the house in the time of King George I, it having been originally erected by John Isham, Esq., in the reign of Elizabeth, and afterwards altered and improved in the time of Charles I from a design by John Webb, the son-in-law of Inigo Jones. The books now discovered were no doubt collected by a more remote possessor of the property — possibly by Thomas Isham, who died in 1605, and whose grandson, John, was knighted by King James I at Whitehall . . . There is every evidence to show that the books have remained in the house from a very remote period, and that no additions of any moment have been made to the library for the last 150 years.

It should be remarked, however, in extenuation of the books in question having for so many years attracted no attention, that the more precious of them being bound in the old common vellum of the period, and without lettering or any outside indication of their contents, would challenge no notice except from a real and curious lover of old, and to most people, uninviting looking books.

Since that first announcement, the "Lamport Find," as it is usually called, has been frequently, and usually inaccurately, referred to in the literature of bibliophily. It seems, therefore, worthwhile to set forth the following account of the Isham books in a volume dedicated to the memory of Dr. J. Q. Adams, for he had under his care in the Folger Library almost a score of Isham-Britwell volumes, several of which he had himself selected for addition to that library which he so ably administered and increased.

Although the family of Isham had dwelt in Northamptonshire longer than any other of the county families, it was not until 1560 that John Isham purchased the manor of Lamport from Sir William Cecil. John Isham, Master Warden of the Mercers Company of London and one of the Merchant Adventurers of Flanders, married Elizabeth, daughter of Nicholas Barker, likewise a Master Warden of the Mercers and believed, although on very slender grounds, to be a relative of Christopher Barker, the Queen's printer. John Isham probably had little to do with the founding of the library, but his son Thomas, who succeeded him in 1595 at the age of 30, although he had been blind since a great sickness which he had at the age of 14, is believed to be the founder of the Lamport Library. There are letters now deposited by Sir Gyles Isham in the custody of the Northamptonshire Record Society at the County Hall, Northampton, which show him ordering books through his son at Cambridge. His heir, Sir John Isham, the first baronet, was something of an Italian scholar and he, no doubt, continued to add to the library. In one of his letterbooks, now in my possession, there is a letter of June 6, 1624, addressed to his London agent, Robert Pearson, in which he says, "and for the Bookes which you write of I should very well like & allow of what you shall do there in. And do desire you to send them downe with the rest of ye thinges which you buy for me by Sherman the waggener of Northampton vpon wednesday the last day of the Tearme."

His son, Sir Justinian Isham, the second baronet, was a man of learning and culture, though perhaps of little humor, for it was he whom Dorothy Osborne described when, a widower with four daughters, he came to court her in 1653, as "the vainest, impertinent self-conceited learned coxcomb that ever I saw." He undoubtedly added considerably to the library, and in 1654–1655 he employed his friend John Webb, the pupil and connection, but not the son-in-law, of Inigo Jones, to rebuild the west front of Lamport Hall.[1] Sir Justinian's second wife was a granddaughter of Thomas Egerton, Viscount Brackley, the founder of the Bridgewater Library, and whether or not the collecting of books is an inheritable characteristic, it is interesting to note how frequently in succeeding generations of both the Isham and Egerton families there have been book collectors.

It was for the next baronet, Sir Thomas, that David Loggan engraved in 1676 "a print of your cote of arms," or rather two plates, for the first one, reproduced in W. J. Hardy, *Book-Plates*, p. 9, has an esquire's helmet and no "bloody hand of Ulster," so that Loggan had to make a new plate which was heraldically proper for a baronet (see Plate VIII, A). The letters which Loggan wrote Sir Thomas concerning these plates are a *locus classicus* in the history of the English bookplate,[2] as the plates themselves are among the finest examples of the "Restoration" style.

Sir Thomas Isham died in 1681 and was succeeded by his brother Sir Justinian, who died in 1730 and was followed by his son, another Justinian. It was the latter, the fifth baronet, who built the library room at Lamport.[3] These two Justinians were learned men and the friends of learned men. The library at Lamport contained many books which they must have collected or which are inscribed to them, but it contained little of importance of a later period; and the number of books which

[1] Webb's drawings are still in existence and together with his letters were published in *R.I.B.A. Journal*, XXVIII (1921), 565–582.

[2] William J. Hardy, *Book-Plates* (London, 1893), pp. 8–11; Walter Hamilton, *Dated Book-Plates* (London, 1895), I, 69.

[3] For a view of the library as it was in 1921, see *Country Life*, XLIX (1921), 677.

had by that time accumulated at Lamport was far greater than could be housed on the shelves of the library proper. In 1921, even after two auction sales and other dispersals, the shelves of that room were still filled with old calf-bound volumes, so that it is understandable if some of the unlettered, vellum-bound pamphlets had been relegated to a lumber room.

As Edmonds has nowhere published a complete list of the rarities which he found in that upper room,[4] it is not surprising that there has been some confusion about the "Lamport Find." At this distance it is probably not possible to determine just which of the numerous valuable and rare books were still on the library shelves and which were in the lumber room, nor is it of much importance. But some notion of the rarities at Lamport can be obtained by various means. For example, Edmonds printed in 1880 an eight-page quarto prospectus entitled *An Annotated Catalogue of the Library at Lamport Hall* (see reproduction of the title from a copy in the author's possession, Plate VII). According to a note at the bottom of the title, "The object of the following pages is to present a List of some of the most rare and interesting Books and Manuscripts preserved in the above Library, full details of which are given in the MS. Catalogue of 520 pages." Where that manuscript catalogue may now be is not known, but about two hundred items are listed in this printed prospectus, and from it one can form a fair notion of how rich the collection once was.[5] In 1877 Sir Charles Isham had lent fifteen of the most important and rarest pieces for the Caxton Celebration at South Kensington and at various times had permitted Edmonds to exhibit the Shakespearian volume at his place of business,[6] so that even then at least part of the collection must have been known to those who followed such matters.

At Puttick and Simpson's, 15 July 1874, Sir Charles had sold a number of the books of lesser literary interest, and through the same auctioneers, 14 December 1886, he disposed of his copy of the second edition

[4] The list of unrecorded works found at Lamport and published in *The Athenaeum*, 11 January 1868, p. 57, is admittedly incomplete.

[5] On page 6 of this prospectus is listed, in a section headed "Fine Arts," a work entitled "Lacework: The True Perfection of Cutworks. Lond. 1598," of which no copy can be traced, although a book of this title was licensed to William Jaggard, 23 January 1598 (Arber, III, 101). It is possible that this work is the original of one section of John Taylor's *The Needles Excellency*.

[6] Edmonds edited four volumes of "The Isham Reprints" (1890–1895), and for the Roxburghe Club, *A Lamport Garland* (London, 1881).

A. Bookplate of Sir Thomas Isham

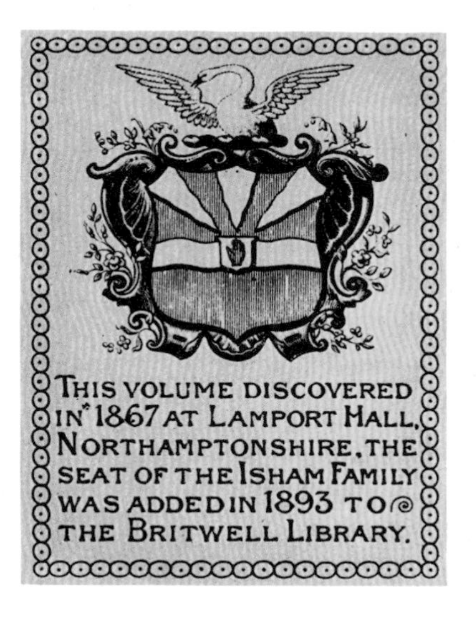

B. Lamport-Britwell label

VIII. Isham and Lamport-Britwell bookplates

of Brereton, which copy was later in the Kalbfleisch, Lefferts, Church, and Huntington collections. In 1893 Wakefield Christie Miller acquired by private treaty 130 of the rarest items (of these more later), while at Sotheby's, 17–18 June 1904, Sir Vere Isham sold 355 lots, including a number of pamphlet collections. At this sale there were sold a number of rarities, such as the unique copy of Lodge's *Rosalynde* (1596), now in the Huntington Library; Ben Jonson's copy of Savonarola's *Triumphus Crucis* (1633), now in the Shakespeare Memorial Library at Stratford; a large-paper copy of François Du Jon's *The Painting of the Ancients* (1638), now in the Folger Library; etc. But this did not end the dispersal of the Isham books, for in 1935 the British Museum purchased from Sir Gyles Isham eight leaves of the Cotton manuscript of Eccleston's *Chronicle*, which Walter Rye had discovered at Lamport in 1879.[7]

The hundred-odd volumes purchased for the Britwell Court Library formed the core of the Lamport Library, whether one regards them from a purely literary or a bibliophilic standpoint. No other copy of twenty of those items is now known, and the majority of them belong to the greatest period of English poetry. Furthermore, all but a few are in the finest possible condition, clean, uncut — some were unopened when found, and many in original vellum, sheep, or calf. The only similar collections with which these books may be compared are those of Sir Robert Gordon and Frances Wolfreston. In 1894, ten Lamport books were sold by Wakefield Christie Miller to the British Museum, together with sixteen Britwell duplicates which the finer Lamport copies had replaced. Five of the Lamport books have not been traced in the Britwell sales. As they were all duplicates of ones already in that library, and as none of them was of any great rarity or value, they were probably privately disposed of. The remaining 115 items were sold in the various Britwell sales from 1910 to 1927, in exactly one hundred lots, for several were still bound together in original vellum. The hundred lots fetched a total of £51,725, which is an amazing sum for a collection of this kind of unillustrated book. Nevertheless, it is not unlikely, even without the competition of Folger and Huntington, that if sold again today they would bring an even larger sum.

Besides making his elaborate manuscript catalogue of the Lamport books, Charles Edmonds labeled all of the unlettered vellum bindings with a small paper label with printed border (2 x 3 inches), on which

[7] See *British Museum Quarterly*, IX (1934), 115–117.

in a copper-plate hand he wrote the author and title. All eighteen of the volumes, containing thirty-three works, which are still in their original vellum, retain these labels. But seventy-two of the books were bound in various colored moroccos by Pratt, with the Miller arms and Wakefield Christie Miller's monogram.[8] And in most of them, whatever their binding, there was placed a bookplate with the Isham arms and the legend, "This volume discovered in 1867 at Lamport Hall, Northamptonshire, the seat of the Isham Family was added in 1893 to the Britwell Library" (see Plate VII, B).

The following list of the Lamport-Britwell books is based upon that published by Reginald E. Graves in *Bibliographica*, III (1897), 418–429, but is supplemented and corrected from manuscript notes in my copy of a privately printed catalogue of "English Poetry in the Britwell Library," as well as from other sources.

S.T.C. 24.5 Abbot, G. A Briefe Description [second edition], 1599. CLEMENTS LIBRARY. Britwell June 1919, no. 1.

S.T.C. 685 Anton, R. Moriomachia, 1613. L. Acquired 1894.

S.T.C. 719a Apuleius, L. The XI Bookes of the Golden Asse, 1582. Untraced. Britwell June 1920, no. 26, sold to "English Collector."

S.T.C. 980 Averell, W. An Excellent Historie, 1581. HN. Britwell Feb. 1922, no. 24. Not unique; J. P. Collier records another in *N. & Q.*, 4th Ser., iii (1869), pp. 5–6.

S.T.C. 1429 Barksted, W. Mirrha the Mother of Adonis, 1607. FOLG. Britwell Feb. 1922, no. 32.

S.T.C. 1484 Barnfield, R. Cynthia, 1595. HN. Britwell Feb. 1922, no. 109, bound fourth with 4268, 12367, and 24097. Unique, cf. title of Reed-Heber-Britwell-Folger copy of first edition reproduced Britwell Cat. 1923, no. 42.

S.T.C. 1556 Basse, W. Three Pastoral Elegies, 1602. HN. Britwell Dec. 1919, no. 2.

S.T.C. 1559 Bastard, T. Chrestoleros, 1598. FOLG. Britwell Feb. 1922, no. 38.

S.T.C. 1695 Beaumont, Sir J. The Metamorphosis of Tabacco, 1602. HN. Britwell Feb. 1922, no. 45.

S.T.C. 3634 Breton, N. Brittons Bowre of Delights, 1597. HN. Britwell Dec. 1919, no. 10. The British Museum received the Luttrell-Farmer-Ellis-Heber-Britwell copy despite Garnett, *Three Hundred Notable Books*, p. 41.

S.T.C. 3648 —— A Diuine Poeme, 1601. FOLG. Britwell Mar. 1921, no. 8 — Harmsworth.

[8] One book, the G. Dawes, was bound in blind-tooled russia, presumably for Sir Charles Isham.

S.T.C. 3649 —— An Excellent Poeme, 1601. HN. Britwell Feb. 1922, no. 76.

S.T.C. 3659 —— Honest Counsaile, 1605. HN. Britwell Feb. 1922, no. 80. The British Museum acquired the Inglis-Heber-Britwell duplicate in 1894.

S.T.C. 3667 —— A Merrie Dialogue, 1603. HN. Britwell Mar. 1923, no. 84. The British Museum acquired in 1894 the Heber-Britwell duplicate.

S.T.C. 3669 —— The Mothers Blessing, 1602. C. H. PFORZHEIMER. Britwell Mar. 1923, no. 82.

S.T.C. 3672 [——] No Whippinge, nor Trippinge, 1601. HN. Britwell Nov. 1919, no. 107. Bound third with 25351 and 14071. The British Museum received the imperfect Luttrell-Britwell copy in 1894, despite Garnett, *Three Hundred Notable Books*, p. 44.

S.T.C. 3673 —— Olde Mad-Cappes New Gally-Mawfrey, 1602. HN. Britwell Mar. 1923, no. 83. The British Museum acquired a Britwell duplicate in 1894.

S.T.C. 3674 —— An Olde Mans Lesson, 1605. Untraced. Britwell Feb. 1922, no. 79, resold July 1927, no. 130. A fragment of eight leaves only.

S.T.C. 3680 —— The Passion of a Discontented Minde, 1602. FOLG. Britwell Mar. 1921, no. 9 — Harmsworth.

S.T.C. 3683 —— The Pilgrimage to Paradise, 1592. HN. Britwell Dec. 1919, no. 8.

S.T.C. 3696 —— A Solemne Passion, 1598. HN. Britwell Dec. 1919, no. 13.

S.T.C. 4268 C., E., Esquire. Emaricdulfe, 1595. HN. Britwell Feb. 1922, no. 109, bound first with 12367, 24097, and 1484.

S.T.C. 4283 C., J., Gent. A Poore Knight, 1579. HN. Britwell Feb. 1922, no. 112.

S.T.C. 4518 [Camden, W.] Reges, Reginae . . . Sepulti, 1600. WESTMINSTER ABBEY. Britwell Dec. 1919, no. 18.

S.T.C. 4985 Chapman, G. Ouids Banquet of Sence, 1595. HN. Britwell Mar. 1923, no. 129. Bound second with 4990 and 17414.

S.T.C. 4990 —— Σκιὰ Νυκτός, 1594. HN. Britwell Mar. 1923, no. 129. Bound first with 4985 and 17414.

S.T.C. 5326 Citois, F. A True and Admirable Historie, 1603. L. Acquired in 1894. Imperfect.

S.T.C. 5956 Craig, A. The Amorose Songes, 1606. FOLG. Britwell Feb. 1922, no. 183 — W. A. White.

S.T.C. 6151 Cutwode, T. Caltha Poetarum, 1599. HN. Britwell Mar. 1923, no. 185.

S.T.C. 6350.5 Davies, Sir J. Epigrammes, [1599]. HN. Britwell Dec. 1919, no. 85. Bound with 22342 and 22358. Unique.

S.T.C. 6351 —— Hymnes of Astraea, 1599. HN. Britwell Mar. 1923, no. 199.

S.T.C. 6566 Deloney, T. Strange Histories of Kings, 1602. HN. Britwell Feb. 1922, no. 230. Unique. Bodleian has no copy.

S.T.C. 6785 Des Portes, P. Rodomonths Infernall, 1607. HN. Britwell Feb. 1922, no. 231.

S.T.C. 6820 Dickenson, J. The Shepheardes Complaint, [1596]. HN. Britwell Feb. 1922, no. 233. Unique.

S.T.C. 7202 Drayton, M. Idea, 1593. HN. Britwell Mar. 1923, no. 226.

S.T.C. 7217 —— Poemes Lyrick and Pastorall [1606?]. N.Y.P.L. Britwell Mar. 1923, no. 233—O. D. Young.

S.T.C. 7231.5 —— To the Maiestie of King James. Second impression, 1603. Britwell Feb. 1922, no. 242.—Clarendon Park.

S.T.C. 7378 [Duwes, G.] An Introductorie, [1539?]. HN. Britwell Mar. 1924, no. 264.

S.T.C. 7521 Edwards, R. The Paradice of Dainty Deuises, 1596. HN. Britwell Dec. 1919, no. 74.

S.T.C. 7525 Edwards, T. Cephalus and Procris, 1595. L. Acquired 1894. A fragment, 4 ll. only.

S.T.C. 7594 Elizabeth, Queen. The Poores Lamentation, 1603. HN. Britwell Feb. 1922, no. 545.

S.T.C. 7606 Ellis, G. The Lamentation of the Lost Sheepe, 1605. HN. Britwell Feb. 1922, no. 270.

S.T.C. 10596 Evans, W. Pietatis Lachrymæ, 1602. HN. Britwell Mar. 1923, no. 261. Unique.

S.T.C. 10686 Faret, N. The Honest Man, 1632. HN. Britwell Mar. 1926, no. 212.

S.T.C. 10771 Fenner, D. A Defence of the Godlie Ministers, 1587. FOLG. Britwell May 1920, no. 181—Harmsworth.

S.T.C. 10798 Fenton, J. King James His Welcome, 1603. FOLG. Britwell Feb. 1922, no. 285—W. A. White. The British Museum acquired in 1894 the B.A.P.-North-Heber-Britwell duplicate.

S.T.C. 10944 Fitz-Geffrey, C. Sir Francis Drake, Oxford, 1596. HN. Britwell Mar. 1923, no. 438. Bound with 17385.

S.T.C. 11058 Fletcher, G. Christs Victorie, 1610. HD. Britwell Feb. 1922, no. 295.

S.T.C. 11158 Ford, J. Fames Memoriall, 1606, ROSENBACH. Britwell Feb. 1922, no. 301.

S.T.C. 11339 Fraunce, A. The Countesse of Pembrokes Emanuel, 1591. C. H. PFORZHEIMER. Britwell Mar. 1923, no. 295. Bound second with 11340 and 11341.

S.T.C. 11340 —— The Countesse of Pembrokes Yuychurch, 1591. C. H. PFORZHEIMER. Britwell Mar. 1923, no. 295. Bound first with 11339 and 11341.

S.T.C. 11341 —— The Third Part of the . . . Yuychurch, 1592. C. H. PFORZHEIMER. Britwell Mar. 1923, no. 295. Bound third with 11339 and 11340.

S.T.C. 11480 Fulwood, W. The Enimie of Idlenesse, 1586. HN. Britwell Mar. 1923, no. 298.

S.T.C. 11638 Gascoigne, G. The Whole Woorkes, 1587. A. A. HOUGHTON, JR. Britwell Mar. 1925, no. 252 — F. B. Bemis.

[Gayton, E.] Chartae Scriptae, 1645. Untraced. Britwell Feb. 1910, no. 124.

S.T.C. 12217 Greene, R. Arbasto, 1584. HN. Britwell Dec. 1919, no. 33. Leaves A3, and C3–4 are from the Charles Davies copy which was acquired in 1894 by British Museum. S.T.C. 12217 and 12218 are identical.

S.T.C. 12244 [——] Greens Ghost, 1626. Untraced. The only copy in Britwell Library sold Mar. 1923, no. 325, now Rosenbach, apparently not Lamport copy.

S.T.C. 12311 Greene, T. A Poet's Vision, 1603. HN. Britwell Feb. 1922, no. 339.

S.T.C. 12367 Griffin, B. Fidessa, 1596. HN. Britwell Feb. 1922, no. 109. Bound second with 4268, 1484, and 24097.

S.T.C. 12504 [Guilpin, E.] Skialetheia, 1598. FOLG. Britwell Feb. 1922, no. 344 — W. A. White. The British Museum acquired in 1894 the Sotheby May 1846–Britwell duplicate.

S.T.C. 12606 Hake, E. Newes out of Powles Churchyarde [1579]. HN. Britwell Dec. 1919, no. 53. The British Museum acquired in 1894 the Freeling-Britwell duplicate.

S.T.C. 12716 Hall, J. Virgidemiarum (Pt. II), 1598. C. H. PFORZHEIMER. Britwell Feb. 1922, no. 349. Bound with 12717.

S.T.C. 12717 —— Virgidemiarum (Pt. I), 1598. C. H. PFORZHEIMER. Britwell Feb. 1922, no. 349. Bound with 12716.

S.T.C. 12751 Har., W. Epicedium, 1594. FOLG. Britwell Mar. 1923, no. 73. The British Museum acquired in 1894 the B.A.P.-Sykes-Heber-Britwell duplicate.

S.T.C. 14029 Hutton, L. The Blacke Dogge of Newgate [1596?]. HN. Britwell Mar. 1924, no. 443. Imperfect.

S.T.C. 14071 I., W. The Whipping of the Satyre, 1601. HN. Britwell Dec. 1919, Lot 107. Bound first with 25351 and 3672. S.T.C. 14071 repeated as 25352.

S.T.C. 14784 Jonson, B. Ionsonus Virbius, 1638. Untraced. There were three copies in the Britwell sales but it could not have been one of them, for that sold Mar. 1921, no. 114, is now Folger (Harmsworth) and bears on verso of title the stamp of the Charterhouse Library; while the other two copies (Feb. 1922, no. 399, and Mar. 1923, no. 386) are described as being in the Britwell Library before 1868 in a privately printed catalogue of the poetry in the library.

S.T.C. 15686 Ling, N. Politeuphuia, 1598. C. H. PFORZHEIMER. Britwell Mar. 1923, no. 65.

S.T.C. 16589 The CL. Psalmes, 1602. FOLG. Britwell May 1920, no. 391 — Harmsworth.

S.T.C. 16658 Lodge, T. A Fig for Momus, 1595. C. H. PFORZHEIMER. Britwell Feb. 1922, no. 440.

S.T.C. 16674 —— Scillaes Metamorphosis, 1589. HN. Britwell Feb. 1922, no. 436.

S.T.C. 16696 Lok, H. Ecclesiastes, 1597. Untraced. Britwell 24 Feb. 1910, no. 136. An imperfect copy, bought by Dobell.

S.T.C. 17091 Lynche, R. Diella, 1596. HN. Britwell Feb. 1922, no. 426.

S.T.C. 17133 M., E. Humors Antique Faces, 1605. FOLG. Britwell Feb. 1922, no. 497.

S.T.C. 17143 M., Jo. Phillippes Venus, 1591. FOLG. Britwell June 1920, no. 198.

S.T.C. 17253 Mandeville, Sir J. Voyages and Trauailes, 1627. FOLG. Britwell June 1919, no. 534 — Harmsworth.

S.T.C. 17385 Markham, G. The most Honorable Tragedie, 1595. HN. Britwell Mar. 1923, no. 438. Bound with 10944.

S.T.C. 17414 Marlowe, C. Hero and Leander, 1598. HN. Britwell Mar. 1923, no. 129. Bound third with 4990 and 4985. Unique; compare reproduction of title in *Britwell Catalogue* and Garnett, *Three Hundred Notable Books*, p. 42, also see Hazlitt, p. 695.

S.T.C. 17414+ —— Hero and Leander, 1598. L. Acquired 1894. Bound with 21535 and 21536. Unique. See note on 17414.

S.T.C. 17454 Marprelate, M. O Read Ouer [1588]. QUARITCH. Britwell May 1920, no. 323.

S.T.C. 17457 —— Theses Martinianæ, [1589]. QUARITCH. Britwell May 1920, no. 317.

S.T.C. 17547 Mary, B. V. The Song of Mary the Mother of Christ, 1601. HN. Britwell Feb. 1922, no. 621.

S.T.C. 17569 Marie Magdalens Lamentations, 1601. ROSENBACH. Britwell Feb. 1922, no. 462.

S.T.C. 17875 M[iddleton], T. The Blacke Booke, 1604. N.Y.P.L. Britwell Mar. 1923, no. 485 — G. Arents.

Milton, J. Paradise Lost, 1667. A. A. HOUGHTON, JR. Britwell Dec. 1919, no. 60 — Seth Terry.

—— Paradise Regain'd, 1671. A. A. HOUGHTON, JR. Britwell Mar. 1923, no. 479 — Seth Terry.

S.T.C. 18369 Nash, T. Haue with You, 1596. C. H. PFORZHEIMER. Britwell Dec. 1919, no. 66.

[Neville, H.] Newes from the New Exchange, 1650. HN. Britwell Mar. 1926, no. 394.

Nevizanus, J. Silva Nuptialis, Paris, 1521. Untraced. Britwell 10 June 1917, Lot 776.

S.T.C. 18511 Newton, T. Atropoion Delion, 1603. QUARITCH. Britwell Dec. 1919, no. 68.

S.T.C. 18546 Nicholson, S. Acolastus His Afterwitte, 1600. HN. Britwell Mar. 1921, no. 180. The British Museum acquired 1894 the Luttrell-Farmer-Steevens-Bindley-Hibbert-Bright-Britwell duplicate.

S.T.C. 18583 Nixon, A. The Christian Navy, 1602. FOLG. Britwell Dec. 1919, no. 69 — Harmsworth.

S.T.C. 18755 O., I. The Lamentation of Troy, 1594. HN. Britwell Mar. 1923, no. 501. The British Museum acquired in 1894 the Caldecott-Britwell duplicate.

S.T.C. 18943 Ovidius Naso, P. The Heroycall Epistles, [c. 1584]. ROSENBACH. Britwell Mar. 1921, no. 195 — R. B. Adam-R. Isham.

S.T.C. 19338 Parry, R. Sinetes Passions, 1597. HN. Britwell Mar. 1923, no. 529. Unique.

S.T.C. 19805 Petowe, H. Elizabetha Quasi Viuens, 1603. D. F. HYDE. Britwell Dec. 1919, no. 77.

S.T.C. 19808 —— Philochasander and Elanira, 1599. L. Acquired in 1894.

S.T.C. 19876 Phillips, J. Vt Hora, sic Fugit Vita, 1591. HN. Britwell Feb. 1922, no. 540. Unique.

S.T.C. 19975 Plato. Platoes Cap, 1604. HN. Britwell Mar. 1923, no. 540. The British Museum acquired 1894 an imperfect Britwell duplicate. According to Hazlitt, the title was in Bagford Collection, query now placed in British Museum copy.

S.T.C. 20169 Powell, T. Vertues Due, 1603. HN. Britwell Feb. 1922, no. 546. Unique.

S.T.C. 20992 Rich, B. A New Description of Ireland, 1610. Untraced. Not located in Britwell sales. The Britwell (Reed-Heber) copy now Folger.

S.T.C. 21120 Robinson, R. The Reward of Wickednesse, [1574]. FOLG. Britwell Mar. 1921, no. 259 — Harmsworth.

S.T.C. 21206 Rogers, R. A Garden of Spirituall Flowers, 1610. FOLG. Britwell May 1920, no. 409 — Harmsworth. Unique.

S.T.C. 21225 Rogers, T., of Bryanston. Celestiall Elegies, 1598. HN. Britwell Mar. 1923, no. 571. Unique.

S.T.C. 21364 Rowlands, S. Aue Caesar, 1603. HN. Britwell Mar. 1923, no. 558. No plate.

S.T.C. 21534 Sabie, F. Adams Complaint, 1596. HN. Britwell Mar. 1923, no. 584. The British Museum received in 1894 the Luttrell-Bindley-Heber-Britwell duplicate. No plate.

S.T.C. 21535 —— The Fishermans Tale, 1595. L. Acquired 1894. Bound with 17414+ and 21536.

S.T.C. 21536 —— Flora's Fortune, 1595. L. Acquired 1894. Bound with 17414+ and 21535.

S.T.C. 21537 —— Pans Pipe, 1595. HN. Britwell Feb. 1922, no. 596. Really only Pt. I of volume which should contain 21537, 21535 and 21536. The title of 21535 is bound with this copy.

S.T.C. 21616 Salesbury, W. A Dictionary, 1547. CARDIFF PUBLIC LIBRARY. Britwell Mar. 1924, no. 677.

S.T.C. 22137 Seager, F. The Schoole of Vertue, 1593. HN. Britwell Mar. 1923, no. 595. Unique.

S.T.C. 22342 Shakespeare, W. The Passionate Pilgrim, 1599. HN. Britwell Dec. 1919, no. 85. Bound with 22358 and 6350.

S.T.C. 22358 —— Venus and Adonis, 1599. HN. Britwell Dec. 1919, no. 85. Bound with 22342 and 6350. Unique.

S.T.C. 22426 Sherley, Sir A. Witts New Dyall, 1604. HN. Britwell Mar. 1921, no. 269.

S.T.C. 22949 Southwell, R. A Foure-Fould Meditation, 1606. L. Acquired 1894. A fragment only.

S.T.C. 23078 Spenser, E. Complaints, 1591. Untraced. The Britwell Library already contained the uncut Heber copy bound uniformly with the Britwell Spensers. The Lamport copy does not occur in the Britwell duplicate sales. The Folger Library has a copy bound by Pratt without Christie Miller arms which might be the Lamport copy.

S.T.C. 23579 Sylvester, J. Monodia (Pt. I), [1594]. HN. Britwell Feb. 1922, no. 647.

S.T.C. 23687+ Tarlton, R. Tarletons Tragicall Treatises, 1578. FOLG. Britwell Feb. 1922, no. 649, a fragment, 8 ll.

S.T.C. 23695 Tasso, T. The Lamentations of Amyntas, 1596. L. Acquired 1894.

S.T.C. 24050 Throckmorton, F. A Discouerie of the Treasons, 1584. Untraced. Britwell Feb. 1910, no. 117.

S.T.C. 24079 Timberlake, H. A True and Strange Discourse, 1603. FOLG. Britwell June 1919, no. 807 — Harmsworth.

S.T.C. 24097 Tofte, R. Laura, 1597. HN. Britwell Feb. 1922, no. 109. Bound third with 4268, 12367, and 1484. British Museum received other Lamport copy.

S.T.C. 24152 Tourneur, C. The Transformed Metamorphosis, 1600. L. Acquired in 1894. Unique.

S.T.C. 24345 Turner, R. The Garland of a Greene Witte, [1595?]. HN. Britwell Mar. 1921, no. 314. Unique.

S.T.C. 24800 Virgilius Maro, P. The Nyne Fyrst Bookes, 1562. CHAPIN. Britwell Feb. 1922, no. 690 — H. V. Jones.

S.T.C. 24918 W., T., Gent. The Lamentation of Melpomene, 1603. HN. Britwell Mar. 1921, no. 317. Unique.

S.T.C. 25082a Warner, W. Albions England, 1597. Untraced. Not in Britwell sales.

S.T.C. 25226 Weever, J. The Mirror of Martyrs, 1601. FOLG. Britwell Feb. 1922, no. 703.

S.T.C. 25351 The Whipper of the Satyre, 1601. HN. Britwell Dec. 1919, no. 107. Bound second with 14071 and 3672. The British Museum acquired in 1894 the Britwell duplicate.

S.T.C. 26014 [Wrednot, W.] Palladis Palatium, 1604. HN. Britwell Mar. 1924, no. 849. Unique.

10

Humphrey Dyson's Library, or, Some Observations on the Survival of Books (1949)

This paper was read at a meeting of the Bibliographical Society of America at Princeton, New Jersey, on June 4, 1949. Jackson's later findings are embodied in footnotes (Bibliography, no. 60).

THE purpose of this paper is not to add to the information, such as it is, that has previously been published concerning Humphrey Dyson,[1] but rather to examine the role of the book collector as exemplified by him. Dyson was a notary public who died in February 1632 and who collected English printed books, particularly those relating to the history of church and state. He placed his signature on the title pages of most of his books, though sometimes he affixed a stamp of his name and profession on the versos of the titles, while in a few cases he had his initials stamped in gold on the bindings. In his will, he directed that his executor, William Jumper, should "have care to put of and sell my bookes to the most profitt that he can." Mr. Jumper, who died ten years later, appears to have sold a large portion of Dyson's library to Richard Smith, Secondary of the Poultry Compter (that is, an assistant to the sheriff, with his office in the Court in the Poultry), for a large number of Dyson's books appeared in the auction sale of Smith's library held by Richard Chiswell in 1682, and the catalogue declares that "a great part of the Rarities" had been gathered out of the library of Humphrey Dyson. One of the lots then sold comprised six notebooks, compiled by Dyson himself, containing the manuscript catalogue of some of his books.

[1] *The Library*, 3rd series, I (1910), 144–151, and *Harvard Library Bulletin*, I (1947), 76–89.

These notebooks were bought by Narcissus Luttrell, and by his heir, Luttrell Wynne, were bequeathed to All Souls College, Oxford. Through the kindness of Dr. Craster, formerly Bodley's librarian and now librarian of the Codrington, I have been permitted to obtain a microfilm of this catalogue, and these observations are based upon a study of it, though for want of time I have had to limit my statistics to the period ending with the year 1600.

That Chiswell's statement of the source of many of Smith's books is correct may be gathered from the fact that a large number of the books listed in Dyson's catalogue have placed beside them the letters "R S" or "S," often with the prices which Dyson had paid altered, always to a somewhat higher figure. In almost all cases the increases in the price are very slight indeed. Frequently a group of books which had cost Dyson a shilling was sold for eighteen pence, or even less. In collections of early English books both in this country and in England one frequently finds books bearing Dyson's signature which are not listed in the surviving manuscript catalogue. Some of these also Richard Smith appears to have purchased, and it would seem that he must have had his pick of Dyson's entire library, and not merely of that portion of which the catalogue is preserved in the Codrington at All Souls.

Dyson's catalogue is divided, a notebook to a sovereign, from Henry VII to Charles I, except for Edward VI. Each notebook is arranged chronologically, an opening for each year, and through the end of the reign of Henry VIII Dyson frequently gave the name of the printer, but thereafter he confined himself to a transcript of the title and a statement of the size. Occasionally he gave the author, but in some cases, particularly of anonymous books, or ones with initials only, his attribution of authorship differs from that now accepted. Altogether, in the portion of these surviving notebooks which I have checked — that is, through the year 1600 — a total of 658 books are recorded, not counting the collections of broadsides. Of these 658 titles no copies are now known of 107. Of the 551 which are known today, I have only identified some 57 copies as having Dyson's name on their titles, but I have no doubt that a large proportion of the remaining items would be found to be represented somewhere by Dyson's copy. Since many of the books are known by only two or three copies, their identification should not be very difficult, although it would involve pestering a large number of librarians, for the books are widely scattered. Altogether there are 67 books which Dyson once had of which only one copy is now known, and it is probable that a large part of these 67 would be found to be Dyson's copies.[2]

Since a very large proportion of the single-leaf broadsides and proclamations of this period which have survived to us have been preserved through Dyson's having gathered them together and bound them in volumes, it is all the more remarkable that this somewhat obscure collector of the early seventeenth century should be responsible also for having preserved to us so many books of that period which are known today only by the copies he once owned. In doing so he exercised not only the proper but the greatest function of a book collector, as a preserver of the records of mankind. Dyson was what we would call today a specialist collector. His interests, as I have said, were in English history, not in English literature. The collection which he formed must have been noted in his own day. He was a friend of Anthony Munday, and Robert Bateman, the bookseller to Charles I, was one of his legatees, so that he was known in bookish circles.[3] When Richard Smith, a man obviously much more wealthy than Dyson, learned of his opportunity to acquire Dyson's books, he would have lost no time in doing so. At Smith's sale many of Dyson's books passed into the collections of Samuel Pepys, Narcissus Luttrell, the Earl of Egremont, Lord Mostyn, and Bishop Stillingfleet. Pepys's books are preserved at Magdalen, Stillingfleet's at Marsh's Library in Dublin, the Egremont books at Petworth (until modern times, when part of them were dispersed), while Mostyn's books were sold only in our century and Luttrell's were kept together until near the end of the eighteenth century and some until only a little over a decade ago. It is therefore obvious that the decisive and crucial moment in the story of the survival of all these books was when they were first acquired by Humphrey Dyson. Because he gathered them — some of them printed in his own lifetime, but many before he was born — made them part of what was then an important collection recognized by his fellow collectors, and therefore made them available to other collectors who followed after him, he belongs in the rank of the great

[2] While I have made no attempt to check all of them, I did do some sample checking by means of the Edwards microfilm facsimiles. Of a dozen or more, nearly all turned out to have Dyson's signature on their titles. I presume that the same proportion would hold for the rest of the unique items. Those who have had any experience with microfilm will understand why I have not attempted to examine all of them.

[3] Although both Dyson and Smith at one time lived in the Jewry, they may not have known each other, for Smith's appointment as Secondary was not until after Dyson's death and he does not mention Dyson in his *Obituary*.

preservers of literature. If Mr. Streeter, our former president and fellow member, could be assured that three hundred years from now over ten per cent of his great collection of Western Americana, not counting broadsides, would be the only surviving copies of important pieces in our own history, he would, I am sure, feel that his collecting had been worth while. And that is what we may credit to the industry and bibliophilic knowledge of Humphrey Dyson, Notary Public.

That Dyson was not wholly successful in ensuring that all his books, which he had so lovingly gathered together, should be preserved, may have been because of his inability to afford the proper binding of large numbers of his pamphlets, for when they were sold in the Smith sale, many of them were bundled together, in lots ranging from 20 to more than 120 pieces, under the heading "Stitched and Unbound." A great many of the items which are marked in his manuscript catalogue with the initials of Richard Smith, and which do not occur by name in Smith's catalogue, must have been included in these bundles. In one lot there were then sold "Several forms of Prayer and Thanksgiving on Sundry Occasions by the appointment of Edward VI, Queen Mary, and Queen Elizabeth, as also by Archbishop Cranmer, to the number of 26." Although this bundle was sold among the unbound collections, the purchaser apparently had it bound, and in the latter part of the nineteenth century it came upon the market again at a country auction and was purchased by W. C. Hazlitt, who broke it up and sold the separate pieces, all with the signature of Dyson on them, either to the British Museum or to Henry Huth. Several of these pieces are unique, and probably would not have been preserved had they not been bound by the purchaser in 1682.

However, while the fact that so many of Dyson's books were unbound may be the reason for their not having survived, it is also probable that the collectors of that day had great difficulty in distinguishing what was really valuable and scarce and what was not, among the 20,000 items in the Smith sale. We cannot read their minds, but we can tell something from the prices which different books fetched in that sale. Of the nine Caxtons which Smith had collected, several of them now identifiable and very fine copies, not one brought more than eighteen shillings, while a copy of Michael Servetus' *De Trinitate* (1531), a book then well known to be scarce, fetched £5/1/0. This last year the Harvard Library acquired a fine copy of the Servetus, which had belonged to Count Hoym, for less than $800, whereas any one of the Caxtons would today fetch a great deal more than that. It is apparent, therefore, that when the collectors of that day could be assured of the comparative rarity and importance of an item, they were ready to pay an outside price for it.

Collectors normally do not care to have a former owner's name signed in ink on the title pages of their books, unless, of course, that signature is a desirable one wherever it may occur, but among many of the greatest rarities of English literature of this period are to be found books which have on their titles the signatures of Myles Blomefield, Frances Wolfreston, Sir Robert Gordon of Gordonstoun, and Edward Palmer. Almost any book bearing one of their signatures is more likely than not to be an item of great intrinsic interest, and no collector in this field need ever be ashamed that his copy of a rare book has one of their names on its title. These signatures have preserved for us the identity of the original collectors who recognized the importance of these books, and who in adding them to distinguished collections gave them a reasonable chance of survival by ensuring that when sold or otherwise dispersed they would come to the attention of collectors and not be thrown away as unconsidered trifles. Once they had been placed in the succession of established collectors, and either gathered in calf-bound tract volumes, or in the morocco of Lewis of the "Black-letter" period, the principal hazards which they would face would be fire, flood, and uninsurable acts of God. Humphrey Dyson's name belongs in the honorable roll I have just recited, and yet it is interesting to note that in the catalogues of the Mostyn and Leconfield sales the books having his signature on their titles are described as having "a signature on title" as if it were a disfigurement.

George Parker Winship, when I was an undergraduate, recommended to me that instead of studying the books that have survived I should spend my time studying the books of which no copy was known. At that time I think I told him that, as the Irishman would say, in order to learn anything about an unknown book you first have to find a copy, but as the years have gone by I have often recalled his recommendation, and now believe that there is a great deal more to it than would first appear. From this list of his own books made so carefully by Humphrey Dyson, we can see that fifteen per cent of the books he then owned are no longer traceable, and they include a number of books of the greatest interest.

For example, Dyson had "A dialogue in verse between Watkyn & Jeffrey of the pride & evell life of Cardinal Wolsey, in octavo [1530],"[4]

[4] *Ed. Note*: Jackson later conjectured that this work might be Bishop William Barlow's *Rede me and be nott wroth* [Strasburg, J. Schott, 1528], *S.T.C.* 1462.6 (formerly *S.T.C.*

for which he paid a shilling. A number of broadsides on the same subject which formerly were Dyson's have been preserved in the Society of Antiquaries, but this book is not known, and perhaps would tell us a good deal about the feeling concerning the Cardinal that we can now only gather from reading between the lines in the State Papers.

A sidelight on Henry VIII might be obtained if we only had a copy of "A Comfortable consolacōn wherein the people may see howe farre greater Cause they have to be gladd for the Joyfull birth of prince Edward, then sorry for the death of Queene Jane, printed in octauo by the K^{es} printer [1537]."[5]

Moreover, a good many items which Dyson collected concerning the rise of the merchant companies, and of the sea fights with Spain, are apparently lost to us forever, as, for example "An Act made 8 Eliz for the Corporacōn of Marchents adventur^{rs} for the discouerie of newe Trades of the Muscouy company, printed in folio," in 1566; "The Marriners booke conteyning godlie & necessarie orders of prayers to be obserued in euery Shipp both for the Master Maryners & all others for the tymes of their voyages printed in octavo 1575";[6] Nicholas Breton's "A discourse in Comendacōn of the aduentures of Captain Drake . . . in octavo [1580]"; "A true discourse of the aduentures & travailes of David Ingram being sett on Shore wth 100 more of his fellowes by Captaine Hawkins in the heathen Countries in 8° 1583," "Newes out of Turkey of the losse of the Shipp called the Mary Martin 1584 in verse in octavo"; "Newes from Turkey A true report in verse of a Seafight in the Straights by 5 shipps of London against 11 Gallies & 2 ffrigatt^{es} of the King of Spaine 1586 in quarto"; and, in the same year, "The aduentures of a Seafight of the Anne Gallant & the Princesse against the King of Spaines shipps . . . in 4°."

Of six satirical epitaphs on Bishop Edmund Bonner published in 1569, only one has survived.[7] And perhaps we would know more about the

---

21427 when ascribed to William Roy), of which Dyson's copy is now in the Bodleian Library.

[5] *Ed. Note*: Jackson subsequently located a copy of this book in the John Rylands Library, Manchester. It was printed by Thomas Berthelet in 1537 and has been numbered *S.T.C.* 18109.5.

[6] This title is recorded in Robert Watt, *Bibliotheca Britannica* (Edinburgh, 1824), II, 686g, as written by Thomas Mors, but no copy has been located.

[7] *Ed. Note*: Jackson eventually identified five out of the six. *S.T.C.* 3817, Thomas Broke, *An epitaphe declaring the life and end of D. Edm. Boner*, J. Daye, [1570]; 3817.4, Broke, *An epitaphe declaryng the lyfe and end of D. Edmund Boner &c.*, J. Daye, [1570]; 3817.7, Broke, *A slaunderous libell (cast abroad) vnto an epitaph*, J. Daye, [1570]; 977, Lemeke Avale, *A*

court of Queen Elizabeth if we had a copy of "The dead mans right or an Apologie in defence of the hono[r] of the Earle of Leicester deceased against the libells & Calumnies of his aduersaries in octauo [1588]."

It would be interesting to compare the 1598 form of "An Apologie of the Earle of Essex against those w[ch] Jealously & malitiously taxed him to be the hinderer of the peace of his Country penned by himself 1598, in 4°" with the well-known book of a similar title but a later date.

These, and many others which could be mentioned, are not now traceable. Probably some of them have survived and will in due course come to notice. But it is apparent that no history of the book production of that period, or even of the social and political or ecclesiastical history of the time, can be written without taking into account the fact that a good deal of the evidence cannot now be examined.

May I conclude my little homily by reiterating that a collector who does not merely buy high spots or books already known to other collectors, but discovers for himself a field which he can cultivate thoroughly, performs thereby a valuable function by bringing into the line of other collectors who follow him books they might never have seen, and so preserves these books for posterity. If he marks his acquisitions, either with his signature, his stamp, or his bookplate, future generations may be given an opportunity of honoring him for the service he has performed, and he will the more successfully accomplish the preservation of his collections if he binds his books or cases them suitably, so that they will be regarded by later generations as being worthy of preservation. Finally, we must recognize that despite all the work of the collectors of the past, a considerable portion of what once was printed no longer exists, and it is possible that the study of such lost books may become a recognized part of bibliographical work, just as the paleontologists are forced to reconstruct beasts whose bones they have never seen. Researches into books that have not survived may prove to be far more fruitful than at first seems possible.

---

commemoration or dirige of bastarde Edmonde Boner, [J. Kingston], 1569; 15033, Thomas Knell, *An epitaph, or rather a short discourse made vpon the life & death of D. Boner*, J. Allde, 1569.

II

Tunc et Nunc: or the Pepys and Taylor Collections of Early English Books on Navigation

(1951)

This paper was contributed to a festschrift in honor of Lawrence C. Wroth, then director of the John Carter Brown Library and an old and respected friend. It reflects Jackson's lifelong interest in the achievements of great collectors; but like all such accounts, it must be judged according to its date. Since 1951 Mr. Henry C. Taylor's collection has continued to grow at a prodigious rate, until now it surpasses the Pepys Collection in the field of early books on navigation. (Bibliography, no. 68).

HOW often does the collector of today wish that he might have attended such and such a sale of the past.[1] If only one could rummage in the shops of Ballard, Osborne, Edwards, and Lilly, what treasures and what bargains one could have! Not only collectors, but booksellers also, mourn the days when "good" books were plentiful and when one could build "great" libraries. No doubt there were in that golden age opportunities when some other collector had done the work and one might at his sale acquire ready-made an important series of books of an author, a press, or a subject. But even then, if one sought to collect what had not been collected, the task was not an easy one.

For more than forty years Samuel Pepys, residing in London, with gradually increasing means — during most of the time quite ample ones

[1] The compiler is much indebted to the kindness of the present Pepys librarian, Mr. R. W. Ladborough, and to Mr. Henry C. Taylor of New York for permission first to examine the books here discussed and then to attempt this comparison.

for the book prices of that day — President of the Royal Society, and friend of the clerisy and the virtuosos, gathered a library which on his death contained almost three thousand volumes. Since many of them were tract volumes or scrapbooks or broadsides, the total number of pieces probably exceeded five thousand. It has been said that if we did not have his diary, Pepys's library would give us an admirable picture of the man and his interests. In a certain sense that is true, for though the bulk of the collection is made up of the learned and useful books of the period, generally in their latest and "best" editions, such as "should be in every gentleman's library," and such as would have been provided by the booksellers of the time to any buyer who did not insist upon forming his own collection, there are a number of sections which reflect Pepys's personal interests and accomplishments. The shorthand manuals, the scrapbook of calligraphy, the broadside ballads, the remarkable series of chapbooks, the Spanish books, the views of London, the naval papers, and particularly the manuals of English navigation, are all very personal accumulations which, though they may in some instances, such as the ballads, have been founded on ready-made collections, were mainly built by his own persistent efforts and were not the result of a chance visit to the bookseller.

There are many books in the Pepysian Library outside these special collections which are remarkable items indeed, such as the nine Caxtons, the thirteenth-century English artist's model-book, the Italian "tear-out" book of confessions, etc., but these were items that caught Pepys's eye at the booksellers' or were called to his attention by friends, not ones that he systematically collected. And while among them are a good many unique books, including some of great intrinsic interest, the importance of the library to scholarship lies mainly in the sections of it which center around his personal interests.

According to Frank Sidgwick, in the nearly ten years of Pepys's diary there are about five hundred references to books, his library, and to booksellers. It is not unreasonable to infer, therefore, that book collecting was certainly one of his major avocations. His later correspondence, though by no means complete, contains many references to his interest in his library, and his careful concern for its preservation indicates that he regarded it as important.

As Clerk of the Acts and Master of the Trinity House, Pepys had a special interest in the history and science of navigation and may even have studied some of the rudiments of it with Master Cooper or on the Tangier voyage. Heterogeneous as are the contents of his library it is perhaps significant that of the more than four hundred books printed in England before 1640, over one in five relates either to voyages and travel or to the science of navigation. We may take it, therefore, as probable that Pepys was not only a good example of the book collector of his time but also that to his collection of English books on navigation he devoted particular attention.[2] It is even more certain that he would have had little competition in this field and that he was a collector of sufficient eminence and means to enable him to obtain the devoted assistance of the antiquarian book-trade of that day, such as it was.

If, therefore, we compare the collection of these books that Pepys gathered with a collection of our own time which has been made during little more than a decade and which is still growing, that of Henry Calhoun Taylor of New York, we shall see that the collector of today, while he may have to pay well for these services, has certain advantages which counterbalance those enjoyed by the collectors of the past. First of all, he can now find out without much labor, from bibliographies and monographs, just what books he needs and their relative rarity and intrinsic importance. Secondly, if he has established himself as an earnest and ardent collector, he will not have to find the books in country auctions or barrows on side streets. The organized book trade of the world will see to it that he is informed of the appearance on the market of items likely to appeal to him and worthy of being added to his shelves.

Comparative statistics, at least when applied to rare books, are generally treacherous, for the volumes enumerated may vary greatly in condition. However, in the present instance we need not be greatly concerned, for the state of nearly all the books in both the Pepys and Taylor collections is very fine indeed. Our real difficulty is in finding a standard of measurement. If, for example, we take the eleven books which Capt. John Smith in his *An Accidence for Young Sea-men* of 1626 recommended for the cabin of a well-found ship, a list which Mr. Taylor has taken particular pains to collect but of which we may assume that Pepys was entirely ignorant,[3] we find that Pepys has only six of the

[2] As evidence of this may be adduced the fact that, contrary to his usual practice of discarding early editions and replacing them with later ones, in this field he collected and kept not only first editions but frequently later ones as well.

[3] Pepys's library contains none of the works of Captain Smith, whereas Mr. Taylor possesses eight of the nine.

eleven, while Mr. Taylor has ten. Although each of them has three of the works in first editions — Pepys, the Wright *Certaine Errors*, the Bourne, and the Wagenaer; and Mr. Taylor, the Tapp, the Cortes, and Wright's *Description and Use of the Sphere* — Pepys has also the 1610 edition of Wright's *Certaine Errors* and the 1592 Bourne, as well as the second and fourth editions of the Norman. To counterbalance this wealth of later editions, Mr. Taylor has a unique copy of the seventh edition of the Bourne *A Regiment for the Sea*, 4to, f. T. Wight, 1601, and a unique third edition [4] of the Aspley *Speculum Nauticum; a Looking Glasse for Sea-men*, 4to, T. Harper, to be sold by G. Hurlock, 1638. The one work which Mr. Taylor does not have represented in any edition, John Davis' *The Seamans Secrets*, is present in the Pepysian Library only in the eighth edition of 1657. On this showing it is evident that the honors go to Mr. Taylor.[5]

It is of interest to note that first editions of the Wright *Certaine Errors*, the Norman, and the Hues, which are in the Taylor collection only in later editions, have recently passed into other American private libraries. Had they been added to the Taylor library, the comparison would have been even more one-sided.

If now we take another list of early English works on navigation to serve as a standard of measurement, we shall find somewhat different results. This list, though admittedly one which could be much improved, has the advantage of not having been used by either of our collectors. It is the one appended to Capt. A. H. Markham's edition of *The Voyages and Works of John Davis* [6] and includes forty-four different books printed in England or in English before 1640, many of them, of course, being translations of foreign works which had previously been printed on the continent. Its greatest deficiency lies in its omission of the minor English works on the compass, a field in which both the Pepysian and the Taylorian libraries have some strength, but it also omits such items as the Aspley and the Tapp, which are included in Capt. John Smith's list, the works of Smith himself, John Skay's *A Friend to Navigation* (1628), and similar books.

A unique second edition of the book is at Jesus College, Oxford: 4to. T. Harper, to be sold by G. and J. Hurlocke, 1632.

[5] Since the above was set in type, Mr. Taylor has been so fortunate as to find a perfect copy, with all the maps, the errata, and the signed blank "A," of the first edition of Wright's *Certaine Errors*, V. Sims, 1599, and also another unique edition, the fourth, of Bourne's *A regiment for the sea*, 4°. T. Este f. J. White, 1584, which swings the balance even more in his favor.

[6] Hakluyt Society, LIX (1880), 355–366.

Of the forty-four books listed by Markham, there are twenty-six in the Pepys library, of which seventeen are first editions; while in the Taylorian there are eighteen, of which eleven are firsts. Although only four of the books in Mr. Taylor's library are not in the Pepys, eleven others which are in neither library have passed through the market during the last fifteen years and are now mainly in American collections, largely private; while ten others which are in the Pepys but not the Taylor have come to American private collections in the same period. Thus, a total of thirty-six out of the forty-four have recently been available, although it would have been a miracle if any one collector had been able to garner them all.

Of course, such a comparison as this is unfair, not only because it ignores the remarkable array of early foreign books on navigation and the superb run of English voyages which are in both collections, particularly in that of Mr. Taylor, but mainly because it makes no allowance for comparative importance as between one item and another. However, it may serve to illustrate the advantages and disadvantages enjoyed by the collectors of the present. Mr. Taylor is not alone in this field, and part of it he must share also with collectors who have no interest in navigation as such but are, for example, eager to obtain books on magnetism because they are fundamental to a collection concerned solely with the history of electricity. Pepys, on the other hand, collected during the first decades of selling books by auction in England, when many of the navigation items he would have been most interested in, if they were sold at all, would have been bundled with miscellaneous tracts. It is doubtful if he acquired any of his books in this subject by merely checking catalogues. But Pepys probably had no competitors!

Early English Books on the Science of Navigation
in the Pepysian Library

S.T.C. 1442 Barlow, W. Magneticall aduertisements, 1616.
S.T.C. 1445 " ". The nauigators supply, 1597.
S.T.C. 3117 Blagrave, J. Astrolabium vranicum generale, 1596 (no map).
S.T.C. 3119 " ". The mathematical iewell, 1585.
S.T.C. 3145 Blundeville, T. A briefe description of vniversall mappes, 1589.
S.T.C. 3421 Bourne, W. Inuentions or deuises, 1578.
S.T.C. 3422 " ". A regiment for the sea, [1574].
S.T.C. 3428 " ". " " " " ", 1596 (bound with STC 13695+).
S.T.C. 5799 Cortes, M. The arte of nauigation, 1572.

S.T.C. 5801 Cortes, M. The arte of navigation, 1584.
S.T.C. 5803 " " " " " " , 1596.[7]
S.T.C. 6459 Dee, J. General and rare memorials, 1577.
S.T.C. 6859 Digges, L. A geometrical practise named Pantometria, 1591.
S.T.C. 11185 Forman, S. The groundes of the longitude, 1591.
S.T.C. 11551 Garcie, P. The rutter of the sea, [1555?].[8]
S.T.C. 11883 Gilbert, W. G. Gilberti de magnete, 1600.
S.T.C. 12425 Guevara, A. de A booke of the inuention of the art of nauigation, 1578.
S.T.C. 13695+ [now identified as part 2 of *S.T.C.* 3427] Hood, T. The marriners guide, 1592 (with Ryther map, bound with STC 3428).
S.T.C. 13697 Hood, T. The vse of the celestial globe in plano, 1590.
S.T.C. 13701 " ". The vse of the two mathematicall instruments, 1596.
S.T.C. 15692 Linton, A. Newes of the complement of the art of navigation, 1609.
S.T.C. 17771 Medina, P. de The arte of nauigation, [1581].
S.T.C. 18648 Norman, R. The new attractive, 1585.
S.T.C. 18650 " ". " " " , 1596.
S.T.C. 21044 Ridley, M. Magneticall animadversions, 1617.
S.T.C. 21045 " ". A short treatise of magneticall bodies, 1613.
S.T.C. 21547 Safeguard. The safeguard of sailers, 1590.
S.T.C. 22592 Skay, J. A friend to navigation, 1628.
S.T.C. 23659 Taisnier, J. A very necessarie and profitable booke concerning nauigation, [1579?].[9]
S.T.C. 24043+ Thornton, Captain. Hereafter followeth the vttermost and course round about all Ireland. 4°. A⁴. (Recto [A4], "This Booke was made by Captayne Thornton and caused to be printed by Thomas Banster Mariner. 1606"). H. Dyson's copy.
S.T.C. 24931 Wagenaer, L. J. The mariners mirrour, [1588].
S.T.C. 26019a Wright, E. Certaine errors in nauigation, 1599.
S.T.C. 26020 " ". " " " " , 1610.
S.T.C. 26057+ Wye, Captain T. A briefe discourse, dedicated to . . . Lord Charles Howarde, in maner of a dialogue, betwene Baldwyne & a Sayler. 8vo. D. Waldegraue, 1580.

[7] The imprint reads: "E. Allde f. H. Astley, by the assignes of R. Watkins, and are to be solde at Sainct Magnus corner [i.e., the address of R. Ballard], 1596."

[8] This copy appears to be unique, but earlier unrecorded editions are to be found: (1) R. Copland f. R. Bākes, 1528, at the Middle Temple Library; (2) T. Petyt, 18 March 1536, at Lincoln's Inn Library; and (3) W. Walley [c. 1545], owned by H. C. Taylor.

[9] The title of *S.T.C.* 5801 states: "Whereunto may be added at the wyll of the byer, another very fruitfull and necessary booke of nauigation, translated out of Latine by the sayd Eden," i.e., this book.

12

The "Lincolne Nosegay" Books

(1953)

This paper, written for a publication of the British Antiquarian Booksellers' Association, reflects Jackson's lifelong fascination with all aspects of the career of Thomas Frognall Dibdin. Jackson tracked down and actually examined all but one of the books in this list. Three locations have been changed in accordance with his subsequent notes (Bibliography, no 77).

THE Reverend Thomas Frognall Dibdin has told of his purchase of books from the Dean and Chapter of Lincoln in more than one place, although not with complete candor, and the Reverend Beriah Botfield has added more details, as well as some perhaps justifiable remarks concerning the alienation of these books.[1] However, it is not generally known that there were at least three sales of books from Lincoln, the earliest being of three Caxtons: the first edition of Cessolis, *The game and playe of the chesse* (c.1475); Le Fevre, *The history of Jason* (c.1477); and the first edition of *The history of Reynart the foxe* (1481). These were bought in 1811 by James Edwards, the bookseller, who sold them to Lord Spencer, and they are now all in the John Rylands Library, Manchester.

The second sale was in 1814, to Dibdin, and the books then sold are the ones to which the cognomen "Nosegay" properly belongs. Of this sale, more later. The final sale was of a miscellany listed by Botfield,[2] which contained several unspecified volumes of pamphlets, including the first editions of Shakespeare's *Lucrece* (1594), and Milton's *Lycidas*

[1] Thomas Frognall Dibdin, *The Bibliographical Decameron*, III (London, 1817), 264, and *Northern Tour*, I (London, 1838), 105–106; Beriah Botfield, *Notes on the Cathedral Libraries* (London, 1849), pp. 268–280.

[2] *Cathedral Libraries*, pp. 271–272.

(1638). It is not quite clear to whom these were sold, although Dibdin states that he had tried to buy them but they were sold "at the prices marked by myself" to one "who in other days — days gone by, never to return — I was as happy as proud to visit, and be visited by."[3] It is not unlikely that this enigmatic reference is to James Edwards, the bookseller, with whom Dibdin had once been intimate, but who had apparently resented some statements made by Dibdin concerning his Sweynheim and Pannartz Livy on vellum.[4] In any case, the third sale was made before 1822, for in that year one of the books at least was sold in the James Perry sale.[5]

To return to the second sale, according to a letter written 17 June 1833 by Mr. R. Garvey, librarian of Lincoln, to Beriah Botfield and quoted by him (*op. cit.*), "the Dean and Chapter thought it expedient to sell all the Caxtons and other early prints, and to replace them with more modern works of which they stood in need." In pursuance of this policy they had agreed in the autumn of 1814 to the sale of twenty titles, bound in six volumes, for five hundred guineas. On 18 August 1814, Mr. Edward James Willson, the then librarian of Lincoln, wrote to Dibdin in Kensington, "I have at length brought your negotiation with the Dean & Chapter so far to a conclusion that the six books are packed up & sent to you by this night's coach to be left with Mr Triphook: these are 1 Cathon; 2 Chronicle; 3 Dictes & Sayings; 4 Fabyan; 5 Scotch bible; 6 Poetical pieces, with Eleanor Rummyng. I tried to get the little Cambridge book thrown in,[6] but could not, indeed there is but one Residentiary here at present, & they cannot do anything separately." On 7 October 1814 Dibdin gave his note at eighty-five days for the purchase price and very quickly thereafter must have published *The Lincolne Nosegay*,[7] an octavo single sheet pamphlet describing the books he had

[3] *Northern Tour*, I, 106.

[4] *Bibliographical Decameron*, III, 14–17.

[5] Part III, lot 601. As Perry was quite ill and unlikely to be buying books from 1817 on, this fits with the 1817 reference to Edwards cited above.

[6] What this volume was is not known, but it might have been the volume of poetical pieces listed by Dibdin (*Bibliographical Decameron*, I, 264) which contained the *Justa Eduardo King naufrago* (Cambridge, 1638), or more likely, as Dibdin relayed to Lord Spencer the news that the Cambridge book was not to be had, it may have been the *Papyrius Geminus* printed at Cambridge by Siberch in 1522, a copy of which is still at Lincoln.

[7] On November 19th following, the British Museum sent Dibdin a form notice demanding a copy and entrance of the book in the Register-book of the Company of Stationers of London, the penalty cited being "Five Pounds and Eleven Times the Price of the Book not entered." The text of the *Nosegay* was reprinted by Botfield, *Cathedral Libraries*.

purchased, in an edition of thirty-six copies which were sold at cost, or three shillings and sixpence each. It was not very long until this little piece had risen considerably in the market, and some time before 1838 a counterfeit edition was produced.[8] The counterfeit may be most easily recognised by the fact that in it the printer's "slug" is omitted on the verso of the half-title and at the bottom of page 16.

According to Dibdin's own account the most desirable copy of *The Lincolne Nosegay* was that which belonged to Sir Francis Freeling. Except that it was bound in "calf extra", it does not appear to have been in any way remarkable. Joseph Haslewood, however, had a copy which later belonged to Michael Tomkinson and finally to the late Colonel C. H. Grey of Cranbrook, Kent,[9] which contained among other items the letter of E. J. Willson, the canceled note of Dibdin, and the British Museum form-letter quoted above,[10] and is perhaps the most interesting of all surviving copies.

According to a note by Haslewood, who was the unofficial recorder of gossip concerning the Roxburghe Club founders, Lord Spencer had purchased the entire *Nosegay* from Dibdin. From the Dibdin letters of this period which, with the permission of the present Lord Spencer, I examined at Althorpe it would appear that the transaction was not so clear-cut as Haslewood thought. The second Earl Spencer was providing the money to pay Bulmer's bills for the Althorpe catalogues and other works which Dibdin was then publishing. Dibdin received no direct reward for his bibliographical labors from Earl Spencer but was expected to profit from subscriptions to his works after his lordship had been repaid the money which he had expended in having them printed. However, at the moment Dibdin had just bought a new house in Kensington and was somewhere between seven hundred and a thousand pounds in debt to Lord Spencer for advances intended for the printer. The exact figures are not available, for the accounts and proposals which were enclosed with some of Dibdin's letters are no longer filed with them.

Essentially, Dibdin's proposal was that the Lincoln copies of the Caxton *Cathon* and *Chronicles* and *Description*, together with the Fab-

[8] According to a note by Dibdin in the *Northern Tour*, I, 106, it was the work of a forger who was responsible for more important fabrications than this.

[9] Haslewood, 1833, lot 384; Tomkinson, 3 April 1922, lot 315.

[10] Col. Grey permitted the writer to have photostats of these items made in 1935. It has not been possible to trace the present owner, and the quotation here made is with Col. Grey's long unused permission.

yan and the Edinburgh Bible, though already represented by slightly smaller copies in the Althorpe Library, should be taken by Lord Spencer and the duplicates disposed of to Mr. Gutch. For example, Dibdin thought the Lincoln Chronicles and Description worth £210, while the Althorpe copies only £186. He likewise proposed that he trade the "Sundrie Smal Werkes in Metre . . . whiche be bounde in a kiver of parchmente," Lots VI-XIX to Richard Heber for a slightly imperfect copy of Caxton's edition of Guillaume de Deguilleville's *Pylgremage of the sowle*, 1483, which Lord Spencer coveted. If successful, he suggested that the *Pylgremage* be valued at £260, "as a way of working out my debt."

Heber was not very eager to conclude the exchange, and it was not until January 1815, while coming down to London in a coach with him, that Dibdin finally concluded the transaction by promising Heber in addition some unspecified pamphlets of Thomas Churchyard which belonged to Lord Spencer.[11] Just how the financial accounting of this trade was handled does not appear, but there seems little reason to doubt that not only was Dibdin's note to the Dean and Chapter met with Lord Spencer's money, but his lordship probably had to pay well for any part he had of the *Nosegay*.

The Heber copy of the *Pylgremage* Lord Spencer later replaced with a complete copy at the Blandford sale and disposed of the imperfect one in his 1821 duplicate sale (Lot 226). It was later at Britwell Court and is now in the Morgan Library. Three of the Lincoln Caxtons, the *Chronicles* and *Description*, now bound separately, and the *Cathon* were sold by Evans, 6 March 1815, together with the Fabyan. They fetched a total of £337 which would have netted the owner just less than £300. It must have been a disappointment to Dibdin, for the *Chronicles* and *Description* together made only one hundred and fifty guineas instead of the two hundred he had predicted. This Evans sale is generally referred to as the "John Roberts, Director of the East India Company sale" to distinguish it from the Leigh and Sotheby sale of the same month of the library of John Roberts of Whitchurch, Bucks. Just how the *Dictes* was disposed of by Lord Spencer is not clear. He already had a copy and did not need the Lincoln one, which can be traced first in the George Hibbert sale of 1829.

Indeed, the only one of the score of books from the *Nosegay* which

[11] According to Haslewood's note, "Furthermore some other volumes of celebrity that did not belong to the *Nosegay* were given in this lumping exchange."

Lord Spencer appears to have retained is the Fabyan (1516), and it is not certain that he retained that, merely that his copy is bound in russia of about that period, possibly by Lewis, and the Lincoln copy cannot be traced elsewhere. It is possible that one of the two copies of the Arbuthnot and Bassandyne Bible now in the John Rylands Library was also the Lincoln copy, although, if so, then Dibdin did not record the imperfections of that copy accurately.

To expect accuracy of Dibdin, however, is futile. He seemed to possess almost a genius for botching his work with exasperating errors which one would suppose could only have been introduced with considerable effort. A good but not an extreme example is the plate in the *Typographical Antiquities*, II, 19, purporting to be of the first page of Machlinia's edition of Canutus' *Treatise on the Pestilence*, the upper part of which is taken from the unique copy of Wynken de Worde's edition in the Cambridge University Library and the lower part from the unique copy of Machlinia's edition, then in Triphook's possession and later in the Spencer Library.

Except for the Bible and the Pilkington, all the books in the *Nosegay* can now be traced (see Appendix), and the latter ought to be easily recognizable, if found, for it should be exactly 170 mm. in height, for that is the measurement of the other tracts once bound with it, which would make it a pretty closely trimmed copy.

Dibdin declared that the Chapter of Lincoln "in most instances got 'Gold for their Brass,' and they have wisely replaced their antiquated treasures by the acquisition of numerous and useful volumes of consultation," a statement which, since he hastened into print with his exulting *Nosegay*, inevitably reminds one of the quotation from Proverbs 20:14, which the late Dr. Rosenbach was accustomed to place at the end of his catalogues. Indeed, he had reason to boast of his bargain if one compares the average price paid for perfect Caxtons at the Roxburghe sale which was held a little over two years before — two years during which the Napoleonic inflation had continued its course — for then the four Caxtons at comparable prices ought to have been worth much more than was paid for the whole *Nosegay*.

Beriah Botfield has given a list of some eighty works of reference, in some three times as many volumes, which were purchased in 1817 from the proceeds of the sales of these irreplaceable books. The great majority are today worth at most only a few shillings a volume, and not that unless the bindings are sound, although three or four, if fine copies, would be worth considerably more. The moral of this tale, therefore, is that regardless of the propriety or legality of sale by an institution of "antiquated treasures" bequeathed it in perpetuity, it is unlikely, when reviewed a century or more later, to appear to have been a thoroughly sound business proposition.

In this instance, if one takes the total of the prices paid for the *Nosegay* books when last sold, and all but four of them have passed through the auction room in this century,[12] one finds that their value as of approximately 1920 was almost exactly fifteen times their cost to Dibdin in 1814, and that includes the incredible bargain of the unique de Worde edition of the *Comunycacyon between God and Man* which fetched only two hundred dollars at the Hoe sale. Their value today would be very much more. If the Dean and Chapter had invested the five hundred guineas in 1814 and had compounded it annually at 3 per cent, they would have had in 1920 very little more than the amount the books brought at their last sale. What will happen to the value of such books in the next hundred years is beyond the province of this paper.

Appendix:
Present Location of the Nosegay *Books*

I. *S.T.C.* 6826 Caxton, *Dictes*, 1477. Hibert–Hanrott–Buccleuch–Carysfort — ROSENBACH PRIVATE COLLECTION [now Paul Mellon].

IIA. *S.T.C.* 9991 Caxton, *Chronicles*, 1480. Roberts–Milner–Higgs–Buccleuch–Carysfort–Rosenwald — LIBRARY OF CONGRESS.

IIB. *S.T.C.* 13440*a* Caxton, *Description*, 1480. Roberts–Milner–Higgs–Buccleuch–Bennett — PIERPONT MORGAN LIBRARY.

III. *S.T.C.* 4853 Caxton, *Cato*, 1483. Roberts–G. W. Taylor–C. Barclay — CHAPIN LIBRARY.

IV. *S.T.C.* 10659 Fabyan, *Chronicle*, 1516. Roberts–? Spencer — RYLANDS LIBRARY.

V. *S.T.C.* 2125 *Bible*, Edinburgh, 1579. See above.

VI. *S.T.C.* 10606 *Everyman*, J. Skot [*c.* 1535]. Heber–Jolley–Britwell — HUNTINGTON LIBRARY.

VII. *S.T.C.* 5605 *Comunycacyon between God and Man*, W. de Worde [*c.* 1500]. Heber–Russel–Hoe — HUNTINGTON LIBRARY.

VIII. *S.T.C.* 78 *Mylner of Abyngton*, W. de Worde [*c.* 1532]. Bound with

[12] For those that have not been sold or cannot be traced, recent prices of comparable copies, such as the Harmsworth Bible, the Harvard Fabyan, and the Clawson *Lusty Juventus* and Pilkington have been substituted.

IX. *S.T.C.* 14128 *Romance of Ipomydon*, W. de Worde [*c.* 1530]. Heber–Britwell — PIERPONT MORGAN LIBRARY.

X. *S.T.C.* 24601 Vaughan, *Dialogue Defensiue*, 1542. Heber–Britwell — HUNTINGTON LIBRARY.

XI. *S.T.C.* 1988 *Bevis of Hampton*, W. Copland [1560?]. Heber–Britwell — HUNTINGTON LIBRARY.

XII. *S.T.C.* 22614 Skelton, *Elynor Rumming*, 1624. Heber–Daniel–Huth — HUNTINGTON LIBRARY.

XIII. *S.T.C.* 1384*a* Barclay, *Eglogues*, H. Powell [1548?]. Heber–Britwell — ROSENBACH PRIVATE COLLECTION [now Arthur A. Houghton, Jr.]

XIV. *S.T.C.* 25148 Weaver, *Lusty Iuuentus*, A. Veale [*c.* 1555?]. Heber — BODLEIAN LIBRARY.

XV. *S.T.C.* 17014 Lydgate, *Churle & Byrde*, W. Copland [*c.* 1565]. Heber–Britwell–Harmsworth — FOLGER LIBRARY.

XVI. *S.T.C.* 1374 Bansley, *Pride of Women*, T. Raynalde [*c.* 1550]. Heber–Britwell–Clawson — HUNTINGTON LIBRARY.

XVII. *S.T.C.* 5241 Churchyard, *Myrrour for Man*, R. Toye [*c.* 1552]. Heber–Britwell — HUNTINGTON LIBRARY.

XVIII. *S.T.C.* 13954.7 Hume, *Flyting*, Edinburgh, Heirs of A. Hart, 1629. Heber–Britwell — CLARENDON PARK (Heber VIII).

XIX. *S.T.C.* 19925 Pilkington, *Briefe description*, 1631. Heber VIII (1836), no. 1857 — untraced.

13

Lucius Wilmerding, 1880-1949

(1959)

A tribute to a great collector and personal friend, this piece was written for a commemorative volume compiled by the Grolier Club (Bibliography, no. 104).

FOR thirty years Lucius Wilmerding was a devoted and beloved member of the Grolier Club; for twenty years he sat on the Council and for five years was President. For much of that time he was Chairman of the Library Committee, and his benefactions to the library include many of its choicest items — as, for instance, the foundation book in English bibliography, Bale's *Illustrium Maioris Britanniae Scriptorum Summarium*, in an elaborate binding made for Edward VI, to whom it was dedicated; the magnificent extra-illustrated set of Dibdin's *Bibliographical Decameron*, which even has the original copper of the canceled plate of Diane de Poitiers in one of the bindings; and an unrecorded broadside of a sixteenth-century list of Italian wines, presumably prepared to sell to novices on the grand tour, now framed and hanging in the Dutch room. And the Grolier was by no means the only library to which he was generous.

To spend an evening with Wilmerding in his library was an unforgettable privilege. First of all, it was a large room lined high with shelf after shelf of morocco and calf of all periods and colors, looking out on that great rarity in New York, a secluded and spacious garden. Hours would pass quickly in examining with him treasure after treasure, deciphering Montaigne's notes written in his diary, puzzling over the identity of the arms on a sixteenth-century French binding, or merely admiring the beauty of the workmanship of an illumination or a binding. His affection for his books and his joy in sharing them with friends who appreciated their beauty, literary importance, and rarity, or their combination of these qualities, seemed to lend an aura of pure bibliophilic pleasure to the occasion.

He was not merely a collector with remarkable taste and judgment who for many years was the foremost American collector of French literature and bindings, he was also an eager student of the unsolved problems which some of his books presented. In the memorable address which he gave to the Grolier Club on "Renaissance Bookbindings," and which was printed in the now much sought catalogue of that exhibition, are recorded a number of important observations and discoveries so modestly set forth that most readers are probably unaware that he first made them. His bibliographical essay on the true first edition of Balzac's *Le Prince* (1631), of which his own large-paper copy ironically fetched merely ten dollars at his sale, was the only one he published, but his penciled notes in many of his books undoubtedly will appear unacknowledged in numerous catalogues.

Many of his greatest treasures were acquired during the years of the depression, when it seemed that he was almost alone in this country in appreciating the kind of book he was then collecting, but he was less interested in the cost of a book than almost any other collector one could name, and he never haggled. The way in which he purchased his marvelous Fugger bindings is typical of him and perhaps reveals why so many booksellers took pleasure in offering him their choicest wares. When these Fugger books were sold in 1933 in Munich, Mr. Wilmerding, unable to examine them for himself and unwilling to trust the reproductions in the catalogue, wrote to a learned London bookseller enclosing his check for some thousands and instructing only that he wanted several of the finest bindings in the sale. His confidence was not misplaced. The bookseller purchased a trunkload of the best and, after the sale, pondered carefully which were the finest of each type, that he might send only the best to the collector who had so generously shown trust in his judgment.

As he was fastidious about the books he collected, so — as indeed do many of the greatest collectors — he devoted attention to his reference books. His copy of the de Boze catalogue was the owner's copy in a superb binding with his arms, from the Holford sale, and he even had such esoterica as the catalogue of the sale of Mérard de Saint-Just. When at one time he became interested in collecting letters of French noblemen of the eighteenth century, he gathered together a set of Almanachs Royaux, nearly all *aux armes*, so that he might learn more about these forgotten figures. In this as in many other qualities he impressed his friends as almost one of the last of the *grands seigneurs*.

It is difficult to convey to one who never knew him how completely without pedantry Lucius Wilmerding was, and how extraordinarily wide were the interests of this cultivated gentleman. Perhaps bibliophiles will appreciate the following observation. He liked Trollope. We have all known Trollopians of different kinds, both those who know the entire genealogy of the Duke of Omnium and the names of all the children of Mr. Quiverful, as well as those who know the comparative rarity of *Ralph the Heir* and *Orley Farm* and all the "points" to be found in them. But Wilmerding was not a Trollope specialist — he merely liked to read him and possessed what, in my experience, is a rarity in private hands, a uniformly bound set of Trollope in the most complete of all forms, the Tauchnitz editions. Let us hope that set is now in the hands of a similar lover of good literature.

If space permitted it would be a pleasure to list some of his greatest books and manuscripts, but I must refrain. He rarely attempted completeness, choosing rather to have a few examples of an author or of a subject, but those of the best of that author or of that kind of book. And his interests changed. At the Ham House sale he passed over many great rarities of English literature which a few years before would have interested him and obtained instead the remarkable copy of the *Hypnerotomachie* (Paris, 1554), bound for William the Silent, and the two little volumes of Rabelais forming the first collected edition (1537). At the Bishop and the Terry sales he selected many more books, for then he could himself examine them and so ranged more widely, choosing only those in the finest condition.

Now his library is scattered. Many of his greatest books have recrossed the Atlantic and are among the most treasured possessions of the great private collections of Europe. Indeed, by this very fact his taste and judgment have been endorsed. In this century, not since the Hoe sale has there been such a reversal of the normal trend of rare books. Probably never again will an American collector be able to gather so many remarkable rarities in so many fields.

14

The Hofer Collection

(1960)

The only man who knows the Hofer Collection better than Jackson did is Philip Hofer himself. This article, written for the "Contemporary Collectors" section of *The Book Collector*, combines a warm personal tribute to an old friend with heartfelt praise of a great collector and a litany of noble books (Bibliography, no. 108).

PHILIP HOFER was born with a highly developed collecting instinct, and it has continued to increase as through the years he has given it considerable exercise. Today if he should find himself in some part of the world where there were no books, manuscripts, or drawings available, he would probably begin collecting portable objects of another type, but always ones which would appeal to a discerning taste. And when he returned to a place where the objects of his particular passion were obtainable, he would immediately begin a systematic and indefatigable tour of all the book and art shops of that region.

He began book collecting before he entered Harvard in 1917 and still has the first book he remembers having bought as a "fine" book, a copy of *Baron Munchausen*, illustrated by William Strang and purchased from N. J. Bartlett of Cornhill, Boston. In recent years he has added to it the original drawings. In college he collected in many fields, including press books and first editions of English literature. Later when these books no longer interested him, or he had finer copies, they were dispersed at auction in 1933. Among the books then sold were fine copies of first editions of Blackstone, Boswell, Fielding, Gibbon, Gray, Pepys, Smollett, and Gilbert White, all in the proper condition, although perhaps the most unusual was Richard Bull's copy of Chesterfield's *Letters* (1774), in contemporary red morocco. That he should have then sold the Chew-Williams presentation copy of Edward Benlowes' *Theophila* (1652), may seem odd in view of his later interest in English 17th-century book illustration, until one realizes that he already had the much finer Bindley copy of that book, the type copy against which, since Lowndes's description of it, all other copies have been measured.

By 1927, when he had proved his ability as a businessman and returned to Harvard to study the history of art in all its forms and thenceforth to devote himself to study, collecting, and teaching in those fields which most interested him, he already had determined that he would build a comprehensive collection which would illustrate the arts of the book, from the earliest times to the present. He has, of course, not limited his collecting to printed books and manuscripts, for his collections of master drawings and prints, unconnected with books, and his activities as trustee or adviser to numerous art museums, are another story which I must not touch at this time. For several years he was in charge of the Spencer Collection of the New York Public Library, an experience which he now regards as of great educational value but which at the time was occasionally frustrating, for some of his finest purchases, all of which were of course offered to the trustees, were quite properly pre-empted by them. Then, after a term as assistant to Miss Greene of the Morgan Library, he came to Harvard in 1938 to establish in the Harvard Library a Department of Printing and Graphic Arts.

This department, the first of its kind, at least in the generous dimensions with which Mr. Hofer has envisaged it, for it is built around his own collection of well over ten thousand books and manuscripts, is designed to make possible the study of the history of the development of the arts of the book, from classical times to the present day, both manuscript and printed, and in all countries both Western and Oriental where those arts have flourished. Since it is located in a library which contains nearly seven million volumes, it is supplemented by countless examples which might, in many cases, have otherwise been chosen for the collection and which, in any case, are available for study and comparison.

This circumstance is of great relevance, for throughout his collecting career Mr. Hofer has been far more interested in quality than quantity, in choice copies of the unusual rather than the rare but well known, in the finest of its kind rather than a complete series. His practice in regard to press books may illustrate this, for believing that most presses tend to a certain sameness, he has chosen from the output of those he regards as important only a few examples of their best and most typical, generally copies on vellum, with drawings and proofs, and in special bindings. But in the case of contemporary presses, in the integrity of which Mr. Hofer believes, he is apt to have a complete series with even, perhaps, some pieces which he has commissioned himself. Of the Ashendene Press books he has a superb selection, many on vellum and in appropriate bindings, but of most other presses, while he may have proofs, drawings, and other ephemera, he is likely to have only a few representative books, whereas the Harvard Library frequently possesses complete runs of ordinary copies.

All collectors are apt to spend more time bemoaning lost opportunities rather than gloating over their triumphs, and Mr. Hofer has often said that he wishes he had acquired more illuminated manuscripts when they were available, at least when they could be acquired for less than the cost of a mansion. However, there has been no time during his four decades of collecting when he had a blind eye for manuscripts, though in the 1930's most of the manuscripts he acquired were calligraphic rather than illuminated. Now he must have some five hundred or more European manuscripts, not counting over a hundred single leaves, nearly half of which are classed by him as calligraphic — the border-line is often difficult to establish — and they range from the eighth to the twentieth century. One hundred and forty of them were exhibited at Harvard in 1955, and the catalogue which was then published gives a better idea of their quality, variety, and interest than anything that might be said in the space here available. However, it is perhaps appropriate to remark that the proportion of liturgical manuscripts is less than is usually found in such collections and that, if the quality is very high, Mr. Hofer has on occasion acquired a fragment if he could not have a complete manuscript. He has likewise gone into fields not often trod by manuscript collectors, such as Polish and Portuguese, and has frequently acquired finely illuminated manuscripts of much later date than the range usually sought by collectors.

In recent years he has collected Ethiopian, Arabic, Persian, Turkish, Indian, Nepalese, Siamese, and Chinese manuscripts and has well over a hundred codices and forty scrolls as well as many fragments of great beauty and importance. A few years ago he began collecting Japanese manuscripts, as he has recounted in *The Book Collector* (Winter 1958) and now has over one hundred and fifty, a third dating from the eighth to the sixteenth century, and the rest of the seventeenth and eighteenth centuries, of considerable iconographic interest and charm.

Incunabula have interested Mr. Hofer only spasmodically — the most important pieces, from an artistic standpoint, are so well known and have been so often studied that, compared to the vast prices they fetch when they are available, they provide less satisfaction than those less known. This, together with the fact that copies are available at Harvard, may explain why on various occasions Mr. Hofer has parted with his copy of the first Latin edition of Breydenbach, or the first Aldine *Poliphilus*, even though he was the first to notice and publish the variations to be found in copies of the latter. (At the same time he avidly collected all the later editions of the *Poliphilus* and now has them complete, including the English 1592 edition.) The hundred and twenty incunabula which he has kept, however, are a distinguished lot and include a relatively large number of unique copies. They begin with the fine Holford copy of the block-book *Apocalypsis S. Joannis*, and among fifteen illustrated Florentine books may be mentioned the unique *Epistole et Euangeli* (c.1500); the Tuppo *Aesop* (Naples, 1485); the *Compania del Rosario* [1485]; the Pinelli–Crofts–Crevenna–Heathcote–Heber copy of *Uberto e Philomena*) (c.1495) (Plate IX), of which only one other is known; the Lorenzo de' Medici, *Canzone per andare in Maschera* (c.1495); and the Cessolis, *Libro di Giuoco di Scacchi* (1493). Among the German books are the immaculate Maihingen copy of the Ulm *Ptolemy* (1482); the Passau *Missale* (Augsburg, 1494), with the crucifixion cut printed in four colors; and the Ingold, *Das Goldene Spiel* (Augsburg, 1472), probably the first illustrated sporting book. Two editions of the Malermi Bible (Venice, 1490 and 1494); the *Psaltir a Posledovaniem* (Cetinje, 1495), a Montenegran incunable of which only one other copy is known; a noble copy, in very fine original state, of the Sarum *Missal*, printed at Rouen, 1497, likewise one of two known; and the Lyell copy of the first Spanish illustrated book, Enriquez Villenas, *Los Trabajos de Hercules* (Zamora, 1483), also deserve recording. But one could go on indefinitely, for each one of his books of this period has been chosen with care either for the illustration or for its fine contemporary illumination or binding.

In the 1920's, when many collectors were still concerned with collecting incunabula by presses, Mr. Hofer was eagerly collecting in the sixteenth century, mainly for the illustrations, and with a catholicity of subject and a breadth of coverage which is truly astonishing and, of

IX. *Uberto e Philomena* (Florence, ca. 1495)

course, today impossible to duplicate. A catalogue of the French books of this period is now in preparation for publication, and perhaps it is less important to give very much detail regarding them.[1] The Geoffroy Torys are not complete but include among more than a dozen volumes of his finest productions several extraordinary ones, such as a copy of the *Heures* (1525), illuminated and bound by the binder of Cardinal de Granvelle, either for the Cardinal or for presentation to Charles V, and the magnificently preserved dedication copy of the 1527 *Heures*, bound in full calf, gilt, "aux armes," for Francis I, as well as one of the very few vellum copies of the 1535 *Diodorus Siculus*. One could go on for pages recording the remarkable books from the presses of Denis Janot, Jean de Tournes, Estienne, Vascosan, and the others, but perhaps a comparison with the C. Fairfax Murray collection of French sixteenth-century books may be more illuminating. That collection contained a few more than five hundred sixteenth-century books, while the Hofer Collection contains some six hundred, of which at least eighty are the same books, often the same copy. While a good many of the Murray books are more remarkable for their literary importance (those, for example, by Bruno, Montaigne, and Rabelais) or for their bindings than for their illustration or printing, there are fewer of this type in the Hofer Collection, and when they occur, they were chosen because they are well printed or illustrated, such as the first edition of the *Marguerites de la Marguerite* (Lyons, 1547); the lovely little first edition of Maurice Scève's *Saulsaye* (Lyons, J. de Tournes, 1547); the unique Ronsard, *Les Figures et Pourtraicts des Sept Aages de l'Homme* (1579–1580); the fine Blanchemain copy of the first collected quarto edition of Ronsard, *Les Oeuvres* (Paris, 1567); or *Les Dix Premiers Livres de l'Iliade* (Paris, 1545), one of the handsomest of French books, in a fine large copy bound in vellum gilt, extra, for Nicholas de Herberay, which later belonged to J. A. de Thou, Montgermont, and Rahir.

If one compares the two collections in general, the Murray Collection contained a larger proportion of early romances and translations in gothic letter, frequently with fifteenth-century cuts, whereas the Hofer Collection has a much larger number of illustrated or finely printed books, many in roman or italic, printed in Paris and Lyons in the middle

[1] *Harvard College Library Department of Printing and Graphic Arts, Catalogue of Books and Manuscripts, Part I: French 16th Century Books*, compiled by Ruth Mortimer (Cambridge, The Belknap Press of Harvard University Press, 1964).

of the sixteenth century, the greatest period of French typography and the one which has had the most influence on later periods. Although both collections have copies of Jean Pelerin dit Viator, *De Artificiali P[er]-spectiva* (Toul, 1505), and the Tory edited edition of Leon Battista Alberti's *Libri de re aedificatoria* (Paris, 1512), the Hofer copy of the first being the Dietrichstein copy and of the second a fine copy in a John Reynes binding, architecture evidently was not a subject of much interest to Fairfax Murray. It is, however, one which has interested Mr. Hofer, and he has acquired fine copies of all the important French architectural books of this period, as, for example, first editions of Sebastiano Serlio's *Il primo [quinto] libro d'Architettura* (Paris, 1545–1547); the first complete French edition, with illustrations by Jean Goujon, of Vitruvius (Paris, 1547); the first French Alberti (Paris, 1553); one of the handsomest books of the time, the first edition of Jean Cousin, *Livre de perspective* (Paris, 1560); a complete run of the works of Philibert de l'Orme (1561–1576); and magnificent copies of the works of Jacques Androuet du Cerceau, one being the de Thou copy, as well as a fine vellum manuscript of du Cerceau. None of the books just listed was in the Murray Collection.

Among the more remarkable of the French books of this period there is room only to mention the de Seillière-Hoe copy of Robert Gobin, *Les Loups Ravissans* (Paris, Verard, c.1503) (Plate X), one of the most powerful and rarest of early French illustrated books; the Gaston III Phébus, *Les Deduiz de la Chasse* (Paris, Verard, c.1507); the apparently unique Rahir copy of the first Denis Janot Aesop, *Les Fables* (Paris, 1542), as well as the equally important Jean de Tournes, 1547 edition; five works of Gilles Corrozet, none of which, by the way, was in the Murray Collection, including the Guyot de Villeneuve–Montgermont–Rahir copy of the very rare *Les blasons domestiques* (1539), and the first edition of Claude Paradin, *Devises Heroïques* (Lyons, J. de Tournes, 1551).

The German books of the sixteenth century in the Hofer Collection are nearly twice as numerous as in the Murray Collection, but many of the more important ones, from the standpoint of illustration, are in both collections. It might, however, be of interest to compare them in relation to the work of one or two artists. Of Hans Weiditz, the Hofer Collection has some eighty books with one or more cuts, just about double the number in the Murray Collection, including the Maihingen copy of the

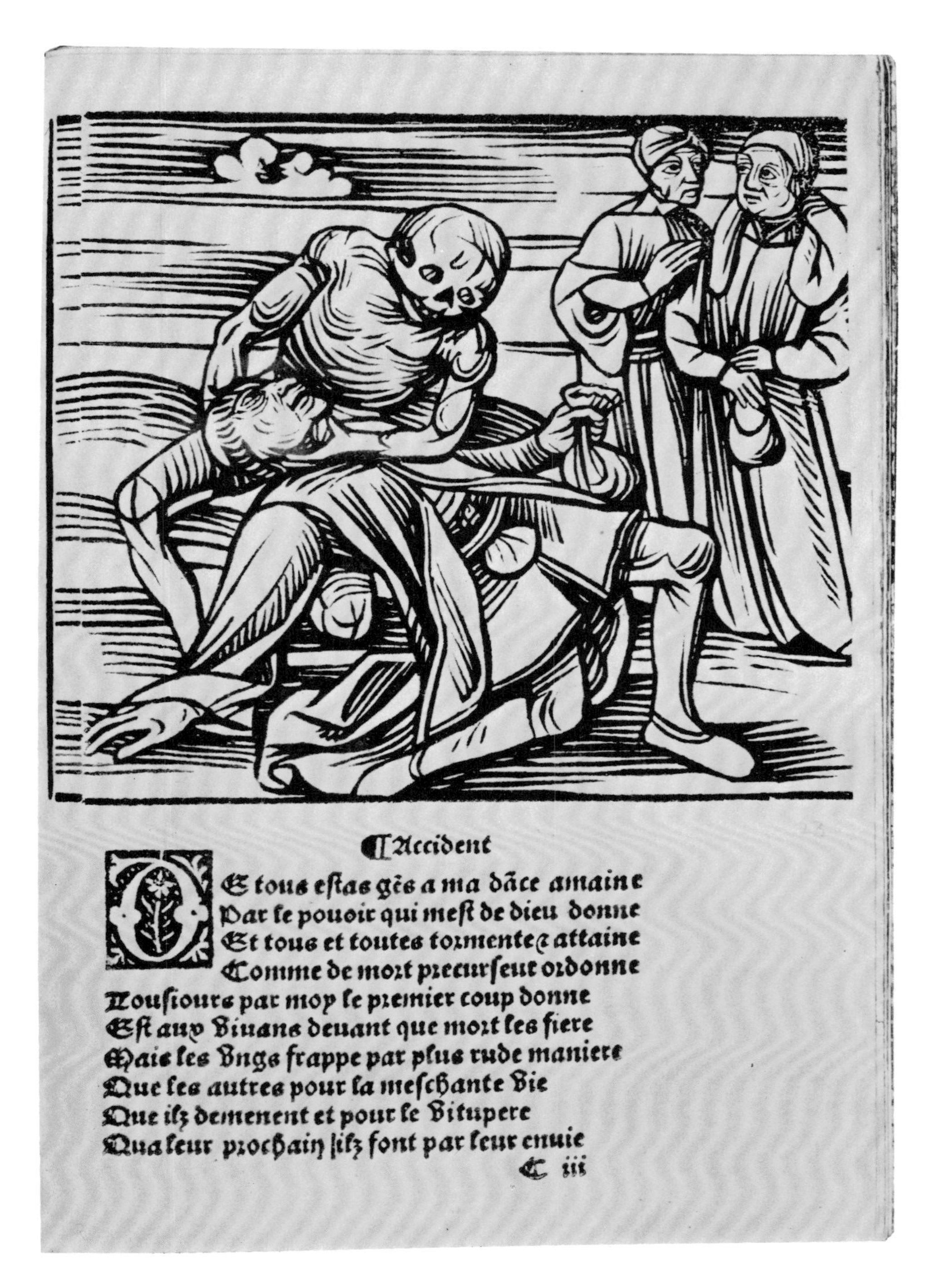

Accident

De tous estas gẽs a ma dãce amaine
Par le pouoir qui mest de dieu donne
Et tous et toutes tormente ꝛ attaine
Comme de mort precurseur ordonne
Tousiours par moy le premier coup donne
Est aux viuans deuant que mort les fiere
Mais les vngs frappe par plus rude maniere
Que les autres pour la meschante vie
Que ilz demenent et pour le vitupere
Qua leur prochain ilz font par leur enuie
C iii

X. Robert Gobin, *Les Loups Ravissans* (Paris, ca. 1503)

very rare Plautus, *Zwo Comedien* (Augsburg, 1518), which contains some of his earliest work, as well as the almost equally rare *Das Buechlin . . . der Gilgengart* (Augsburg, 1520), the Prince d'Essling copy. Of Albrecht Dürer, the two collections are more nearly equal in number, both having nearly all the important books, but the Hofer Collection has both the Latin and the German 1498 editions of the *Apocalypsis*, the only such pair in America, as well as the 1511 edition which was the only one in the Murray Collection, and while both collections have the *Befestigung der Stett* (Nuremberg, 1527), the Hofer copy is one of two known (the other being now in Australia) with the folding cut of the siege. Hans Baldung Grien is represented by thirteen books, which include most of the important ones with his illustrations, such as Ulrich Pinder's *Der beschlossene Garten des Rosenkranzes* (Nuremberg, 1505), in a fine monastic binding from S. Erentrude's at Nuremberg; his *Speculum Passionis* (Nuremberg, 1507), with the arms of Nuremberg on the binding; and the Marcus von Lindau, *Die sehn Gebote in diesem Buch* (Strassburg, 1516). Among over twenty books with cuts by Lucas Cranach there should be mentioned an early Luther Bible (Wittenberg, 1523–1524), and the *Missale Pragensis* (Leipzig, M. Lotter, 1522) (Plate XI), which is likewise noteworthy for the full-page frontispiece of three saints now attributed to Grünewald, and (if the attribution is correct) the only woodcut by this most remarkable of German artists. Among a number of volumes with cuts by Hans Schäuffelein, perhaps the rarest is a copy in original binding with the super-libris of the nunnery of Nonnberg, Salzburg, of Hans Leonrodt's *Hymelwag* (Augsburg, 1517). Of the seven or eight books with cuts by Hans Burgkmaier the Hofer copy of the Melchior Pfintzing, *Theuerdank* (Nuremberg, 1517), is a very fresh and clean one on vellum, bound for the Emperor Charles VI in an eighteenth-century imitation, a most unusual specimen, of a sixteenth-century blind-stamped binding.

One can only suggest the variety and importance of this section by remarking that it ranges from the Strassburg *Ptolemy* of 1513, with the Lorraine map printed in three colors, to a volume containing five embroidery pattern books (Frankfurt, 1564–1575), mostly unrecorded, bound for Princess Anna of Saxony in the style of Jacob Krause. Many of the books in this period, however, illustrate the German taste of that time by being hand-colored, often heightened with gold, and in the fine plaque or enamel bindings of the period. Among examples of this type

XI. *Missale Pragensis* (Leipzig, 1522)

there may be mentioned the Petrus Apianus, *Astronomicum Caesarum* (Ingoldstadt, 1540); a "Royal" copy of the great two-volume Wittenberg Bible (1551, 1550); the Strassburg *Josephus* of 1578; and the rare privately published two volumes on surveying by Paul Pfinzing von Henfenfeld, *Methodus Geometrica* and *Soli Deo Gloria* (Nuremberg, 1598–1599), the Lichtenstein copies. Along with these last Mr. Hofer has a fine manuscript by Pfinzing on perspective, and his copy of Cyprian Leowitz's *Eclipsium Omnium* (1554), is accompanied by the original manuscript with miniatures in gold and colors from which it was derived.

The Italian sixteenth-century books in the Hofer Collection number almost five hundred and are a very distinguished lot, for they include most of the well-known illustrated books as well as many unique or very rare ones which are less well known. All, or very nearly all, of the books which have cuts after Titian are represented here, including the rare chiaroscuro cut in Pietro Aretino's *Stanze in Lodi di Angela Sirena* (Venice, 1537). The *Epistole: & euãgelii volgari hystoriade* (Venice, 1512), the Huth–Dyson Perrins copy, contains the only known woodcut after Marc Antonio Raimondi, and the *Oscuri Passi del l'Opera Ionica di Vitruvio* (Mantua, 1558), contains a brilliant and almost unknown engraved frontispiece featuring Hercules, signed by Giorgio Ghisi after a design by G. B. Bertano, the author of the book (Plate XII).

The apparently unique copy of G. P. Ferraro's *Opera nuova historiata di Christo* (Milan, 1563), contains a series of impressions of the famous fifteenth-century "Specchio di Anima" Lombard cuts. The real first edition (dated 1 March 1508) of the *Libellus de Natura Animalium*, printed at Mondovi, is an important bestiary and a rare one formerly supposed to be unique. Among a fine selection of Francesco Marcolino imprints there may be mentioned the Didot copy, on vellum, of his *Officium Beate Marie Virginis* (Venice, 1545); and copies of the first and second editions of his *Le Sorti* (1540 and 1550), with the woodcut title signed Joseph Porta apparently based on Raphael's "School of Athens" fresco or a study for it. (Three manuscripts of this text — Italian, French, and German — evidently prepared for later editions of it, are also in the collection). A similar work, Sigismondo Fanti's *Triompha di Fortuna*, is here in both the first, 1526, and second, 1527, editions. Among several editions of Domenico Fontana's *Della Trasportatione dell'Obelisco Vaticano* are two variant copies of the first edition (Rome, 1590), one of which is in a fine contemporary silver and gold binding.

XII. G. B. Bertano, *Oscuri Passi del l'Opera Ionica di Vitruvio* (Mantua, 1558)

Among some thirty-five Florentine woodcut books of this century are several which are unique and a number which are very important, including eighteen "Rappresentazioni." Miss Anna Hoyt, who is making a study of the Florentine woodcut books, has stated that the Hofer Collection supplemented by those in the Harvard Library and the Boston Museum of Fine Arts furnishes a greater concentration of both quality and quantity than is to be found elsewhere in America. As examples only, there may be cited the Frezzi *Quadriregio* (1508), the *Fior di Virtu hystoriati* (1511), Petrarch's *Triomphi* (1518), *Le Dodici Fatiche di Hercole* (1550) — from Fairfax Murray — and (1568) — from Huth, Boccaccio's *Ninfale Fiesolano* (1568), and the *Contrasti Viva e Morto* (1572).

Among a number of books of which the literary interest is as great as the artistic there may be mentioned the Beckford–Montgermont copy of the Valgrisi 1562 edition of *Orlando Furioso*, in red morocco with the arms of Anibal, Count Altemps; the first Girolamo Porro edition of the same book (Venice, 1584), the Didot copy bound for Méry del Vic; the Ashburnham–Hoe copy of Pietro Bembo's *Lettere* (Rome, 1548), the only known copy on vellum, in a fine contemporary gilt binding; a thick paper copy of Ludovico Dolce's *Le Trasformationi* (Venice, 1533), bound possibly for Cardinal Granvelle, as well as a blue paper copy of the same book; and two colored copies heightened with gold of the Tasso, *La Gierusalemme Liberata* (Genoa, 1590), which was probably the inspiration of the colored copies of the London 1591 Harington *Ariosto*, the Lady Arabella Stewart copy of which on large paper is also in the collection.

The bindings in this section are particularly fine, for besides a good many of the typical Aldine style there are unusual bindings, such as one for Pier Luigi Farnese, with his upright device, the Britwell–Wilmerding copy of Giovanni Villani, *Croniche* (Venice, 1537), which is remarkable also for having a woodcut putto after Titian; and the dedication copy bound for the Emperor Rudolph II of Bernardo Parthenius, *De Poetica Imitationi* (Venice, 1577), formerly in the Wilmerding collection, in a painted vellum binding of great charm, the equal of, though quite different from, the best in the Pilloni library.

The Spanish and Portuguese sixteenth-century books number one hundred and seventy. They include the collection, fifty-seven volumes, of J. P. R. Lyell, the only ready-made collection which Mr. Hofer has ever acquired. To that collection he has added many books of very great distinction, as, for example, a vellum copy of Ludolphus de Saxonia, *Aqui se acaba el vita Xpi* (Alcala de Henares, 1502), which, while only part four of the *Vita Christi*, is a very handsome volume; a copy of an otherwise unknown edition of Andreas de Li, *Repertorio de los Tiempos* (Valencia, 1501); the Herédia copy, printed on vellum, of Jacobo Marquelles, *Commentaria* (Barcelona, 1505); and an apparently unique *Passionarium Oxonense* (Burgo de Gama, 1562), with the title printed in four colors. An extraordinary pair are the Fernandez de la Gama, *Copilacio delos establecimientos dela orden dela caualleria de satiägo del espada* (Seville, 1503), and the Portuguese *Regra: statutos: & diffincoes: da ordem de Sanctiagno* (Sebutal, 1509). Among other notable Portuguese books there may be cited the Huth–Brooke–Harmsworth copy of the first edition of *Marco paulo* (Lisbon, 1502); a very fine copy in the original vellum envelope-binding of a beautifully illustrated *O compromisso de confraria de Misericordia* (Lisbon, 1516) (Plate XIII), printed in red and black; and a fine copy in the original Portuguese dark green morocco, gilt, of the *Coronica do Condeestabre dom Muno Alurez Pereyra* (Lisbon, 1554), attributed to Fernao Lopez. It was from the full-page woodcut in this book that a recent Portuguese postage stamp was taken.

The Dutch and Flemish books of this period number well over a hundred volumes and are representative of all the major artists who were employed in the Netherlands. A number of the cuts of that most famous of Dutch woodcut books, the *Chevalier Délibéré* of 1485, are found in the William Morris copy of the *Vitaspatrum* (Leyden, 1511). Lucas van Leyden cuts appear in the Utrecht *Missale* (Leyden, 1514), and in the *Cronycke van Hollandt* (Leyden, 1517), which also has *Chevalier Délibéré* cuts. The Huth copy, one of five known, nearly all the others imperfect, of the Alardus Amstelredamus, *Passio domini nostri Jesu Christi* (Amsterdam, 1523), contains a large number of cuts by Jacob Corneliss (van Oostzanen). Among other illustrated books of particular interest may be mentioned the Willems copy of the Columna, *Historie van de Destruction van Troyen* (Antwerp, c.1501), and what appears to be the only known copy of Cornelius van Hoorn, *Epitome* (Utrecht, 1537). The Antwerp 1503 and 1536 editions of Ludolphus of Saxonia repeat many cuts from the fifteenth century editions; and the Hofer Collection contains fine runs of the usual illustrated books, such as those of Goltzius, and the liturgical, botanical, entrée, and emblem books printed

Fol. j.

¶ Do compromisso ⁊ regimento dos officiaes da sancta confraria de Misericordia.

Dom Manuel per graça de Ds Rey de Portugal ⁊ dos alguarues daquem ⁊ daalem mar em affrica Senhor de guynee ⁊ da conquista. nauegaçam ⁊ comercio de Ethiopia. Arabia. Persya ⁊ da Jndia. ¶ A quantos esta nossa carta virem: fazemos saber. que pollo prouedor ⁊ officiaes da confraria da Misericordia desta muy nobre ⁊ sempre leal çidade de Lyxboa. nos foy apresentado huũ compromisso que pera bõa gouernança da dita cõfraria per elles era feito de que ho trelado de verbo a verbo he o q̃ se segue.

¶ Prologo.

Eterno immenso ⁊ todo poderoso senhor Ds. padre das misericordias: começo meo ⁊ fim de toda bondade. açeytando as prezes ⁊ rogos de alguũs justos ⁊ temẽtes a elle. quis repartir cõ os pecadores parte da sua misericordia. E em estes deradeiros dias inspirou nos coraçoões de alguũs boõs ⁊ fiees xpãaos. ⁊ lhe deu coraçam: siso: forças ⁊ caridade: pera ordenarẽ hũa jrmandade ⁊ confraria. sob titulo ⁊ nome ⁊ emvoeaçam de nossa senhora a madre de Ds virgem Maria da Misericordia. pella

a

XIII. *O Compromisso de Confraria de Misericordia* (Lisbon, 1516) by Plantin. Of less obvious relevance but present in distinguished copies are the Dutch, Latin, and French editions of Abraham Ortelius' atlases of 1572, 1595, and 1598; a fine set of first editions of Jan van der Noot; and a magnificent copy, with the cuts heightened with gold, of Hieronymus Natalis, *Adnotationes et Meditationes* (Antwerp, 1595), bound in elaborately tooled red morocco for Colbert, with the arms of Count Hoym let in, and later in the La Vallière and Beckford collections.

The Swiss sixteenth-century books again number well over a hundred and include a very remarkable representation of the book illustration and decoration of Hans Holbein, including all or nearly all his title borders and sets of initials, all but one of the original editions of the "Dance of Death" (the exception being the 1542 Latin edition). He also has thirty-nine out of forty of the "Dance of Death" proofs (Von Lanna's first and preferred group of thirty-six among them). The Old Testament cuts are there in the Latin editions of 1538, 1539, 1544, 1547 (two variant copies), as well as the Spanish 1543 (two variant copies) and the English 1549. The English Holbeins are also well represented and, among many others which might be mentioned, such as the *Grynaeus*, there is a fine impression of the first state of the "term" portrait of Erasmus. Among the earlier works of importance is the second edition of La Tour-Landry's *Der Ritter vom turn* (Basle, 1513), which repeats the Dürer woodcuts of the 1493 edition; the two first issued of Wimpheling's *De fide concubinarum in sacerdotes* (Basle, c.1501 and c.1503), with woodcuts by the Master D. S. who also illustrated the fine *Missale Saltzburgensis* (Basle, 1510); and two copies, one colored and the other uncolored, of the *Von der Zurstörung der Bapstums* (Basle, c.1550). Along with several handsome Gesners, Erasmuses, Fuchses, and Bibles there should be mentioned a magnificent series of Vesalius, including both the Latin and German first editions of the *Epitome* (Basle, 1546), as well as the first and second *Fabrica* (Basle, 1543 and 1555), all in original pigskin.

The English books of this period include most of the more important ones, such as Cunningham's *Cosmographicall Glasse* (1559); Recorde's *The Castle of Knowledge* (1556); a first *Geminus* in original vellum; a superb Saxton's Atlas, from the Hoe sale, colored and heightened with gold, and in a fine original London binding; and the Britwell copy of Tottell's *Boccaccio* (1554), with the two magnificent "Dance of Death" cuts. A vellum copy of the second "Morton" Missal (Pynson, 1520), and two copies, one on thick-paper quarto, the other on large-paper folio, the latter noted above, with contemporary coloring, of Harington's *Ariosto* (1591), are all that can be recorded by name. It is a small but select group of about forty items. Of Scandinavian books there is room only to mention the first Swedish Bible ("Gustavus Vasa's") (Uppsala, 1541 [1540]), and the first Danish Bible ("Christian III's") (Copenhagen, 1550). Seven or eight illustrated books printed in Cracow include Matthias de Miechow's *Chronica Polonorum* (1521), *Crescentius* in Polish [1549], and the *Herbarium Polonicum* (1568). Among a similar number of Czech books there are Wenceslaus Hajek, *Kronyka Czeska* (Prague, 1541), and the *Machsor Rosch Haschanah* (Prague, 1533), complete. Another unusual volume is the *Mishneh Torah* printed in Constantinople in 1509, with a fine title border first used in Ixar in Spain in 1487.

Mr. Hofer very early realized that the seventeenth century was a neglected area that, so far as book illustration was concerned, had never been widely explored by collectors. As many of the finest of Baroque books are very large, it still remains a field that few private collectors dare enter. A measure of his success and the variety and quality of these books may be seen in his own *Baroque Book Illustration* (Harvard University Press, 1951), which has reproductions from some one hundred and fifty books then in his collection. Mr. Hofer's seventeenth century books now total some thirteen or fourteen hundred volumes, for since his survey was published, he has acquired many books that might have been included in it had they been on his shelves when it was prepared. His territorial coverage in this century, ranging from Japan to Peru, makes a proper survey impossible. However, it may be said that he has all the illustrations by Rembrandt and practically all, if not all, the books with illustrations engraved after designs by Rubens, Poussin, and the other major seventeenth-century artists who designed illustrations for books, including many rare Callots.

What Mr. Hofer's pioneer treatise does not reveal is the special quality of many of the volumes in this part of his collection, their binding, provenance, and often the freshness of their condition. One of his two copies of the Duke of Newcastle's *Methode* (Antwerp, 1658), for example, is a presentation copy in fine contemporary morocco from the Beckford and Rosebery collections; one of three variant copies of Antoine de Pluvinel, *Maneige Royal* (Paris, 1623), has the arms of Louis XIII and was later in the Rochefoucauld and Earl Grey collections. The

Philostrate of 1614 is in full red morocco with the arms of Guillaume du Vair, while the 1629 edition is likewise in red morocco with the chiffres of Peiresc, du Vair's great friend; and the *Ovid* of 1619 is Gaston d'Orléans', in full morocco. Hieronymo Tetios, *Aedes Barbarinæ* (Rome, 1642), is in contemporary green morocco with black inlay having the arms of Elizabeth, the Winter Queen, and was later in the Colbert collection. The *Breviarium Romanum* (Antwerp, 1614), with ten full-page engravings after Rubens, is in red morocco with the arms of Cardinal Scipione Borghese. *Le Pastissier Français* (Amsterdam, 1655), is in a mosaic binding by Thibaron and belonged to Elizabeth, Duchess of Manchester; and so it goes with volume after volume. *Les Tapisseries du Roy* (1670), part of the *Cabinet du Roy*, is accompanied by twenty-four exquisite gouaches with gold emblems on vellum by Jacques Bailly (Plate XIV) which evidently were the source of many of the designs in that book. Indeed, among Mr. Hofer's seventeenth-century books there are numerous royal copies and as many books bound in contemporary morocco "aux armes" as in calf.

When one thinks of illustrated eighteenth-century books, one inevitably envisages French illustrated books of the "Fermiers Generaux" type in original citron morocco, *à l'oiseau*, *aux armes*, *avant lettres*, *et avec les dessins originaux*, of a fairly restricted type. Mr. Hofer's eighteenth-century books, which number nearly three thousand, have relatively few of this kind beyond the great monuments — his "du Régent" *Longus* (1719), the first typical French eighteenth-century "illustrated book," is in a Derome binding with ticket, and his *Monument de Costume* (1789), the Edward Arnold copy in a Chambolle-Duru binding is a much better than average copy of this last of the "de luxe" books. He has chosen rather to collect only the best of the fête books, generally in presentation bindings, many "Voyages pittoresques," the great illustrated books of palaces and churches, and especially the books of architecture and ornament of which he has a number of very fine copies. More particularly, he has chosen to collect the little known but frequently remarkable books of science printed in France during this century when even pictures of clocks, monkeys, or shells were made with taste and verve. There are many drawings and a half-dozen manuscripts to support them.

This does not mean that a French collector would not find examples of great interest and importance of the type of illustrated book which he

XIV. MS. Emblems by Jacques Bailly, ca. 1670

would expect in such a collection, for Mr. Hofer has, to name only a few, thirty pencil and two large wash drawings (for Ariosto) by Fragonard, two wash drawings and one red, black, and white crayon by J. M. Moreau le Jeune, over ninety pen and wash drawings by Gravelot (Plates XV, XVI), six drawings by Chodowiecki, all done for books, copies of which are in his collection.

The English works of this period are of course not as numerous as the French but include a considerable number of fine Bewick drawings, proofs, and original woodblocks, a number of Blakes, including *America* and the *Vision of the Daughters of Albion*, as well as drawings and proofs, a splendid series of the works of Thomas Martyn in presentation copies or on vellum, and many unusual architectural books often in bindings of great merit. As an example of the unusual item may be cited Thomas Pennant's own copy of his *Arctic Zoology* (1784), with many fine drawings in the margin by Moses Griffith; and a red chalk drawing by Alexander Pope, with directions to the engraver, for the frontispiece to the 1745 edition of his *Essay on Man.*

The very strong section of German books includes, to list only a very few, not only Giuseppe Galli Bibiena's *Architetture e Prospettive* (Augsburg, 1740), but also an unpublished volume containing hundreds of pen and wash drawings by him; the Bridgewater set of colored proofs on vellum of J. C. Brand's *Cris de Vienna* (c.1775); the Sebright copy in contemporary morocco of the six-volume Marc Eliéser Bloch, *Ichtyologie* (Berlin, 1785), with fine hand-colored plates; the Langton–Sykes–Thorold copy of Frederick, Lord Baltimore's *Gaudia Poetica* (Augsburg, 1770); the Paul Hirsch copy from Schloss Arklitten of Goethe's *Das Romische Carneval* (Weimar, 1789), on large paper, hand-colored, apparently the only one known; G. Lambranzi's *Theatralische Tantz-Schul* (Nuremberg, 1716); and a fine copy in contemporary binding of that most magnificent collection of colored views of Vienna by Karl Schütz and Johann Ziegler (Vienna, 1794–1796).

For many years Mr. Hofer has been interested in Italian eighteenth-century illustrated books and has built up his Piranesi collection with drawings, early impressions, and variant states, and has obtained nearly all the sets of prints and books illustrated by Canaletto, Piazetta, Tiepolo, and the Bibienas, and very special copies of books printed by Bodoni. Only recently, however, has he collected the more obscure and little-known artists and engravers. Now with a collection approaching some five hundred eighteenth-century pieces one can see that they really possess a charm and interest that hitheto has been little appreciated. They are nearly all on fine Italian paper, are often uncut, with generally an elaborate engraved title or frontispiece and often if no other illustration, vignettes and cul-de-lampes which fit the typography, and if not in morocco or inlaid bindings generally in the striking block-printed wrappers peculiar to Italian books of this period.

There is not space enough to describe the Dutch, Spanish, Scandinavian, Slavic, Turkish, and other illustrated books of this century except to say that they contain many of great interest, such as the earliest Dutch experiments in color printing, and a number of the noblest volumes of Spanish typography, these last nearly all in fine Spanish bindings.

For the nineteenth century, from the mass of finely printed or illustrated books which exist, Mr. Hofer has chosen with great discrimination several thousand — I confess not to have counted them — of which the bulk are French or English. To them he has in a great many instances added original drawings for the illustrations, as, for example, four of the famous Delacroix wash drawings for the *Faust* (Paris, 1828), of which Goethe wrote so enthusiastically; the Prudhon drawing for the frontispiece accompanies the Longus, *Daphnis et Chloe* (Paris, 1803); and three large chalk and wash drawings by Doré for Énault's *Londres* (1876) accompany an India paper copy of it. Besides more than a dozen other Dorés there is one of the original woodblocks of his *Rabelais*; while among more than a dozen books illustrated by Toulouse-Lautrec, including the rare *Yvette Guilbert*, as well as a nearly complete set of proofs of the c.1894 edition, there are two variant copies of Jules Renard's *Histoires naturelles* (1899) with four pencil drawings, large and small, for it. Several of the books printed by Didot are unique, printed on vellum or otherwise distinguished. The Levaillants are large-paper, the Redoutés have accompanying drawings, as does *Le Bon Genre*. The famous *Chants et Chansons de la France* (1843) is accompanied by a large group of the original drawings, and *Paul et Virginie* (1838) is present in every possible state accompanied by proofs and woodblocks. Daumier has long been a favorite of Mr. Hofer's, and I have counted at least thirty-five titles, including most if not all the periodicals to which he contributed — the Fabre, *Nemesis Medicale* (1840), is there in wrappers, boards, and contemporary morocco — but I do not know how many proofs and other odd pieces there may be, though I do know there

XVI. Engraving by Scotin after Gravelot for Gay's *Fables* (London, 1738)

XV. Original drawing by Gravelot for Gay's *Fables* (1738)

are at least a half-dozen woodblocks and one great lithographic stone. Likewise the Gavarnis, Grandvilles, and Johannots are well represented. There are all the books illustrated by Manet; the André Gide, *Le Voyage d'Urien* (1893), with plates by Maurice Denis, is a presentation copy to Oscar Wilde; and among other notable volumes of the new art may be mentioned Bonnard's *Parallèlement* (1900) and Vuillard's *Paysages et Interieurs* (1899).

The English books are equally distinguished with many special copies, frequently on vellum, printed by Bulmer and Pickering; and there are rows of the great color-plate books of Ackerman, Alken, Daniel, Girtin, and Nash. The *National Fields Sports* is accompanied by two Alken drawings. Frederick Nash's *Paris and its Environs* (1820) is accompanied by sixty-eight drawings. Malton's *Oxford* in original parts is accompanied by drawings, while to the complete array of the books of Thomas Shotter Boys are added some three hundred drawings of all sizes and kinds. The John H. Clark, *On Landscape Painting* (1827), has all the original drawings — but the list must stop. A strong collection of the books of the 1860's has added letters of the brothers Dalziel and drawings of A. B. Houghton and Sir J. E. Millais. There are about one hundred and fifty drawings by Hugh Thompson and others for Macmillan's "Cranford" series.

There are several sets of drawings by Rowlandson for *Dr. Syntax*, *The Dance of Death*, *The Dance of Life*, *The English Spy*, and *The Microcosm of London*. Among some fifty Lear drawings and manuscripts are ones for his *Nonsense Books*, *Alphabets*, *Corsica*, *Greece*, and so on, together with a strong collection of presentation copies of his books. Westall is represented by his watercolors for Crabbe's *Poems*, and H. K. Brown by the original drawings for Lever's *Our Mess* and *The Daltons*. But there is not room to catalogue them all, for there are few books that one might expect to find in such a collection which are not there, as well as an unusual array, including drawings, relating to the Great Exhibition of 1851, the beginnings of photography, and many other subjects such as botany, ornithology, the industrial revolution, paper making, and the reproductive printing processes.

The German nineteenth-century books include representative collections of Senefelder, Wilhelm Busch, including the first *Max und Moritz*, Adolf Menzel, Heinrich Hoffman, including the rare first *Struwwelpeter* (1845), and many others. Typical of the unusual book

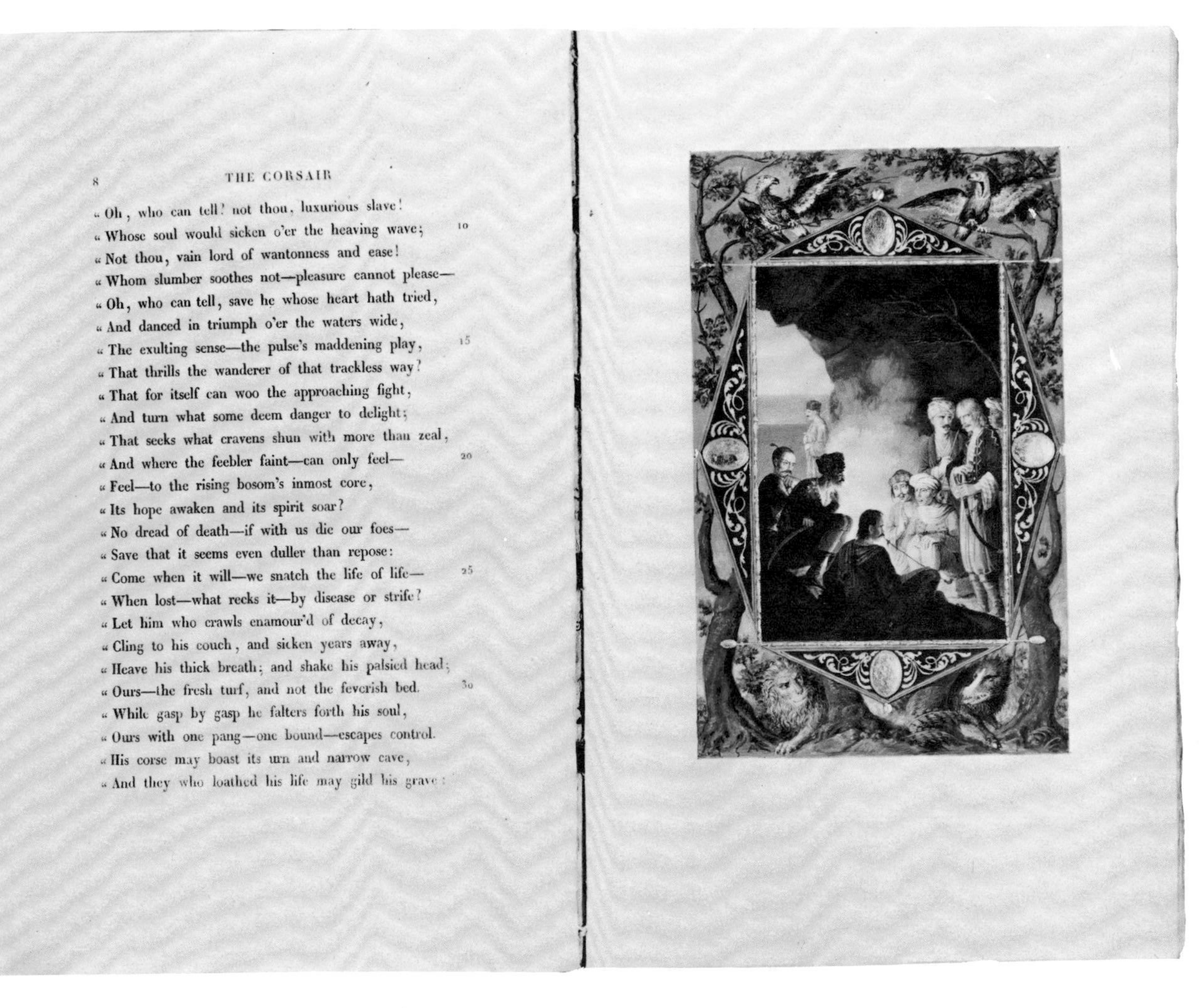

8 THE CORSAIR

« Oh, who can tell? not thou, luxurious slave!
« Whose soul would sicken o'er the heaving wave; 10
« Not thou, vain lord of wantonness and ease!
« Whom slumber soothes not—pleasure cannot please—
« Oh, who can tell, save he whose heart hath tried,
« And danced in triumph o'er the waters wide,
« The exulting sense—the pulse's maddening play, 15
« That thrills the wanderer of that trackless way?
« That for itself can woo the approaching fight,
« And turn what some deem danger to delight;
« That seeks what cravens shun with more than zeal,
« And where the feebler faint—can only feel— 20
« Feel—to the rising bosom's inmost core,
« Its hope awaken and its spirit soar?
« No dread of death—if with us die our foes—
« Save that it seems even duller than repose:
« Come when it will—we snatch the life of life— 25
« When lost—what recks it—by disease or strife?
« Let him who crawls enamour'd of decay,
« Cling to his couch, and sicken years away,
« Heave his thick breath; and shake his palsied head;
« Ours—the fresh turf, and not the feverish bed. 30
« While gasp by gasp he falters forth his soul,
« Ours with one pang—one bound—escapes control.
« His corse may boast its urn and narrow cave,
« And they who loathed his life may gild his grave:

XVII. Byron, *The Corsair* (Milan, 1826). Copy on vellum illuminated by G. B. Gigola in this collection is a beautiful copy of Goethe's *Hermann und Dorothea* (Braunschweig, 1822), with illustrations partly printed in color. The collection of Russian illustrated books which consists of about one hundred titles, as well as drawings and manuscripts, is remarkable for condition, for most of these copies came from the imperial libraries. Among many which deserve mention is a set of A. Agin's lithographic illustrations for Gogol's *Mertvyia Dushi* (1846) in the original eighteen parts with wrappers.

From the smaller national collections of this period there may be noted Andrasy's *Les Chasses et le Sport en Hongrie* (Pest, 1857); *The Corsair of Lord Byron* (Milan, 1826) (Plate XVII), printed on vellum and exquisitely illuminated by G. B. Gigola, one of three copies so treated; a royal copy of *Colección de las Vistas de los Sitios Reales Litografiadas* (Madrid, 1827–1832); F. Waldstein and P. Kitaibel, *Descriptiones et Icones Plantarum Rariorum Hungariae* (Vienna, 1802–1812); the De Jonghe copy of G. L. Lahde, *Das tagliche Leben in Kopenhagen* (Copenhagen, c.1807); the original drawings for C. G. Svedman's "Costumes of Sweden," c.1820; and a really superb copy of Fielding Lucas, Jr.'s *Progressive Drawing Book* (Baltimore [1828]).

From the twentieth century Mr. Hofer has gathered almost as widely as from earlier periods, and his holdings include not only most of the great classics of modern book illustration but also many ephemera which only a trained eye would see were worthy of preservation. Early in 1961 there was held at the Boston Museum of Fine Arts an exhibition of "The Artist as Illustrator: 1860–1960," largely based on Mr. Hofer's collection. The catalogue shows how very strong the collection now is.[2] In surveying it for this article, I could not find lacking any of the books of the masters of modern book illustration of which I had any knowledge, including Rouault, Matisse, Picasso, Braque, Dufy, Derain, etc., and their greatest works are almost always present in their finest form, as for example Picasso's *Buffon* (Plate XVIII), which is one of five printed on Japan "super nacré," with a suite on "Chine" and the rejected plate, in a fine inlaid binding by Creuzewalt and supplemented by the *Eaux Fortes*; Rouault's *Réincarnation du Père Ubu* (1932), one of thirty; Dufy's *Bestiare* (by Apollinaire), the artist's own copy, with original drawings and manuscript material; or Kredel's *Das Blumenbuch* (1930),

[2] *The Artist and the Book*, compiled by Philip Hofer and Eleanor M. Garvey (Boston, 1961).

XVIII. Buffon illustrated by Picasso (Paris, 1942). Extra plate *hors texte*

in every form, including one of two copies with quotations from the Bible inserted on every page in Rudolph Koch's calligraphic hand.

Some idea of the variety and extent of the books of the present century may be obtained by listing a few of the artists whose drawings are to be found — the books for which they were made and many others like them are all in the collection: Artzybasheff, Beerbohm, Boutet de Monville, Calder, Demuth, Disney, Dulac, Gill, Gooden, Kent, Legrand, Müller, Newell, Rackham, and many others. The shelves devoted to the Americans, W. A. Dwiggins, Bruce Rogers, and Rudolph Ruzicka, all contain many drawings, proofs, and mock-ups which are outstanding.

Besides these general collections which have been so cursorily described, Mr. Hofer has a number of subject collections only a few of which can be noted. His calligraphic collections contain both manuscript and printed works. A selection of his manuscripts which range from the anonymous "Modus Scribendi" (Melk, c.1440) to the twentieth century was shown at the Grolier Club in 1958, and those who saw that exhibition could judge of his success in gathering outstanding examples of all periods. One feature of this section which should be mentioned is the more than fifty modern manuscripts by the best of twentieth century calligraphers, which Mr. Hofer has commissioned, a practice which if more frequently observed might keep this great art flourishing. His printed writing-books number more than three hundred, and while this is not a great quantity, they are remarkable in many instances for the condition of the copies — his *Pacioli* (1509) is in a fine contemporary blind stamped binding (the copy chosen for the Grolier Club publication), as are his *Neudorffer* (1538) and his *Wys* (1549). His *Van de Velde*, 1605, is in a fine cut-vellum binding, and his *Rossi* (1598), the dedication copy, is in a silver binding, having the author's portrait repoussé. He has the *Fanti* (1514) in original vellum, six sixteenth-century editions of Arrighi, and three of Tagliente. His *Juan de Ycars* include the first of 1548, and those of 1550, 1553, and 1566. To do justice to this collection would take a full chapter.

Likewise to describe in a paragraph Mr. Hofer's type specimens is hardly possible. They include the first Fell specimen of 1693 and other Oxford specimens of 1629, 1685, and 1768. Caslon and his successors are represented by specimens of 1740, 1764, 1785, 1789, 1796, and 1805, while Baskerville is there in the 1757 broadside, and Wilson and Fry are well covered. The Fournier *Manuel* (1769) is present in the original wrappers decorated with type ornament, and there are fine copies of his oblong *Modèles* (1742), *Caractères* (1764), and *Traité historique* (1765), while the Gillé specimens of 1773, 1778, and 1815 are present in original boards, and that of 1808 is the Eugène de Beauharnais copy which has many pages on variant colored papers, in a superb straight grained morocco binding "aux armes." A dozen Bodoni specimens are there in original royal morocco, and there is one of two complete sets of all Papillon's type ornaments and vignettes. But if one listed all of Mr. Hofer's type specimens that would have meaning to anyone but a specialist, one would not have done justice to them, for frequently it is the odd little book, of which one has never heard and for which one would search a long time without finding another copy, that makes this, like so many other parts of this collection, so delightful to browse in.

Though they are not shelved together nor anywhere listed as a group, there are many subjects which have particularly interested Mr. Hofer and which perhaps would have been as good a means of surveying this vast accumulation as the chronological conspectus here used. For example, he has collected bestiaries, and particularly *Aesops* of all periods, and an account of them, beginning with his thirteenth-century English Hugo de Folieto, "De Bestiis," and including his unique vellum copy of the Verona 1479 *Aesop*, variant and very fine Barlows, with a drawing, and ending with the Leonard Baskin, *Horned Beetles* (Northampton, 1958), one of thirty copies, would give a reasonably good idea of the scope of the whole collection. An even better conspectus would be obtained if one merely told of the books in this collection which have remarkably fine bindings. Mr. Hofer has often said that he does not collect bindings as such, and this is true in the sense that he is not interested in a fine binding on a dull edition of the *Sainte Semaine*, but in the Baltimore Exhibiiton of 1957–1958 there were forty-one exhibits under his name, besides a few among Harvard's entries which had been given by him. This was far more than any other American collector except, of course, those of Mr. Raphael Esmerian. Among the bindings in Mr. Hofer's collection belonging to classes not before mentioned are two Romanesque bindings of the twelfth and thirteenth centuries, two very early European gold tooled bindings, a Ferrarese printed binding of the fifteenth century, and the famous Gruel triple dos-à-dos.

To collect in such a wide field, a very considerable bibliographical reference collection is a necessity, and Mr. Hofer has accumulated several thousand of such tools. Like nearly all the great collectors, however, he has not regarded these books from a purely utilitarian standpoint — his Bayle's *Dictionarie* was Mme. de Pompadour's, his *Brunet* is on thick paper, his copies of the Fairfax Murray *Catalogues* are Davies' own annotated ones, and so on. In writing this necessarily superficial account of Mr. Hofer's collection, I have often been reminded of the joy with which he has greeted a new acquisition, particularly one of a, to him, new kind of book, how quickly he has mastered the literature about it, if there was any, and how quickly he turned with equal pleasure to a still newer volume. May this joy continue to be his for many years to come.

15

Selections from Houghton Library Reports

Much of Jackson's energy went into collecting books for Harvard, and much of the time he could devote to writing had to be allocated to his series of twenty-three annual reports. The vast influx of material and the necessity for compression did not often allow him scope to reveal his full knowledge of the books he noted. These four excerpts represent his obiter dicta on the business of a library keeper, and appraisals of a collection, a field, and a friend (Bibliography, nos. 36, 40, 70 and 79).

(1944–1945)

AS the first of these reports was issued in the year which saw this country take up arms, so the present one covers a period during which the war in Europe ended. Already it is apparent that, despite the frightful destruction of books in battle and particularly during the early days after occupation, many books have survived and will in all likelihood come on the market. But only a prophet can say whether that market will be an orderly one, whether the inflation which obviously threatens will run, or be allowed to run, its course and thus prevent institutional buying, or whether the losses by war, together with the drain of generations of foreign sales, will cause the raising of nationalistic barriers against the export of old books — a locking of the barn after the horse is stolen that must arouse the sympathy of all those who believe that the preservation of the records of a nation's past is important if that nation is to look to its future with courage and understanding. It does not need a prophet, however, to state that unless in the future there is a general disintegration of the public and institutional libraries of Europe, similar to the despoiling of the monasteries, the Napoleonic looting of Europe, or the merchandizing of the tzarist libraries by the Amtorg, this is the last generation which will be able to accumulate important collections of the books of the more distant past. May Harvard have the wisdom and means to take proper advantage of this opportunity.

(1945–1946)

THE desire for completeness is a frequent passion of collectors and librarians and oftentimes becomes an end in itself, completeness for completeness' sake. There are few things as satisfying as checking off the last item on a list of an author's publications, of the pamphlets in a controversy, or of the productions of a particular press, and it is a pleasure which is not wholly self-indulgent, for it means that there, in one place, are all the works which a student of that subject may need. This year the Harvard set of the books presented to the Roxburghe Club was completed. It is a series which contains a number of volumes of very great usefulness to scholars in many different fields, and yet it should be confessed that most of the items until recently lacking were among the least intrinsically important, though perhaps the most difficult to find. Now, however, any scholar who comes here to work may be certain that whatever Roxburghe Club volume he needs is available, whether it is one of the magnificent reproductions of medieval illuminated manuscripts or one of the not very scholarly reprints of English black letter rarities presented to the club in its early days and not otherwise available.

It is true that we spend a good deal of time, money, and effort in the more or less systematic filling-in of the gaps in our collections of the authors and subjects in which we are particularly strong, and derive a deal of satisfaction when we can write "Finis" to a list of desiderata, now happily "acquisita." But, while we conceive such endeavors to be the librarian's duty and pleasure, they are not all or even the first. When he finds it possible to obtain an important book, hitherto unknown, or the only recorded copy, he is adding not just to his own collection but to the sum total of knowledge, for while it is a great convenience to scholars to find in one place a complete, or nearly complete, array of the books which they need, it is of far greater importance to them to find items nowhere else available.

Curators of rare books have often received envious comments about the ivory tower life they must lead and of what a pleasant existence it must be to spend one's days reading beautiful old books. They are to be envied, certainly; but in reality most of their time is spent scrabbling for the means to pay for the books they have hardly time to catalogue, much less read. At this moment of history, when civilization is threatened as it has not been for centuries, although their task may be pleasant, it is likewise an important one, for they are gathering the records of the past, which are necessary for man's knowledge of himself. Indeed, our present struggle is not just for survival but to ensure that the accomplishments of the human mind and spirit may not be lost in another dark age.

(1951–1952)

THE year ending 30 June 1952 saw the completion of the first decade of the Houghton Library. During these years the Harvard collections of rare books and manuscripts have increased by over 75,000 volumes and many, many thousands of letters. Of the nearly 400 incunabula acquired, almost all are intrinsically important and many are either unique or the only ones in this country. Nearly 3,000 books printed on the continent of Europe in the sixteenth century were added in this period, and they include a large proportion of rare and important items. Over 10 percent of the 1,645 books printed in England before 1640 which have been added to the library during this decade are either unique or unrecorded. In later periods it is possible to say of many authors, including some who may be described as prolific, that all their printed works known to bibliographers are now on Harvard's shelves. The use made of the rare books and manuscripts at Harvard has more than doubled in the same period.

. . .

The Hauslab-Prince Liechtenstein Map Collection

THE Harvard Map Collection was founded early in the nineteenth century upon the Ebeling and Warren collections, which were particularly strong in American maps, and under the guidance of Justin Winsor most of the fundamental atlases of the early geographers were acquired. In recent years additions of early maps have been spasmodic, though from the Matt B. Jones collection and other sources notable items have been received. This year, through the generous gift of Stephen W. Phillips, '95, and Curt H. Reisinger, '12, the cartographical collection of Prince Liechtenstein was purchased. This addition of over 150 wall and sheet maps, two-thirds of which are of the sixteenth century, brings to Harvard one of the world's great collections of Renaissance maps. A good many of these maps are unique, and very few of them are to be found in any other American collection. Over thirty are wall maps extending to as many as a dozen sheets, and two are manuscript, a portolan chart of the Mediterranean by Vesconte Maggiolo dated Naples, 24 August 1513, in its original tin chart-case, and a portolan of the East and Gulf coasts of North America and the northern part of South America by Nicholas Comberford, dated 1659.

There are three of the rare pilgrim maps of Europe printed in Nuremberg in the last decade of the fifteenth century and the first of the sixteenth, attributed to Erhard Etzlaub, which are among the earliest sheet maps to have been printed. Included in the dozen sixteenth-century world maps are several which are unique, such as the Vespucci, Vopell, Oronce Finé, and Rosaccio; while among the five sets of printed gores for globe are also several unique ones, of which the Ingolstadt terrestrial globe, which is dated about 1518, is one of the earliest to name America and is remarkable for its coverage of cartographical information of that date.

The Liechtenstein maps were for the most part collected by General von Hauslab, and although half of them were printed in Italy, they contain a large number of rare maps of Eastern Europe — nine, for example, being Russian. They also include seven detailed maps of cities, including Moscow, St. Petersburg, Warsaw, and Vienna. The names of their makers are enough to start one's imagination traveling — Herberstein, Vavassore, DeMongenet, Mercator, Hondius, Kyrilov, and Blaeu. A score or more of them were recently lent to "The World Encompassed," an exhibition held at the Baltimore Museum of Art, and some thirteen of those shown are reproduced in the catalogue of that exhibition. Several of these maps have never been reproduced, although obviously representing stages of importance in the growth of man's knowledge of the world, and it is certain that scholars for generations to come will find much worthy of publication in the study of the maps in this collection.

. . .

The Rosamond B. Loring Collection of Decorated Papers

ONE cannot tell of this collection formally. Though the books and boxes of papers are the same books and papers, somehow they have lost a special brightness which they had when one looked at them with Mrs. Loring. This is the collection which she made and which as a collection has apparently only one or two rivals anywhere. And yet to enumerate its parts is not enough, knowing that no longer will one hear her explain just how or where this or that book was obtained, or how oddly this signed sheet of Dutch gilt turned out to match the piece used as an end paper in a Boston tract obtained years before. To those who did not know her the collection will doubtless be a monument to an enthusiastic student and amateur of decorated papers, the source from which her own books on the subject were derived and from which in all probability many other monographs will come. But to her friends, and they are unnumbered, it will not seem, when viewed all tidied up on library shelves, such a den of adventure and glorious fun as it did in her upper room on Gloucester Street.

To catalogue the collection will not be an easy task, for though here and there are books which are great books in themselves regardless of their bindings, many others are of little interest except for the clothing which they wear. Waifs, odd volumes, and even cripples stand side by side with noble tomes such as a Jenson Bible or Franklin's *Cato Major* (1744), uncut in a decorated wrapper. Among several hundred works in embossed board bindings of the early nineteenth century one will look quite a while to find any author or title of which one has ever heard or which is of any importance except as a binding. But among the more than fifteen hundred pieces there are treasures to be found, like the thin little quarto *Les oeconomicques de Aristote traslatees . . . par Sibert Louuenborch* (Paris, C. Wechel, 1532), which was unknown to Brunet, though now in the Bibliothèque Nationale, and which is here because of its bright embossed gold eighteenth-century wrapper; and when they are all listed and described, no doubt they will be found to include many books which will be of use to scholars who know nothing of paste or marbled papers.

The cataloguing of the fifty boxes of sheet papers, ranging from the sixteenth-century Persian marbled ones to those of the twentieth century made by Ruzicka and Cockerell, will be a simple matter, for though they number in the thousands, they were all beautifully sorted and arranged by Mrs. Loring herself. Before his death, her husband, Augustus Peabody Loring, Jr., '08, whose pride in the collection was as evident as his devotion to the collector, had arranged an endowment which will make possible occasional additions to the collection. Already two most unusual sample books have been found which, if only Mrs. Loring could look at them with us, would afford hours of pleasure in identifying the sources and finding examples in use on bindings.

(1953–1954)

EACH year as we look over the accessions of the past twelve months, the old truism comes to mind that in the field of rare books and manuscripts one can only collect what is available. No matter how carefully we may plan or industriously check our *lacunae*, there is no way by which we can be certain that during a given period any particular rarity will come upon the market. But each year we can be sure that books and manuscripts for which we never hoped, and, indeed, of whose very existence we were often ignorant, will be offered and that some of them may be added to the Harvard Library.

All bookmen are familiar with a phenomenon which may not be limited to the collecting of books, viz., that when an unexpected rarity appears, it is often followed shortly by others of similar kind. For example, last year there was reported the gift by Mr. Louis H. Silver of the first book printed from movable type on the continent of Africa, a book so uncommon that Richard Garnett stated that he did not believe three copies could be traced. This acquisition prompted a review of just what were the first books printed on the seven continents and was also evidently the catalytic agent which brought to Harvard this year two other books in that category.

The First Books of the Seven Continents

The introduction of printing into a continent or a country is an important cultural landmark and the first products of such a press will always have an historical and intellectual as well as a sentimental interest. Although the Spanish government permitted the establishment of printing in its colonies only with reluctance, the need for handbooks of religious instruction which could be used for the conversion of the natives invariably overcame the fear of what else the press might produce. In the Western Hemisphere a press was set up in Mexico City by Juan Pablos, an agent of Juan Cromberger of Seville, in 1539 and, after some difficulty and delay, produced three books, fragments of two of which were seen in the last century but cannot now be traced, according to both Henry Wagner and Lawrence C. Wroth. The earliest surviving product of this press is therefore the *Doctrina breue* prepared by Juan de Zumaraga, first Bishop of Mexico, and printed at his expense, being completed 14 June 1544, although the title is dated 1543. A very fine copy of this book, in its original blind-stamped calf binding, possibly the finest in condition of all the surviving copies, was this year presented to the Harvard Library by Curt H. Reisinger, '12. This copy comes from the library of the late Sir R. Leicester Harmsworth.

The first press in South America was established in Lima by Antonio Ricardo, who moved there from Mexico City in 1580. He also found that the way of the prototypographer is seldom smooth, and it was not until 13 February 1584 that permission was given him to commence printing. He thereupon began a *Doctrina Christiana* in the Spanish, Quichua, and Aymara languages which had recently been prepared by José de Acosta and other learned Jesuits. While he was at work on this book, an order came from Philip II that the alteration in the calendar, which had been made by papal decree of Gregory XIII in 1582, should be proclaimed in his vice-royalty of Peru, which meant dropping ten days from the month of October in the year 1584. On 14 July 1584 the Real Audiencia in Lima ordered that the *Pragmatica sobre los diez dias del año* should be printed and copies sent to all the cities of the province. Presumably, Ricardo stopped printing the *Doctrina* and printed the four folio pages of the *Pragmatica*, for a copy of it was discovered in the John Carter Brown Library by the late George Parker Winship endorsed with a date of proclamation which apparently indicates that its printing antedates the completion of the *Doctrina*. The J. C. Brown copy was, until recently, thought to be unique, but this past year another very fine copy was discovered in the library of the Marquis of Bute and was likewise presented to the Harvard Library by Mr. Reisinger.

If there be any question as to whether the *Pragmatica* precedes the *Doctrina*, it is not a matter of great concern so far as this library is concerned, for, with the *Pragmatica*, Mr. Reisinger also gave a copy of the *Doctrina* (1584), bound with the *Confessionario para los curas de Indios* (1585) and the *Tercero cathecismo* (1585), in contemporary gilt-tooled limp vellum with gilt gauffered edges, so that the first four publications issued in South America are now on Harvard's shelves in extraordinary condition.

The earliest surviving book printed in North America and the first book printed in South America were thus both acquired this past year. It may therefore be of interest to survey what are the other first books printed in the several continents. The first book printed in Europe is at the moment a matter of some debate. It seems likely, however, that the primacy of the Gutenberg Bible as the first substantial book to be printed in Europe will be sustained. The Hoe-Widener copy of the first issue, on permanent display in the Harry E. Widener Memorial Rooms, is a remarkably fine one. The first African book is the *Commentary on the book of prayer* by Dãvid Abũdraham printed in Fez in 1516, mentioned above. The first surviving book — though at least the fourth recorded — printed in Asia in the Western manner is the *Compendio spiritual da vida Christãa* (Goa, 1561) of Dom Gaspar de Leão, of which the only known copy is in the New York Public Library. A much more important book was printed at Goa two years later, viz., Garcia da Orta's *Coloquios dos simples, e drogas* (1563), of which one of the very rare copies is in the Harvard Library, as well as the unique copy of the first book printed in Asia in an Indic language, the *Doctrina Christam en lingua Malauar Tamul* (1578), concerning which, see *Harvard Library Bulletin*, VI (1952), 147–160. This last was likewise presented by Mr. Reisinger. The first surviving printing in Australia is a broadside printed by a convict named George Hughes, *Instructions for the constables of the country districts*, dated 16 November 1796. The only known copy is in the Mitchell Library. The first book printed in Antarctica is the *Aurora Australis* [1908], which was printed by members of Sir Ernest Shackleton's expedition in an edition of ninety copies, bound in boards from empty provision cases, and produced under conditions of great difficulty. For example, it was found that the only way of keeping the printing ink in a fit state to use was to have a candle burning under the inking-plate. A copy of this book was given to the library in 1946 by Donald McKay Frost, '99, and mentioned in the report for that year.

16

The Revised S.T.C.: A Progress Report

(1955)

Jackson's great life-work was his collaboration with F. S. Ferguson on the revised *Short-title Catalogue of Books Printed in England, Scotland and Ireland and of English Books Printed Abroad 1475–1640*. Although he wrote this article for *The Book Collector* at an early stage of his project, it fairly represents his methods and the results he achieved, and it may still serve as a foretaste of the whole work, which continues toward completion in the hands of Miss Katharine F. Pantzer (Bibliography, no. 87).

WHEN I was asked for a report on the progress of the revision of the *Short-title Catalogue*, I had to wait until I could find a weekend which could be devoted to compiling the statistics which would make such a report intelligible. Now, back at the spot — Williamstown, Mass. — where I first saw the newly published *S.T.C.* (and immediately had it interleaved and bound) and with a bag filled with the great loose-leaf folders of the so-far accomplished revision — about the first fifth, i.e., well into the letter *C* — and between well-remembered walks in some of the loveliest of New England hills, I have managed to read over the first four thousand numbers, a segment sufficient, I hope, to give some idea of what has been accomplished.

Before telling of that, however, it would perhaps be proper to mention briefly what we, i.e., F. S. Ferguson and I, are attempting to do in this revision. First of all we are checking every item, authorship, spelling of title, size, attribution of printer, if anonymous, and date, if undated, and location of copies — five copies for Great Britain and five for North America, with plus signs for each if more are known. In some cases it has not been as yet possible to determine to which edition or issue a particular copy may belong. In that case it is recorded with an asterisk which will, of course, be removed when the proper identification has been made.

In these first 4000 more than 220 are ghosts, i.e., the copies listed are not in the libraries named, are merely parts of other books or are already recorded, more properly, under other numbers. In this last category there are many duplicate entries; indeed, a number of triplicate ones and even one or two quadruplicates.

The identification of printers and the establishing of dates, at any rate for books in the British Museum, the Bodleian, the Cambridge University Library, or passing through the London market, has been assumed by Ferguson as his particular burden. He has done extraordinary work in this field, aided by A. F. Johnson for some of the continental presses, and by A. F. Allison and D. M. Rogers for the recusant ones. As for the spellings, sizes, etc., the nine thousand books at Harvard, if relevant, are always checked against bibliographies, the Folger cards, the various catalogues, and the Edwards microfilms. A number of books have the sign of the shop where they are to be sold, but not the name of the bookseller, in their imprints. In such cases the bookseller is noted in brackets.

If the book is unique, either Ferguson or I have had it in our hands, or seen a photostat or microfilm of it, or a description of it has to be requested, sometimes at the expense of half a dozen letters. Although the Bodleian has numerous genuinely unique books, many of them not recorded, a good many that are so listed in the *S.T.C.* turn out merely to be "analytic" entries. Consequently, Strickland Gibson and L. W. Hanson have been invaluable in checking not only the books in the Bodleian but scores of others in the various Oxford colleges.

The drudgery of checking the original entries (though sometimes exciting by reason of the fact that an entry oftentimes blossoms into two or more editions, hitherto unrecognized) and the method of interpolating the new entries and canceling the old may be illustrated by comparing the original record of the editions of *The answeres of some brethren* (*S.T.C.* 68–70) with the revised version.

68 The answerers of some brethren of the ministerie to the replyes of the ministers and professours of divinitie in Aberdene; concerning the late Covenant. 4°. *Aberdene, E.*	68 The answers of some brethren of the ministerie, to the replyes of the ministers and professours of divinitie in Aberdene; concerning the late Covenant. 4° in 2's. *Aberdene,*

Raban, 1638. L.D^{2}.G^{2}.DUR^{5}.	*E. Raban*, 1638. L. DUR. E^{2}. E^{8}. YK*.+; F.BO^{3}*.PN^{2}. Ends on I2. "Raban" in roman.
	68.1 [Anr. ed.] 4° in 2's. *Aberdene, E. Raban*, 1638, L.G^{2}. Ends on I2. "Raban" in italic.
69 [Anr. ed.] Answers of some brethren of the minitserie [*sic*.]. 4°. *Aberdeen, E. Raban* 1638. L.A.E^{3}.M.	69 [Anr. ed.] 4°. *Aberdene, E. Raban*, [*Edinburgh, G. Anderson*], 1638.L.A.D.E^{3}.M.;F.HD.Y. Ends on E2. Misprint in title, "minitserie."
	69.1 [Anr. ed.] 4°. *Aberdene, E. Raban*, 1638. L. Ends on E2. Misprint corrected.
	69.2 [Anr. ed.] 4°. [*Edinburgh? J. Wreittoun?*] 1638. O^{6}.C^{10}.E.M. YK.+; F. HN. BO (imp.). HD. U.
70 [Anr. ed.]; also Duplies of the ministers and professors. 2 pts. 4°. *R. Y*[*oung*]., *H. M. Printer for Scotland*, 1638. Ent. 9 no. L. O(pt. 1).C.	70 [Anr. ed.] Also, duplies of the ministers and professors. 2 pts. 4°. [*London*], *R. Y*[*oung*]., *H. M. Printer for Scotland*, 1638. Ent. 9 no. L. A. C. D. E. + ; F. HN. HD. ILL. N. +

Or the *Antidotarius* (*S.T.C.* 675–678):

675 The antidotharius, in the whiche thou mayst lerne how thou shalt make playsters, salves, etc. [Sig. B iii, catchw. "in Aurium."] 8°. *R. Wyer*, [1530?] L.	675 Now 675.4
	675.1 The antidotharius, in the whiche thou mayst lerne howe thou shalte make plasters, salues, oyntmēt. 8° in 4's. *R. wyer*, [1535?] WIS.
	675.2 [Anr. ed. In title "oyntemēt."] 8° in 4's. *R. wyer*, [1536?] L. (Formerly 677)
	675.3 [Anr. ed. In title "oyntement."] 8° in 4's. *R. Wyer*, [1540?] O.
	675.4 [Anr. ed. In title "oyntementes" and "shalt."] 8° in 4's. *R. Wyer*, [1542?] L.; AML (imp.). (Formerly 675)

675a [Anr. ed. Sig. B iii 'aureum.'] 8°. *R. Wyer*, [1538?] O.	675a [Anr. ed. In title "oyntementes" and "shalt." Fleur-de-lis and pansy ornaments on title.] 8° in 4's. *R. Wyer*, [1545?] G.; HN.
676 [Anr. ed. Sig. B iii "Au."] 8°. *R. Wyer*, [1538?] L.O.	676 [Anr. ed. In title "oyntementes" and "shalte."] 8° in 4's. *R. Wyer*, [1548?] L.O.
677 [Anr. ed. In title "plasters"; Sig. b 3 catchw. "Aureu."] 8°. *R. Wyer*, [1542?] L.	677 Now 675.2
678 [Anr. ed. In title "plaesters."] 8°. *R. Wyer*, [1545?] C.	678 [Anr. ed. In title "oyntementes," "shalt" and "plaesters."] 8° in 4's. *R. Wyer*, [1550?] L^{16}.C.; BO^{4}.

Or of *Adam Bell* (*S.T.C.* 1806–1813):

	1805.7 [Adam Bel, Clym of the Clough, a. William of Cloudesle.] 4°. [*W. de Worde*, 1510?] E(frag.).
1806 [Adam Bel, Clym of the Clough, a. William of Cloudesle.]. 4°. *J. Byddell*, 1536 (2 jn.) C(frag).	1806 [Anr. ed.] 4°. *J. Byddell*, 1536 (2 jn). C(frag.).
1807 [Anr. ed.] Adambel, etc. 4°. *W. Copland*, [1550?] Ent. to J. Kýnge, 1557–58. L.	1807 [Anr. ed.] Adambel, . . . 4°. *W. Copland*, [c. 1565]. Ent. to J. Kynge, 1557/58. L.
1808 [Anr. ed.] Adam Bell, etc. 4°. *J. Roberts*, 1605. Ent. 31 my. 1594. O.	1808 [Anr. ed.] Adam Bell, . . . 4°. *J. Roberts*, 1605. Ent. 31 my. 1594. O. B2^{v}. l. 1: "lightly on theyr."
1809 [Anr. issue] 4°. [*W. Jaggard f. J. Roberts*, 1605?] C(imp.).	1809 [Anr. ed.] 4°. [*J. Roberts*, c. 1605.] C(imp.). B2^{v}.l.1: "lightlie on their."
1810 [Anr. ed.] 4°. *W. Jaggard*, 1610. Ent. 29 oc. 1615. O.	1810 [Anr. ed.] 4°. *W. Jaggard*, 1610. Ent. 29 oc. 1615. O.
1811 [Anr. ed.] 4°. *T. Cotes a. R. Cotes, sold by M. Trundle*, 1628. Ent. to T. a. R. Cotes, 19 jn. 1627. O.	1811 [Anr. ed.] 4°. *T. Cotes a. R. Cotes, sold by M. Trundle*, 1628. Ent. to T. a. R. Cotes, 19 jn. 1627. O.
	1811.5 [Anr. ed.] 4°. [*T. Cotes a. R. Cotes?* c. 1630.] O (lacks tp). B3, l.8: "They Maior."

1812 [Anr. ed.] 4°. *T. Cotes a. R. Cotes, sold by F. Coules*, 1632. L.	1812 [Anr. ed.] 4°. *T. Cotes a. R. Cotes, sold by F. Coules*, 1632. L.
	1812.3 [Anr. ed.] 4°. [*T. Cotes a. R. Cotes?* c. 1635.] HD (lacks tp). B2^{v},l.1: "Sheriff."
	1812.6 [Adam Bell. The second part.] 4°. [*f. J. Wright?* 1608?] Ent. to Wright 24 se. 1608. O (lacks tp).
1813 Adam Bell. The second part. 4°. *f. J. Wright*, 1616. Ent. 24 se. 1608. O.	1813 [Anr. ed.] 4°. *f. J. Wright*, 1616. O.
	1813.3 [Anr. ed.] 4°. *f. J. Wright*, 1630. HD.

The really pleasant part, of course, is in finding and recording new titles and, to a lesser degree, new editions of already recorded titles. Of the former, if my addition is correct, in the first 4,000 numbers we have added 336 new titles, or 8.4 per cent. Pollard predicted that not more than 10 per cent would be found omitted, and yet, though the numbers of new ones which occur are diminishing, it is obvious that there are many yet to be recorded. Of new editions or issues, in the first 4,000, there are 832 or 20.8 per cent. If these percentages hold, there will be something over 2000 new titles and over 7500 new editions and issues in the revised edition of the *S.T.C.* It seems not improbable that these percentages will increase, though not greatly, for the new titles, because more and more frequently when an "unrecorded" title is reported we find that we already have another copy listed. However, our own labors and those of others, particularly H. M. Adams, Miss M. S. G. Hands, L. W. Hanson, J. C. T. Oates, and F. B. Williams, Jr., will doubtless continue, by parthenogenesis, to proliferate editions as we progress with our examination of the recorded ones.

There are, of course, many dull passages where the corrections are slight, except for added copies, and few new titles or editions; but occasionally an author turns out to have been meagerly represented, as, for instance, John Andrewes:

587 The anatomie of basenesse; or the foure quarters of a knave. [Anon.] 4°. *f. R. Redmer*, 1615. Ent. 26 jn. O.; HN.	587 The anatomie of basenesse; or the foure quarters of a knave. [Init. J. A.] 4°. [*H. Lownes*] *f. R. Redmer*, 1615. Ent. 26 jn. O (2).; HN.

588	Andrewes caveat to win sinners, 12°. *J. Wright*, 1631. L.	588	Andrewes caveat to win sinners. 16° in 8's. *f. J. Wright*, 1631. L.P.
		588.5	Andrewes golden chaine. 8°. *f. J. Wright*, 1637. O^{6}.
589	Andrewes humble petition unto Almighty God, declaring his repentance. 8°. *J. Wright*, 1623. Ent. 26 jy. 1630. Assd. by N. Okes. L.	589	Andrewes humble petition unto Almighty God, declaring his repentance, 16° in 8's. [*G. Eld*] *f. J. Wright*, 1623. Ass'd. by N. Okes to Wright. 26 jy. 1630. L.
590	Andrewes resolution to return to God by repentance. 8°. *N. Okes*, 1621. Assd. by N. Okes to J. Wright, 26 jy. 1630. O.	590	Andrewes resolution: to returne unto God by repentance. 12°. *N. Okes*, 1621. Ass'd. by N. Okes to J. Wright, 26 jy. 1630. O.
		590.5	[Anr. ed.] Andrewes repentance, sounding alarum, to return from his sins unto Almightie God. 8°. *f. J. Wright*, 1631. P.
591	The brazen serpent, a sermon. 4°. *G. P*[*urslowe*]. *f. T. Thorp*, 1621. L.O.	591	The brazen serpent, a sermon. 4°. *G. P*[*urslowe*]. *f. T. Thorp, sold by E. Wright*, 1621. L. L^{13}. O. C^{2}. D. + ; F. HN. BALT. Y.
592	A celestiall looking-glasse. 8°. *N. Okes*, 1621. Assd. by N. Okes to J. Okes, 2 au. 1630. O.	592	A celestiall looking-glasse. 12°. *N. Okes*, 1621. Ass'd. by N. Okes to J. Okes, 2 au. 1630. O.
		592.1	[Anr. ed.] 8°. *f. F. Coles*, 1635. D.
		592.2	[Anr. ed.] 8°. *N. a. J. Okes*, 1638. O^{6}.
593	[Anr. ed.] 8°. *N. a. J. Okes*, 1639. L.	593	[Anr. ed.] 8°. *N. a. J. Okes*, 1639. L.
594	Christ his crosse. 4°. *I. Barnes*, 1614. O.	594	Christ his crosse. 4°. *Oxford, J. Barnes*, [*sold by the author*], 1614. O. ELY.; PN^{2}.
595	The converted mans new birth: describing the direct way to heaven. 12°. *N. O*[*kes*]. *a. I. N.*, 1629. Ent. to John Okes, 18 se. 1635. L.	595	The converted mans new birth: describing the direct way to heaven. 12°. *N. O*[*kes*]. *a. J. N*[*orton*]., 1629. Ent. to J. Okes, 18 se. 1635. L.
		595.1	[Anr. ed.] *J. N*[*orton*]., 1634.

	L^{11} (S.P.D. 1625–49, p. 486, no. 23) (title only).
	595.2 [Anr. ed.] 8°. *N. a. J. Okes*, 1639. O^{6}.
	595.4 A most necessary caveat from God, to beware of his rod. 8°. *N. Okes*. 1627. O^{6}.
[Under "Subpoena":]	
23417 A subpoena from the high imperiall court of heauen. 8°. *W. White*, 1617. Ent. to J. White, 26 no. 1616. O.	595.6 A subpoena from the high imperiall court of heaven. [Anon.] 8°. *W. White*, 1617. Ent. to J. White, 26 no. 1616. O. (Formerly 23417)
23418 [Anr. ed.] 8°. *J. White*, 1618. C.	595.7 [Anr. ed. Anon.] 8°. *J. White*, 1618. C. (Formerly 23418)
23419 [Anr. ed.] 8°. *J. White*, 1620. HH(sig. A. only).; HN.	595.8 [Anr. ed. Anon, except for acrostic.] 8°. *J. White*, 1620. F. HN. (Formerly 23419)
	595.9 [Anr. ed. Anon, except for acrostic.] 8°. *A. Mathewes*, 1623. F.

Or James Balmford:

1334 Carpenters chippes; or simple tokens of unfeined good will. 8°. *f. R. Boyle*, 1607. L(title-page only).	1334 Carpenters chippes; or simple tokens of unfeined good will. 8°. *(F. Kyngston)* [1] *f. R. Boyle*, 1607. Ent. 18 de. 1606; ass'd. by E. Boyle to N. Bourne, 30 jn. 1625. L. D. DUR^{5}.
[Under B., I.:]	A modest reply. 1623. *See* 1336.
1044 A position maintained before the late Earle of Huntingdon. 8°. n. p. 1600. L.	1334.5 A position maintained before the late Earle of Huntingdon. 8°. [n.p.]. 1600, L. O^{17}.; COR. Reprinted in 1334. (Formerly 1044)
1335 A short and plaine dialogue concerning the vnlawfulnes of playing at cards. 8°. *f. R. Boile*, [1593]. L.; HN. [Under N.:]	1335 A short and plaine dialogue concerning the vnlawfulnes of playing at cards. 8°. [*T. Orwin?*] *f. R. Boile*, [1593]. L.; HN.

[1] Parentheses used to indicate colophon imprints.

18324 To the maior, aldermen, a. inhabitants of N. A dialogue ag. playing at cardes a. tables. s.sh.fol. *f. R. Boile*, [1590?] L.	1335.2 [Anr. ed.] To the maior, aldermen, a. inhabitants of N. A dialogue ag. playing at cardes. s.sh.fol. *f. R. Boile*, [1593?]. L. L^{5}. (Formerly 18324)
	1335.4 [Anr. ed.] s.sh.fol. [*R. Field*, c. 1595]. HD. Reprinted in 1336.
1336 [Anr. ed.] 8°. *Imprinted f. R. Boile* 1593, *reprinted* 1623. Assigned by Ellen Boyle to N. Bourne, 30 jn. 1625. L. O.	1336 A modest reply to certaine answeres which Mr. Gataker giveth to arguments in a Dialogue. 8°. [*Ellen Boyle?*] 1623. Ass'd. by E. Boyle to N. Bourne, 30 jn. 1625. L. O. O^{8}. D. E. + ; HN. BO. BO^{5}. LC. Title to the Dialogue has imprint: *f. R. Boyle* 1593, *reprinted* 1623.
	1336.5 A short catechisme, verie necessarie to be learned of all christians. [Anon.] 8°. *J. Roberts*, 1597. COR.
1337 A short catechisme, comprizing the principall points of the Christian faith. 8°. *F. Kyngston f. R. Boyle*, 1607. Assigned with 1336. L.	1337 [Anr. ed.] A short catechisme, comprizing the principall points somewhat corrected and augmented of the Christian faith. 8°. *F. Kyngston f. R. Boyle*, 1607. Ass'd with 1336. L.
	1337.5 Sixth ed. 8°. *F. Kyngston f. R. Boyle*, 1610. E^{2}.
1338 A short dialogue concerning the plagues infection. 8°. *f. R. Boyle*, 1603. Assigned with 1336. L.	1338 A short dialogue concerning the plagues infection. 8°. [*R. Field*] *f. R. Boyle*, 1603. Assigned with 1336. L. O. C^{10}. D.; HN. COR.
1339 Three positions concerning the Lords day, etc. 8°. *F. Kyngston f. R. Boyle*, 1607. Ent. 18 de. 1606. L. DUR^{5}.	1339 Three positions concerning the Lords day. 1607. = secondary title of 1334.

It is great fun when a gap-toothed series of numbered editions can be completed, as for example with Nicholas Byfield's *Marrow of the oracles of God*, where before only seven editions were listed and now we have filled in the gaps with the first, third, fifth, and eighth editions. Sometimes the job is not quite completed, as in the case of Lewis Bayly's *The practise of pietie*, where although twelve numbered editions have been inserted, including the first, as well as seven unnumbered ones or variant issues of ones already recorded, yet at least fifteen numbered editions remain to be found, i.e., if they were actually published.

We have devoted a good deal of time to attributions of authorship but have left the entries under the original heading, merely inserting a cross-reference, unless the evidence seemed indisputable. The identification of the originals from which the English translations were made has perhaps provided most of the transfers such as the new entries under Matteo Bandello, which include the titles and editions formerly recorded as *S.T.C.* 10791–2, 87, and 3812–4; or the identification of *S.T.C.* 191, *The description of the countrey of Aphrique* (1554), as a translation from the French of J. Boemus. Cross-references are now given for translators and editors so that the revised edition of the *S.T.C.* will give a full account of the contribution of such prolific translators as Edward Aggas, Arthur Golding, and Anthony Munday, as well as many others whose names do not occur at all, as main entries, in the original edition of the *S.T.C.*

There has, however, been some general reshuffling, such as the Newsbooks, which are all being gathered under that heading, and academic theses, which are being put under the university and college where they were given. For example, under Aberdeen, King's College, and Marischal College, there are now listed thirty-two theses, of which all but six were formerly scattered under the names of the proponents or the presiding officers, often with no indication of where they had been presented. Also, under Book-plates, arranged alphabetically but without numbers, and not included in the additions totaled above, are forty-six different bookplates, a number which may well be much increased before publication. Occasionally the transfer is caused by the necessity of assembling in one place the various editions or translations of one original, as in Saint Bernard's *Dialogue*:

1908	A compēdius & a moche fruytefull treatyse of well liuynge. *Tr.* T. Paynell. 8°. *T. Petyt*, [1545?] L.C.	1908	A compēdius & a moche fruytefull treatyse of well liuynge. *Tr.* T. Paynell. 8°. (*T. Petyt*), [c. 1545]. L.L^{2}.C.; F.Y (forged col. dated 1541).

1909 The complaint or dialogue betwixt the soule and the bodie of a damned man. *Tr.* and put into metre by W. Crashaw. 12°. *G. P[urslow]. f. L. Becket*, 1616. Ent. 10 ju. 1613. O.

[Under Crashaw:]

6019 A manuall for true catholicks. 12°. *G. P[urslow]. f. L. Becket*, 1616. O.

6025 Querela sive, dialogus animae & corporis damnati. 8°. *Ex. off. G. Eld sumpt. L. Becket*, 1622. Eng. tr. ent. to L. Becket, 10 jn. 1613. HN.

6026 [Anr. ed.] 12°. *J. B[eale]. sumpt. L. Becket*, 1632. C.

1908.5 Dialogue betwixt the soule and the body of a damned man. *Tr.* and put into meeter [by W. Crashaw.] *Lat. a. Eng.* 8°. *N. O[kes]. f. L. Becket*, 1613. Ent. 10 jn. O.; F(–Latin title). Latin title reads: "Querela sive, dialogus," etc.

1909 [Anr. ed.] The complaint or dialogue, . . . Now published by W. Crashaw. (A manuall for true catholicks.) *Lat. a. Eng.* 12°. *G. P[urslow]. f. L. Becket*, 1616. O. LINC.; HN. HD. (Pt. 2 formerly 6019)

1909.3 [Anr. ed.] *Lat. a. Eng.* 12°. *G. Eld f. L. Becket*, 1622. HN. (Formerly 6025)

1909.6 [Anr. ed.] *Lat. a. Eng.* 12°. *J. B[eale]. f. L. Becket*, 1632, 31. L. O^{28}. C. (Formerly 6026)

Whenever a transfer is made, a tracer is inserted under the original number and that number is not employed for a new title or edition, however convenient it might be. When an original entry is found to represent two or more editions of the same date or no date, one of them is usually left with that number and the others interpolated according to date or presumed order. Likewise when a number is canceled for any reason other than transfer, that reason is given, as, for instance:

113 = frag. of 104
574 Printed c. 1680.
844 = 846
3557–61 Not English. [A Latin book pr. abroad.]

Whenever a new title is found, particularly an anonymous one, it is scrutinized with some skepticism and checked against the date file and Morrison's *Index of Printers*. If not examined personally by Ferguson or myself, its collation must be obtained to determine if it might be part of a book, and its entry in the Stationers' Register searched. If its title page appears to be a cancel, then a photostat of an opening or two must be obtained to determine if it is an issue of an otherwise recorded item, etc. Perhaps our most constant annoyance is the collections of sermons, either the "nonce" collections made up of the sheets of previously separately issued sermons (sometimes not always the same ones), with a prefixed general title, or collections printed with part titles and separate signature sequences so that they might have been separately issued. The problem then is to find copies of the parts bound separately, in original bindings or in contemporarily bound collections of miscellaneous sermons, or, after checking the recorded copies, to relist the separate publications as merely parts of the collected edition.

Now as to when we may be through, I can only say that, aside from vacations and holiday-interrupted weeks, we are now progressing at the rate of nearly a page and a half a week or roughly some fifty pages a year. As there are nearly five hundred pages yet to go and not many parts, except the Proclamations, where we can reasonably expect to increase our pace, it will be a decade at least before we are finished, i.e., well before Ferguson's ninetieth birthday, when presumably he will wish to slow down a bit. However, as we hope to start printing when we have finished the first third or so, the new *S.T.C.*, which with the extended titles, locations, and added matter will be double the size of the old one, ought to be published about that time.

I wish it were possible to record here the countless librarians, booksellers, collectors, and sometimes merely conveniently traveling or situated friends who have answered innumerable questions about particular books. I fear that some of them may now wince a bit when they see a letter from me in the morning's mail. Perhaps, however, you will permit me to say that we are always delighted to hear of the location not merely of the unique and unrecorded titles but also of any books that belong in this period. If booksellers would let us know, or ask the purchasers to let us know, when unique or very rare books have passed through their hands, it would be a great service.

17

Bibliography & Literary Studies

(1962)

This lecture was delivered before the School of Librarianship at Berkeley and the School of Library Service at Los Angeles, California. It embodies in greatly expanded form some of the ideas that Jackson expressed in an unpublished talk, "Our Libraries and the Future of Bibliography," before the Friends of the Bodleian Library, Oxford, on June 23, 1959 (Bibliography, no. 118).

BIBLIOGRAPHY has often been defined, frequently by a description of its fundamental purposes and functions. Its utility has been extolled, usually to the converted; and it would seem that to devote another evening to this topic would be repetitious and unprofitable. However, this is the topic which has been assigned, and I shall endeavor to deal with it, mainly by specific examples which may be, at any rate largely, unfamiliar to you.

For our purposes this evening may we use as a definition of "bibliography," "the art of looking at a book objectively, as a physical object." "Literary studies" will be presumed to include both literary and historical studies, for despite the opinion of some of the newer critics, they are related, and it is sometimes disastrous to ignore that relationship. There are some problems in literature and history which are bibliographical and which can be solved efficiently and convincingly only by bibliographical methods. It is the failure to recognize these problems as bibliographical, that is, the necessity of looking at the book or books involved objectively, that has caused the waste of scholarly effort in the instances presently to be described.

Each year as I interview graduate students who wish to take a course in bibliography, which for the last twenty-odd years I have offered at Harvard, I assure them that taking such a course will not make them bibliographers — that will only be possible by looking at, really looking at, thousands of books, many thousands of books, and making themselves familiar with what is normal and what is phenomenal in at least one period of publishing history. However, I do assure them that perhaps, if they are attentive, they may at the end of the course be able to recognize the difference between a literary and a bibliographical problem and, if they properly prepare themselves, may be able to solve it if it is a bibliographical one, or refer it to a bibliographer who can. As an example of this I have often cited a not too recent book by an eminent historian, a colleague and friend of mine, on the Marian exiles. In this book there is a long chapter regarding Bishop Aylmer's *An harborowe for faithfull subiectes* (1559), which says on the title that it was printed in "Strasborowe." After what undoubtedly was a laborious search of the registers of aliens in various cities of Europe, my friend traces the wanderings of Bishop Aylmer in 1559 and records that he was apparently in several cities of Germany in that year, but not in Strassburg. His final conclusion is that the book might have been printed in any one of the various cities which the author had visited but that it probably was not printed in Strassburg.

Now, a glance at the book would have shown that it has distinctive types, ornaments, and initials that to someone familiar with such things would probably be identifiable. There are many people who would be able to say offhand that the book was English printed, and certainly there are several who, with very little effort indeed, could positively identify the ornaments and initials and testify that the book was printed in London by John Day. This was a bibliographical problem which, if approached in a bibliographical way, would have been solved with certainty and dispatch.

Sometimes the difficulty has been not in the failure to look but in looking at the wrong thing, a corrupt edition or a facsimile which is inadequate. The classic example of this last was pointed out by the late R. W. Chambers in his edition of A. J. Wyatt's *Beowulf*. You have doubtless all seen the charred and crinkled Cottonian manuscript of that prime work of Anglo-Saxon literature in the British Museum. Most scholars, however, have perforce had to use Zupitza's fascimile of it, which although an excellent one is, as Chambers observes, no substitute for an examination of the manuscript itself, for that manuscript has to be turned in many ways and examined under many lights before the stroke of a letter can be distinguished from some accidental crease.

An American scholar thought he saw in the facsimile an erased word, *heado*, in an admittedly defective passage (ll.62–63). Later when Chambers examined the original manuscript and held it up to the light, all the dim marks, which in the facsimile (and at first sight in the manuscript also) look like fragments of an erased word, turned out to be nothing more than strokes of a word on the other side of the leaf, which, as so often in the Beowulf manuscript, show through the parchment. The discussion of the "erased word" and of the theories built upon it was the subject of seven contributions to a philological journal consisting of about ten thousand printed words. Chambers, disregarding the misspent labor of the scholars, remarked only, "It is painful to think that the time of skilled compositors should have been thus wasted."

It might have been more polite to mention my own sins of failure to look at the proper original before casting stones at others. However, this platform is not a confessional, and you may be so indulgent as to accept my statement that the following is by no means the only one I might cite, but is chosen in the hope that this correction may be noted by some of those who may have been misled by my stupidity, and that I am duly penitent. In the Pforzheimer Catalogue, I (1940), 71–72, I rather elaborately described two states of the fine engraved title of the "He" Bible which principally consisted of variations of the vowel signs of the Tetragrammaton at the top. These states were based on a comparison of the collotype reproduction of a British Museum copy in A. F. Johnson's *A Catalogue of Engraved English Title-pages* and the Pforzheimer and other copies. The earlier state, known to me only in the Johnson facsimile, does not exist. It consists merely of slight variations introduced into the photographic reproduction — a far more common occurrence than generally recognized — and not to be found in the British Museum copy from which that reproduction was made. This failure to look at the original will probably continue for generations to plague the literature concerning this great book and, like Spielmann's "fly-speck" variant of the Droeshout Shakespeare portrait, be a ghostly nuisance which cannot be destroyed. *In nobis nulla est salus.*

Doubtless you can all recall instances of fruitless discussion of textual cruces based on misreadings or corrupt texts. One which has often been cited is of Yeats' "soldier Aristotle" on which a long and subtle exposition of the meaning was once published. It turns out, however, that it is a corruption in the American edition of what Yeats wrote and published in the original English edition, "solider Aristotle." It is not just critics, however, who have been thus misled by failure to confirm the authority of their texts, but also editors. The learned journals have had a number of articles in recent years telling of the repetition in edition after edition of errors, even to the confounding of the order of whole chapters, in classic texts of the nineteenth and twentieth centuries. One happy restoration which may not be familiar to you was performed by my colleague, Professor Harry Levin, when editing a translation of Flaubert's *La Légende de Saint Julien l'Hospitalier*, where, in describing the peaceful chateau of Julien's parents, nearly all editions, including those presently being published, say that the moats were full of water, "les fosses étaient pleins d'eau," whereas Flaubert had actually written "pleins d'herbe," full of grass, and these words appear on a page of the manuscript which is reproduced in the Conard edition. The compositor, however, apparently preferred water to grass, ignoring the peaceful setting, the unlowered portcullis (*herse*), and the pigeon which, a few pages later, Julien rushed through the briars to pick up in the moat.

At this point it may be proper to repeat a warning of the almost inevitable humiliation which may be the lot of an editor who reproduces the original, or any part of it, alongside his transcript of it without proofing it with the greatest care. A. W. Pollard has stated that he did not believe the scholar existed who could transcribe without error a single page of a sixteenth century manuscript. Presumably, he meant at a single try. Even E. Gordon Duff, that paragon of bibliographers whose accuracy and industry are unmatched, in his Caxton Club biography of William Caxton in transcribing four lines from Wynkyn de Worde's poem about Caxton, which he reproduced on the opposite page, made nine changes, not counting punctuation. It is true that they are mostly modernizations, but some are the reverse, such as "fyrste" for "first" in the original. If this *helluo librorum*, in Dibdin's phrase, can do that, it behooves us lesser mortals to take very great care we do not do even worse things of this nature.

We are accustomed to thinking that the bibliographical method of looking at books, as distinct from the mere listing and categorizing of them, began with Bradshaw and Blades, and that the sudden interest of literary students in bibliographical matters began with the proof of the false dating of certain of the Jaggard quartos by Greg, Pollard, and Neidig. But the eighteenth and early nineteenth centuries produced a number of bibliographical works which in their competent resolution of complex matters may be favorably compared with the best work now being done. A very good example of this is Thomas Bennet's *Essay on the XXXIX Articles* (London, 1715), which not only examines a number of located copies of the various editions, all with the same date, but puts them in order of publication, not only from textual but also bibliographical evidence. Such a task would today be undertaken only with the aid of innumerable microfilms and xerographs and might daunt even Dr. Todd. The results would differ from those of the Reverend Thomas Bennet only in that there are now traceable one or two editions which his diligence failed to discover. Dr. John Griffiths published in 1859 a study of the editions of the Elizabethan homilies, many of which bear the same date or no date. The latest listing of the editions totals sixty-nine, of which twenty-six were not recorded in the first edition of the *Short-title Catalogue*, but of these last Dr. Griffiths knew quite a few and even himself possessed three or four which, with the whole of his magnificent collection of these homilies, are now in the library of Wadham College, Oxford. Both of these are studies that would today be regarded as not merely laborious but sound and perspicacious.

Since the great revival of bibliographical studies toward the end of the nineteenth century, at least in the bibliography of incunabula and of English books of all periods, there have been enormous advances made so that at times some of the younger scholars have complained that little remains to be done. This of course is nonsense. We have only begun. The tasks before us are challenging, and their completion will be rewarding. Even in the case of the great monuments of literature there are still bibliographical problems to be solved. It was only a few years ago that David F. Foxon discovered a new way of viewing the tangled problems of the first issue of the *Lyrical Ballads*, a problem that had certainly been discussed in a dozen catalogues and articles. He used the tympan pinholes in a way that had never until then been explored. Not long before that Dr. William B. Todd, using watermarks among other evidence, reordered the variant copies of the second folio of Shakespeare, completely altering a sequence that had seemed immutable. And so it goes; each generation always has and always will find new evidence and new methods of viewing problems which have hitherto been insoluble or which have been accepted as proved on evidence which can be demonstrated to be inadequate.

Traditionally the order of the two unauthorized editions of Sir Thomas Browne's *Religio Medici* (1642) was first the longer edition of 190 pages and 25 lines to a page and second the contracted one of 159 pages and 26 lines to a page. In 1924 Mr. Geoffrey Keynes reversed this order on the evidence of the state of the engraved titles of the Bodleian and Osler copies, all of which were in their original bindings. His new order was accepted and for a generation had a marked effect on the price which these two editions fetched on the rare book market, not only in the auction rooms but more particularly in the booksellers' catalogues. Keynes' evidence, even if true for the copies he cited, was irrelevant, for the state of these engraved titles might in some cases have only an accidental relationship to the relative order of the two editions. Those titles would have been printed on a rolling press, probably in another shop, and which state was bound with which edition would have been subject to all the accidents of combination and permutation one could imagine. In 1948 Miss Elizabeth Cook examined the question once again and proved from purely internal grounds that the formerly accepted order was the proper one — a reversion which Sir Geoffrey has graciously acknowledged to be correct.

If I ask to be permitted to confine my remarks about the nature and extent of bibliographical work which needs to be done to the field with which I am most familiar, viz., English printing to 1640, it is not because I am unaware of the needs of other literatures and other periods. Indeed, the earlier periods of French literature and the minor items of American literature have been perhaps less adequately studied than have the early English ones.

Students of eighteenth and nineteenth century literature with their plethora of documentation often speak condescendingly of the tasks of students of earlier periods who oftentimes cannot say whether the man whose published work they are studying was tall or dark or had a stammer, whereas they are familiar even with the gossip and table-talk of a Pope, a Boswell, a Coleridge or a Thackeray. Nevertheless, those who work in those earlier periods know the satisfaction which comes from gathering hard-won information about their less documented subjects. For example, Mr. Robert Birley recently identified an early seventeenth-century Eton binder with distinctive tools — including the Stephanus device — as a drunkard named Williamson. The other day Dr. William E. Miller kindly sent me some notes regarding stationers in the records of St. Giles Cripplegate which he had compiled last summer. Among ones of even greater moment were some regarding the christening and burial of the children of a Vincent Williamson, "stationer and boke-binder," who married Elizabeth Dawson in December 1584 and who probably is the man whose bindings can now be identified in many libraries and who appears without his Christian name in the Eton records.

When the revision of the *Short-title Catalogue of English Books 1475–1640* is finally published, we hope in some four or five years, there will have been added to the record more than ten thousand new titles and editions. We shall not have reached perfection by any means, for new titles and new editions are still being discovered every week. However, some measure of the present coverage may be given by the so-called lost books in Richard Robinson's manuscript *Eupolemia* which has been studied by Vogt and McKerrow and many others. Of the nineteen books there listed, three according to previous accounts had not survived. All three are now known and recorded. It is true that relatively few of the new titles will be of intrinsic literary importance, although a number will fill gaps in the contemporary reporting of history. Perhaps, except statistically, it is of no great moment to literary studies to have multiplied the known number of editions of a book no longer regarded as very interesting. But is it so? Let us take, for example, Nicholas Ling's *Politeuphuia, Wits Common wealth*, a collection of sententious aphorisms which formerly was known in seven editions before 1640, but which can now be shown to have been printed at least twelve times before that date. It would not be a frivolous topic for a doctoral thesis to investigate the influence of this little book which in a century was republished nearly thirty times. In the original *Short-title Catalogue* there was recorded only one edition of Martin Billingsley's *The pens excellencie or the secretaries delighte*, 1618. Now it can be shown to have survived in at least eight editions printed before 1640, which makes it one of the most popular and possibly the most influential writing books of that period. One might well take a second look at Richard Harvey's *An Astrological discourse upon the coniunction of Saturne & Jupiter* (1583), formerly known by two editions, but now by five editions printed within the same year. A sixteenth century book that sold presumably over six thousand copies in twelve months must have had a considerable impact on the reading public of that day.

Although the distinguishing, locating, and recording of these proliferating editions is no doubt a menial form of bibliographical labor, it has a very great utility in studies of the history of ideas. If in this period, 1475–1640, more than a third new titles and editions than were formerly known will have been added, it is obvious that scholars will have a better measure of what at that time was available to readers, and what publishers thought was salable.

Of course, the next step in this bibliographical preparation for literary and historical studies will be the identification and listing of those books which were published but of which no copies can now be found. The search for these titles will not only be rewarding but will involve skillful use of all kinds of evidence, literary, historical, and bibliographical. The entry of a title in the Stationers' Register is, of course, no proof that that book was actually printed, but an entry plus other evidence creates a very strong presumption. For example, John Wolf entered 11 September 1587 for an edition of a lace-pattern book by Frederico de Vinciolo to be printed "aswell in Englishe as in French." No copy of this Wolf edition has been traced — lace books are notoriously subject to destruction by their users — although a copy of a Paris, 1587, edition printed by Jean Le Clerc is in the British Museum. But if Wolf did not print it he, or someone else, had at least two of the fairly elaborate blocks of the Paris edition copied. One, the title-compartment, showing two ladies making lace, was used at Eton by John Norton in 1610, and another block, a laurel wreath, was used twice by Adam Islip in his edition of Holland's Livy, 1600.

Sometimes the illation is more bibliographical, as is the case for a separate contemporary edition of Ben Jonson's masque, *The Newes from the New World* (1621), which rests on the typographical similarity of the titles of the three other Jonson masques of which separate editions do exist, printed evidently for the use of the nonprofessional court masquers, and the manner in which those titles and that of *The Newes from the New World* were reprinted in the 1640 Jonson folio.

The search for these "lost" books will involve a consideration of the factors which have caused the preservation of some books and the apparently complete destruction of others. Among these factors is one which hitherto has not been given the attention it deserves for its role in the survival of the books of the past, viz., the obscurity of the original publisher or even merely the remoteness of his shop from the main publishing centers. Just as today it is difficult for a small publisher away from the major centers to persuade the jobbers and booksellers to stock his productions, so, in the sixteenth and seventeenth centuries, a publisher whose shop was on London Bridge or in Smithfield, away from Fleet-street and St. Paul's, evidently found it difficult to call his wares to the attention of the normal buyers of books whose purchase of them would have put them on permanent institutional shelves or in the stream of collectors who, generation after generation, have passed their books, by auction or otherwise, from one to another. That this obscurity or remoteness is an important cause of the failure to survive can be measured by the frequency with which, when hitherto unrecorded books are discovered, they turn out to be the production of publishers whose recorded output is very slight or who were not recorded as having published any books. Even, in some cases, they are found to have been published by men so obscure that they are unknown to the dictionaries of publishers.

When, with all its omissions and errors, the record of the surviving books of this period, 1475–1640, is completed and the relevant index of printers and publishers has been prepared, it will be possible to undertake a systematic study of the books printed in each shop. The types, ornaments, and initials can be recorded and their transfer from printer to printer traced. The printing habits, methods of signing, headlining, and general typographical practice of each printer can be noted, and from all these studies there will most likely emerge other less bibliographical ones concerned with the literary, social, and economic content of the production of various periods or even of single printing offices. While hundreds and even thousands of anonymously printed books will, in the revision of the *Short-title Catalogue*, have been ascribed to particular printers, this work has rarely been done other than on an ad hoc basis and will doubtless be in need of verification, or correction, as the result of an examination of all the books printed in each shop.

Some of these bibliographical investigations will no doubt be undertaken with no larger end in view than the establishing of the truth — in other words, bibliography for bibliography's sake. In the words of a learned Warden of Wadham College, "If any shall suggest, that some of the inquiries here insisted upon do seem too minute and trivial for any prudent Man to bestow his serious thoughts and time about, such persons may know, that the discovery of the true nature and cause of any the most minute thing, doth promote real knowledge, and therefore cannot be unfit for any Man's endeavours who is willing to contribute to the advancement of Learning." Sometimes, however, these minute investigations do have broader implications. Thomas Dekker's *West-ward Hoe* (1607) is anonymously printed but it has throughout the ornaments and initials which belonged successively to James Roberts and William Jaggard, one or other of whom must have printed it. In 1906 Henry R. Plomer first stated that "in or about 1608" Roberts sold out his business to Jaggard, and this statement is repeated in McKerrow's *Dictionary*. An investigation of Roberts' signed work shows that from 1594 on he had a method of printing the signatures of the first leaf of each quire which was peculiar to himself, at least as a consistent method, during the remainder of his activity as a printer. As *West-ward Hoe* is not signed in this way, it must have been printed by Jaggard. Indeed, it can from this evidence be shown that it was during the autumn of 1606 that the business was transferred and that it occurred half-way through the printing of a book, viz., Robert Greene's translation of Jean de Flores' *A paire of turtle doves* (1606). We can now state that any book which contains these ornaments and is dated 1607 or 1608 was printed in the shop of William Jaggard.

Since writing the above, I have had an opportunity to compare at the Huntington Library a microfilm of the British Museum copy of Henry Constable's *Diana* (1584) with the Huntington copy of the same date. They belong to two different editions, though very closely reset. Both state on their titles that they were printed by James Roberts, and literary scholars have for some time conjectured that they actually were printed about a decade later than the date they bear, viz., about 1594. Since the first leaves in each quire in both of them are signed with a full stop only, and no numeral, in Roberts' peculiar manner which he first employed in 1594, the literary evidence can now be confirmed with this bibliographical testimony.

I have cited these minuscule matters merely to indicate that in bibliography it is the concinnity of demonstrable facts that makes possible, sometimes, more general dicta.

Far too often in recent bibliographical studies, particularly those using the newer techniques of type shortages, compositor identification, printing order of formes, etc., one reads phrases in which the words "likelihood," "probable," "apparent," etc., recur with alarming frequency. These papers have been prepared with vast labor — one is sometimes informed of the exact number of pieces of type, which on a given day were in a particular box of the compositor's case — and one can well imagine innumerable manuscript tables which were prepared to confirm the more striking examples which are printed. We seem to be looking over the compositor's shoulder, watching his every movement, or assisting the pressman as he turns his piles of paper to begin perfecting them. But do we really know so much? Did our compositor suffer that day from a surfeit of beer? Did the pressman really have his mind on what he was doing and was he not thinking of his domestic troubles? They were not automatic machines — and even if they were, the number of times the machine which packages my cigarettes put the ribbon inside the wrapper instead of outside would give one reason to be wary.

The late R. W. Chapman wrote some wise words regarding arguments which are based on a group of probabilities each of which depends for its support upon a preceding one, and I cannot do better than to quote him: "even when the odds are three to one in favour of certain theories, it is perilous to make two such odds depend one upon the other. Two three-out-of-four chances are only just more than even odds ($3/4 \times 3/4 = 9/16$). If you add yet another three-out-of-four chance *depending upon the preceding two*, the odds have definitely turned against you ($3/4 \times 3/4 \times 3/4 = 27/64$). Yet how many plausible arguments depend upon the exponent getting our consent to one position as probably true, and then proceeding to further steps, and demanding our final assent to the whole concatenation, because at no one stage can we prove probability against him."

But to turn again to our topic, the future of bibliography and literary studies. The kind of bibliography to which I refer has little to do with the "science fiction" developments of "information retrieval," "data processing," or "reference arrays" with their punch cards and computation machines. However, I firmly believe that photographic instruments can and will be developed which will aid greatly in the solution of many of the major bibliographical problems which lie almost unexplored and certainly unsolved.

For example, generations of incunabulists have distinguished over three hundred black letter fonts used in Germany alone in the fifteenth century, and over eight hundred fonts of roman type in the same century, really half-century. It would have taken an army of expert punch-cutters to have cut in steel the several hundred thousand punches which would have been needed if all these types belonged to different punches. To identify the printers, it was necessary to distinguish these fonts. But if we are to have a true picture of the spread of printing, it will be necessary to reassemble them into families of fonts all cast in varying sizes from matrices made from a much smaller number of sets of punches. A good "eye for types" was sufficient for the incunabulist of the past. The future scholar will need precision photography which will enable him to compare, letter by letter, in controlled enlargement on a measured grid, all the letters of every possibly related font.

We have only begun to study the initials and ornaments used by the printers of any period of the past. In English printing before 1640 the number is large but not uncontrollable. The problem really lies in distinguishing between the frequent copies which belonged sometimes to the same printer but more often than not to other printers, to trace their successive owners, and to date the stages of their deterioration. Already there is available a microfilm enlarging machine which will reproduce an enlarged positive of a frame in four seconds. Admittedly the enlargements do not have the sharpness of definition which must be obtained before one can really rely on them, but this gadget will, at any rate, serve to record all the ornaments in the stock of a given printer. (Having just acquired one of these machines, I may be overly optimistic.) The next instrument, which has not yet been developed but which obviously is well within the capabilities of our technicians, is a variable-apertured camera, with an aperture extending let us say from one to five inches — larger cuts would have to be taken in sections — similar to the one used to prepare the reprint of the British Museum Catalogue now being published, equipped with a built-in scale which would be reproduced beside the image, and with a self-developing film similar to the Land camera. With these two devices and the ability to develop an indexing system capable of controlling their output, a scholar without a laboratory and in a relatively short time could recheck the printer identifications of past bibliographers and solve a large part, if not all, of the problems of anonymous printing which have hitherto been insoluble.

All students of the English Renaissance, and I suppose of other periods, have dreamed of a new edition of the *Dictionary of National Biography* because of the enormous amount of new information, the innumerable corrections of dates and other factual data, which have been noted in the last sixty to eighty years, and because each generation must reappraise and reinterpret the history of the past. When Professor F. B. Williams' index of the preliminary matter in English books before 1640 and the revised *Short-title Catalogue*, with its thousands of cross-references, have been published, there will be available two tools which should be of considerable value to this undertaking. As a bibliographer I do not desire to exaggerate the importance of the contribution which bibliography can and will make to this and other literary and historical studies of the future.

Perhaps I can best state the thesis I have this evening tried to bring to your attention, and thus end my discourse, by quoting a sentence from Erasmus' introduction to Laurentius Valla's *Adnotationes* on the New Testament, Paris, 1505: "In minimis versatur, sed sine quibus nemo evasit maximus; nugas agitat, sed quae seria ducant," which may be translated: "He is occupied with the smallest things, but such as the greatest cannot afford to neglect; he deals with minute points, but such as have serious consequences."

18

The Importance of Rare Books and Manuscripts in a University Library

This is surely the classic statement concerning the position occupied by rare books and manuscripts in a research library. No piece of Jackson's writing occupied more of his concentrated thought and effort. It was prepared for a symposium on university libraries at the opening of the Lamont Library; when he was called upon to repeat its delivery under other circumstances in 1961 and 1964, he found no reason to alter it in any material way (Bibliography, no. 59).

THIS generation has witnessed a phenomenal growth of rare book collections in American university libraries. In the past such libraries have usually had a reserved section which contained a miscellany, including some real rarities, inferno books, and many other items which were neither rare nor important but merely fragile or difficult to administer either because of their size or material or because they really were not books at all but curiosities. Now, in most of the larger university libraries special departments have been established for the preservation and administration of rare books, and the relative growth in size and expense of these departments has frequently been greater than that of the libraries of which they are a part. This evening let us consider whether this expensive growth is justified by the utility of these books in our educational processes.

But first, may we pause to define what a "rare book" is? The term is often an embarrassment to those whose lives are spent mainly in the study and care of such books, for, far too often, to the layman it appears to have a connotation of triviality and superficiality which we believe to be unwarranted. "Uncommon" or "seldom found" is only one meaning of the word "rare" and, although the one which perhaps first comes to mind, is neither the traditional nor the proper one when used in the phrase "rare books." The *Oxford Dictionary* gives as one of the definitions of the word "rare": "unusual in respect of some good quality; of uncommon excellence or merit, remarkably good or fine; distinguished," and, aptly enough, as the earliest use of the word in this sense instances William Caxton's prologue to the *Book callid Caton*, 1483: "There was a noble clerke named pogius . . . whiche had in the cyte of Florence a noble & well stuffed lybrarye whiche alle noble straungers comynge to Florence desyred to see. And therin they fonde many noble and rare bookes. And whanne they had axyd of hym whiche was the best boke of them alle, and that he reputed for best. He sayd that he helde Cathon glosed for the best book of his lyberarye." A "rare book" is then a book which either has been regarded for generations as an intrinsically important one or, if a little-known book, may be so regarded when its virtue has been recognized.

It has been often observed by bookmen that a volume which has only its rarity to commend it, even one which is so "rare" as to be unique, may well be worthless. It is only when in varying degrees intrinsic worth, condition, and rarity are combined that one has a "rare book." For example, a telephone book of New York City for even one of the later years of Edwin Arlington Robinson might well be scarcer and more difficult to find today than a city directory of the later years of Franklin's life, and yet the telephone book would hardly fetch ten cents. It may well be that a hundred years from now the scholars of that time will recognize the usefulness of our current telephone books and then they may be sought after as avidly and pertinaciously as we now seek the city directories of one or two centuries ago. Then, because their worth has been recognized, they will be "rare books"; because they will be uncommon they will be doubly valuable; and because the paper on which they are printed is of a poor quality, ones in good condition will have an added virtue.

In a consideration of rare books in university libraries, it is pertinent to examine what role, if any, they may have in solving the educational problems of our generation. Our educationists rightly regard "the capacity for research as a test of ability in scholars and a guarantee of soundness in teachers," and they recognize that in the humanities there is a disciplinary tradition as severe and exacting as that of any of the sciences, and indeed even more venerable. The sciences of epigraphy and paleography, the newer procedures of bibliography, the patient assembling of data in history and biography, textual criticism — these are the time-proved methods and processes of humanistic scholarship, and scholarship will not remain sound unless training in such disciplines is fairly widespread. And in all of these disciplines the access to original material, often, of course, rare books or manuscripts, is essential if the training is to be maintained at a level which will enable the younger scholars to advance beyond their teachers. How easy it is for humanistic scholarship to become static without access to research material may perhaps be illustrated by the phenomenon observable among many of the most competent of our Indic scholars, who can read any printed text in that field but can hardly identify even the language of a palm-leaf manuscript, ancient or modern.

In the past, many of our scholars received their training in these sciences in Europe as part of their graduate work, and it is to be hoped that in the future an even larger number will be granted the opportunity for study in the libraries, muniment rooms, and seminars of Europe. These larger numbers may be an impediment, however, for if our students arrive without some familiarity with the material they are to use, they will at best lose much valuable time, and will often be denied access to the muniments and manuscripts they wish to see because they will be unable to convince the custodians of those documents that they are sufficiently competent to be entrusted with them. This, of course, is particularly true in those fields involving the use of early manuscripts, for all the wealth of such material that has crossed the Atlantic in the past three or four generations does not equal the riches to be found in London, Paris, or Rome, while of muniments we have only scattered examples, useful for training but hardly suitable for research.

Nevertheless, the American paleographers trained by Rand at Harvard and Lowe at Princeton, to name only two, although they have perforce had to begin with facsimiles, have had available sufficient original material with which (I was going to say, to try their teeth) — with which to try their prentice skill, so that many of them have gone on and bid fair to equal their masters. And the difference between learning with facsimiles only and having original material to work with suggests the predicament of a man who, never having heard an orchestra or an organ, tries to understand Bach from the score alone. To some of you this may sound merely sentimental, but the limitations of photographic reproduction are too well known for me to discuss at this time. However, I may say that, useful, indeed indispensable, as such aids to scholarship are, they cannot, in many cases, be substituted for the originals without grave danger of error.

In printed books the relative strength, in many fields, is not so overwhelmingly unbalanced. There are many subjects and authors of which the holdings of American universities are as complete, or more so, than those of any one foreign library, as, for example, the early Mexican printing at the University of Texas, or the law books at Harvard, the Goethe collection at Yale, or the Petrarchs at Cornell, to name only a few. In these and many other subjects and authors, the scholar can find one or more university collections which have virtually all the printed books and pamphlets that belong in a complete collection of that subject or author, together with all the relevant reference material. A student of John Locke, for example, can find at Harvard every book by Locke known to his bibliographer, as well as probably most, if not all, of the printed commentary, certainly a more nearly complete collection than exists in any one library in England. (If, having used that, he wishes to carry his researches further, he must then go to the Bodleian to use the Lovelace collection, to the Public Record Office, and the other manuscript archives of England.) So it is in countless fields; the resources of American university libraries for scholarly work in the humanities and in the history of science, so far as the printed materials are concerned, are already rich. In spite of many gaps and many weaknesses, there are few fields in which there are not some representative books with which our scholars can become familiar with the problems, textual or bibliographical, peculiar to their subjects.

It is true that these resources are not very evenly divided among the universities of the country, and probably never will be, in spite of the large sums of money presently available to some of the newer state institutions. In general, there would appear to be no very close correlation between the age of university libraries or their total budgets, on the one hand, and their strength in rare books, on the other. Far more important, it would seem, is the presence on their faculties, on their governing boards, in their libraries, or among their alumni of men who have recognized the value of such material.

George Lyman Kittredge is still remembered by many of us present here today, a giant among scholars, the bibliography of whose writings occupies more than a hundred pages, and whose influence upon scores and hundreds of living scholars cannot be measured. It is conceivable, however, that posterity may conclude that his greatest contribution to scholarship lies not in his own writings or in the innumerable men whom he trained to his own rigorous standards, but in the ballad and folklore collections which, on the foundations laid by F. J. Child, he built at Harvard, without the aid of any special grant, fund, or any other means than his own insistence that, however meager the book funds might be, those books must be acquired. These collections are not now being used in the same way and for the same purposes that Kittredge used them. Studies in ballad literature in the Child-Kittredge-Rollins tradition are not at the moment in fashion. However, these collections are in constant use by the students of the American folk ballad and those studying ballad music. It is, perhaps, not proper for a mere librarian to say whether this is a better use or not, but I refer to it in order to call your attention to the fact that a collection of rare books, even one severely restricted in scope, may be used for many different purposes by many different students. Each generation must rewrite and reinterpret the history of the past, and the critical standards of each generation always have been and always will be different.

We have observed that neither age nor endowment is necessarily a coefficient of the wealth of rare books in university libraries, but age apparently does have some relation to the type of material collected, for the newer libraries in general have tended to collect books and manuscripts of more recent periods and, in particular, to specialize, though by no means exclusively, and with some notable exceptions, in American books and manuscripts. These fields cannot be said to have been neglected by the older institutions, as witness Yale's great Aldis and Coe collections, but the preference for the later and the American among the younger libraries has obviously, judging by the results, been both wise and fruitful, for thereby they have often gathered material that is not elsewhere available. Brown University is without a peer in printed Americana before 1800, though it can hardly be said to have deserved its good fortune through any effort of its own, but Michigan and Virginia have, by the vision of their librarians and, doubtless, a great deal of hard work, as well as good fortune going in one case under the name of Clements and in the other under the disguise of McGregor, done wonders in that earlier period. The collections of historical material, mainly of a somewhat localized interest, which are to be found in such libraries as that of Duke, the University of Texas, and the University of California, the Bancroft collection at Berkeley and the Cowan at Westwood, are important and growing. Furthermore, they are in a large measure not elsewhere duplicated and therefore will increasingly draw to themselves the attention and attendance of scholars from far beyond their local communities.

In other fields besides local history, the emphasis upon the more recent past has reaped a rich harvest, since it is often possible to acquire more nearly complete documentation than is possible for the earlier periods. The collections which are strong in both books and manuscripts are not restricted to those of American origin, such as the Lanier collection at Johns Hopkins, or the Cable collection at Tulane, but include foreign ones, such as that of Leigh Hunt at the University of Iowa, or of Keats at Harvard. In these, and in many similar collections, it is possible for the scholar to find the major part of the relevant material. Indeed, collections of this type, whether or not they include a large proportion of an author's manuscripts or of his correspondence, insofar as they do contain important unpublished material are among the most useful for a university library, since they afford material for scholarly work on both a large and small scale. For example, during one recent summer twelve different scholars were at work on the Emerson collection at Harvard, for periods ranging from a few days to the full three months.

The possession of such collections entails responsibilities for their proper preservation and administration which ought not to be lightly assumed; for whenever there is concentrated in one institution any considerable number of important books and manuscripts, the world of scholars has, justly or not, come to expect not only that reasonable access will be given, but that a competent staff will be provided to answer the questions of those who cannot come to the library, and that there will be available cameras for photostat or microfilm reproduction, as well as some at least of the scientific aids, such as ultraviolet lamps and microfilm reading machines, for those who make use of the collections in person. These facilities, together with proper storage, now normally expected to be air-conditioned if the library is in a large city, means for adequate repair and binding, and cataloguing more or less accommodated to the kind of books and manuscripts collected, are all rather costly and only justified if the collections are of genuine scholarly use. In the larger research libraries with important and growing collections of rare books and manuscripts, the provision of such facilities may, and in many cases does, cost as much as 10 per cent of the total budget.

The larger research libraries which possess not only original source material but also vast reference and periodical collections, often in the ratio of one to fifty, are without question obligated to provide the apparatus and the skilled personnel to which I have just referred. Whether institutions which are unwilling or unable to assume the cost of providing such aids are acting in the best interests of learning in general if they accept the custodianship of important material of this nature is a question which perhaps ought not to be dogmatically answered. But all too often it happens that unique material, which would be of use to scholars from a distance and indeed is eagerly sought by them, is kept in libraries without photostat equipment and even without facilities for its proper use or care. While perhaps the tendency today is to make scholarship too easy, this particular hardship is not merely an exasperation but sometimes a virtual denial of access.

The adequate housing of rare book collections is an expensive business, but it has often proved to be well worth the cost in the attention which it draws not only from scholars but from collectors and the public in general. Usually the books themselves can be utilized as part of the decorative scheme, and the facilities for their exhibition and use provide a constant demonstration of their importance. It will be interesting to observe the effect of the newly constructed rare book reading room and stack in the Harvard Law School upon the support given to that extraordinary collection by the average law school graduate, who until recently has had little means of knowing how rich are the antiquarian resources of the library where he spends so many hours of his graduate years. This "window dressing" use of the rare books of a great research library, though unrelated to the primary purpose of their acquisition, is one which it would be foolish to ignore.

There is much misunderstanding and ignorance concerning the cost of rare books. The knowledge which laymen acquire comes usually from newspaper accounts of spectacular auction sales, often reported without the background details which would explain why such prices are occasionally paid, mostly by private collectors and in relatively restricted fields. Not many institutions indulge in such activities, and when they do, the publicity which results often does more harm to the cause of scholarly rare book collecting than may at first glance seem likely. Generalizations about the cost of rare books, particularly in relation to university acquisition, are admittedly very difficult to make. Yet it may be observed that almost any field of rare books in which it would be worth while for a university library to collect is likely to contain a few items which will, if obtainable at all, cost many times the prices at which most of the other books can be obtained. The high-priced ones are likely to be either the key books, or natural or artificial rarities, which the library will either have to forgo or obtain by the aid of private donors who have become interested in the completing of the collection.

Further, any book which is being avidly collected at the moment would seem a poor choice for an institution. In general, this would rule out most, if not all, contemporary "collected" authors, for two reasons: first, because of the uncertainty of their future importance and the cost of keeping as rare books such questionable gambles; and, secondly, because if they are now popular among collectors, it is likely either that the price will fall when they are no longer fashionable or that the institution may be given one of the collections currently being formed. As an example, when Galsworthy was at the height of his reputation, the Harvard Library spent a fair sum in acquiring two of the four John Sinjohn books in rather less than the most desirable condition. Since then, not only have these books dropped greatly in price, but on several occasions much finer copies have been offered to the library as gifts. It is true that most rare books, except some of those valued mainly because of their beauty, were once relatively inexpensive, and that if we only knew what will be valued by those who come after us, we might save our successors a great deal of money and effort, but it is unlikely that we should have had the prophetic eye to buy for sixpence or less, a hundred odd years ago, a *Necessity of Atheism* or a Bristol *Lyrical Ballads*, and it is equally unlikely that we shall now be more percipient.

Again, institutional libraries may occasionally be custodians for posterity of books in remarkably fine and fragile condition. If the state of such items should be unique, or of such rarity that it would be extremely difficult to find other examples, their use for normal scholarly purposes may be precluded, in order that they may be preserved physically as bibliographical "type specimens." It might be said of libraries acting as custodians of such books, in Pope's now anachronistic words, that they "value books as women men, for dress." Therefore, it would be the negation of the normal reasons for the acquisition by university libraries of rare books if they were sought always in the finest condition, in "original boards," in "immaculate wrappers," etc. Inevitably every rare book collection will receive a number of such books, and the extra care that their preservation will entail will usually be sufficient responsibility, so that libraries are well advised not to seek to have all books in such fine condition that if opened at all they will unavoidably be damaged.

All custodians of rare books have been told frequently by otherwise apparently competent and tolerant scholars that they have no use for "first editions," as if they were speaking of tiaras or suits of armor of a feudal aristocracy, with which they, as modern democrats, would have no truck. I venture to say that among the most useful and certainly the most used books in the collections of our university libraries are those of which there never was a second edition, or at any rate no modern reprint. They are the books which must be studied in order to understand the background and meaning of greater books; they are the ones which are necessary for studies in the history of ideas; and it is by extracting the essence of innumerable books and pamphlets of this character that the history of many periods, since the fifteenth century, is being drawn in truer and more just proportions. Oftentimes such books are traceable in only a single copy, at least in any American library, and therefore, because of their irreplaceability, they are properly cared for among the "rare books," even though, particularly in fields outside those most popular with private collectors, they may not be more costly than the average work of modern scholarship.

It would be convenient to have assembled together in each of our university libraries the greatest monuments of literature, science, art, and history, but of all books they are the ones which can be most easily located in other libraries. They are the ones which have been studied most in the past (though by no means has there been discovered all that this or future generations of scholars might find on a re-examination of them). And they are the ones which have been reproduced in facsimile most frequently and which therefore are available in a partially satisfactory form.

It cannot be said that these great monuments will be consulted frequently by scholars; indeed, in this respect they belong in the category to which librarians hesitate to assign any book, viz., that of "little used."

It is unlikely, for example, that anyone during the past decade has consulted, for a scholarly purpose, the magnificent Van Antwerp copy of the first folio of Shakespeare now in the Harry Elkins Widener Collection. But it has been frequently exhibited, and doubtless numbers of people have been moved by the sight of a copy of the book which alone has preserved twenty of Shakespeare's plays. In this way the volume has earned its board and keep many times over. But it has likewise had an imponderable and almost unanalyzable utility. For it is surely not by mere size that libraries are known throughout the world of scholars but by the quality of the books on their shelves. If libraries are to be ranked at all, an invidious task which I have no intention of attempting at this time, it must be both by the completeness of their collections and by the number and importance of their books which are of the first rank or which are nowhere else to be found. Further, it is by the possession of these great books that the special collections and resources of the libraries become known, and also, by a curious magnetism peculiar to rare books, that other books of like importance are added to them, according, it would seem, to the principle laid down in the Parable of the Talents.

In the year 1543 there were published books by Copernicus, Vesalius, and Ramus, each one of which is important in the story of man's intellectual advance, for together they broke the chains which had bound man's speculative and scientific growth to the Ptolemaic, Galenic, and Aristotelian doctrine. On occasion in the Harvard Library, copies of these books are exhibited together, and the student, young or old, who pauses to look at them in the case and who is not stirred by the sight of them — the neat quarto of Copernicus, the magnificently illustrated folio of Vesalius, and the beautifully printed little octavo of Ramus — such a one, I say, can have only the vaguest knowledge of the revolution in men's thoughts inaugurated and marked by their publication in the same year. There before him lie not mere relics in the history of thought, but a copy of the veritable book, fresh from the printer, which Copernicus saw on his deathbed; of the tome which Vesalius labored with Van Calcar for several years to produce; and of the volume which was condemned by the king and the Sorbonne and eventually cost Ramus his life. It was with these types, these woodcuts, and this paper that first, in 1543, were published these books which ended man's thralldom to the ancient science and made possible the advances of the modern age. One could continue, indefinitely, the catalogue of similar books now treasured in many university libraries of our country. At any moment the sight of any one of them may be the spark which will kindle in some young scholar the desire to unravel the complex which makes them important for mankind and set forth on a scholarly adventure which may result in one more solid addition to the structure of man's understanding of his past.

But, it may be objected, this is all antiquarian, it is looking backward, and despite Thucydides' dictum that "an exact knowledge of the past is a key to the future which in all probability will repeat or resemble the past," the concepts of our scholars should be in terms of the present and the future. I need not repeat to you the truism that though the conditions of life may change, sometimes with vertiginous speed, human character itself alters slowly, it would seem almost imperceptibly. This "new world" of ours, despite the addition of the fears and hopes which accompany the advances in nuclear physics, will still be inhabited by men and women, who, if there is any civilization worthy the name, will be concerned with what "we instinctively call the higher interests," who will be curious about the whole drama of life, if only because it may reveal important data concerning our present and future.

And in this "new world" it is obvious that the role to be played by America will be a leading one. If it is to be guided by something more than pure opportunism, it will be because our statesmen will be provided by the scholars of our country with a far more complete and surer understanding of the background of culture and history of the peoples of the world with which to judge the wisdom of our present and future policy. Some of the scholarship upon which these decisions may be based will seem, and in fact will be, remote from the situation presently to be dealt with. John Jay Chapman once referred to the hegemony, in his day, of the English universities in all branches of Greek scholarship as merely another manifestation of British imperialism. If our country is to be adequately armed for the great opportunity which is ours, an opportunity which is the antithesis of imperialism, but nonetheless epochal, it will demand American leadership in all fields of learning. We do not fear that our scientists will be denied the instruments and laboratories which they need. So in the humanities it is to be hoped that our libraries will be able to fulfill the needs and demands of our scholars. If they do, it will be found that rare books and manuscripts form one of the most useful and most important parts of their resources. In Chaucer's day a library might be merely "twenty bookes, clad in blak or reed," but there is much truth, *mutatis mutandis*, in his familiar lines:

> For out of olde feldes, as men seyth,
> Cometh al this newe corn from yer to yere,
> And out of olde bokes, in good feyth,
> Cometh al this newe science that men lere.

The "science" to which he referred is, of course, *scientia*, learning in general, and scholarship will always be dependent on "olde bokes" for much of the wisdom which surely will be needed in the world we face today.